INSIDERS' GUIDE®

OFF THE BEATEN PATH® SERIES

Off the Beaten Path®

THIRD EDITION

philadelphia

A GUIDE TO UNIQUE PLACES

KAREN IVORY

INSIDERS' GUIDE®

GUILFORD, CONNECTICUT
AN IMPRINT OF THE GLOBE PEQUOT PRESS

The prices, rates, and hours listed in this guidebook
were confirmed at press time. We recommend,
however, that you call establishments to obtain
current information before traveling.

To buy books in quantity for corporate use
or incentives, call **(800) 962–0973,**
or e-mail **premiums@GlobePequot.com.**

Text design by Linda Loiewski
Maps created by XNR Productions, Inc. © Morris Book Publishing, LLC
Illustrations by Carole Drong
Spot photography throughout © Andre Jenny/Alamy

ISSN 1544-7413
ISBN-13: 978-0-7627-4210-3
ISBN-10: 0-7627-4210-0

Manufactured in the United States of America
Third Edition/First Printing

Acknowledgments

I would like to thank my Globe Pequot editor and friend Mary Norris for her confidence and support. I have great appreciation for the Greater Philadelphia Tourism Marketing Corporation (www.gophila.com) and the Independence Hall Association (www.ushistory.org), which both offer informative, entertaining Web sites. Thanks to the friends who offered up their favorite Philly places, with a special nod to Anne Buchanan and the Weiss and Castelli families for agreeing to go on field trips. I'm also grateful to Janet Israel for her culinary contributions and to the members of my writing group for their continuing encouragement. And special thanks, as always, to my husband, Phil, and my daughters, Katie and Susannah, with whom I have loved going off the beaten path in Philadelphia, or anywhere for that matter.

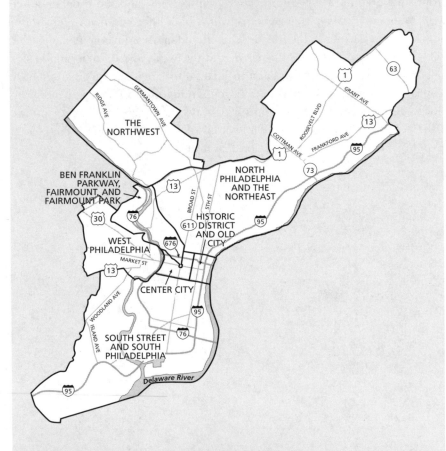

Contents

Introduction vii

Historic District and Old City 1

Center City 35

South Street and South Philadelphia 65

Benjamin Franklin Parkway, Fairmount, and Fairmount Park 87

North Philadelphia and the Northeast 111

The Northwest 135

West Philadelphia 167

Appendix: Annual Events 187

Indexes 193

General Index 193

Restaurants 200

Lodging 201

About the Author 203

Introduction

What a difference a decade makes. In case you haven't heard, Philadelphia is hot. Forget all those other cities that have been coasting on their good reputations for years. Philly is shedding its outdated rep as the butt of bad jokes. In fact it's the new "it" city, at least according to *National Geographic Traveler* magazine, which crowned Philadelphia America's "next great city" in 2005. *USA Today* touts Philly as going "from Rocky to Rockin'," and even the august *New York Times* has noticed there's something in the air, declaring that the City of Brotherly Love has become hip enough to be considered New York's "Sixth Borough."

The message is getting out. The number of visitors grows every year, and more and more people who experience the city are deciding to stay. While many downtown areas have seen declining populations, the number of people moving into Center City Philadelphia is up 11.5 percent in the past five years with no sign of stopping. One reason is that the city has something for everyone. As the only U.S. city chosen to host a Live 8 webcast concert, Philadelphia was able to bask in the glow as images of the city were beamed around the world. The filming of reality television program *The Real World* in Old City let the MTV crowd see just how hip the city has become. The spate of articles touting Philadelphia talk about the city's growing appeal to young people, but it's not just the Xs and Ys being drawn here. Retail spaces are at near capacity, and arts organizations are expanding throughout the Philadelphia area—a recent study showed the number of cultural nonprofits doubling in the last ten years. The city has also gotten respect for its decision to go wireless citywide, offering free high-speed Internet access for all residents, businesses, and visitors.

In addition Philly's growing reputation as a mecca for upscale restaurants and ethnic food appeals across the age spectrum. One new trend in the city is the older empty-nest set taking advantage of the boom in downtown condominiums and culture to leave the suburbs behind for all the city has to offer.

To be sure, it wasn't always this way, and all of this praise only goes so far in convincing the locals that the accolades are legit. This is, after all, the city that once promoted itself with billboards proclaiming "Philadelphia Isn't as Bad as Philadelphians Say It Is." For a long time Philadelphia seemed to define itself by what it was not: It was not Washington, just a few hours south on Interstate 95, and it was not New York, just 100 miles north on the New Jersey Turnpike. Still, there are those here who say, "Yes, we're not New York or Washington, or even Baltimore for that matter—that's exactly the point!" We are Philadelphia, and there are wonderful things to do here and it's a great place to live. Though the city may take some hits from its urban neighbors, Philadelphia's location is one of its greatest assets. It's a plus that Washington, Baltimore, and New York are just hours away by an easy drive or train trip. And within an hour and a half, you can be swimming in the Atlantic or skiing the slopes of the Poconos.

Not everyone who lives here is so anxious to get out of town. There's an amazing amount to do and see in Philadelphia, and the longer you live here, the more you discover. To begin with, the city is vast, stretching from the northeastern neighborhoods, referred to collectively as the Great Northeast (practically all the way to Trenton, New Jersey), to the southern tip, almost to Wilmington, Delaware. You can drive that stretch for almost an hour and still be within the Philadelphia city limits.

In a city that big, there are lots of hidden nooks that hold wonderful, uniquely Philadelphian treasures: houses that still have bullet holes and bloodstains from the Revolutionary War; churches where the graveyards hold statuary worthy of a museum; an abandoned prison that's become a venue for the arts; hidden museums in the former homes of wealthy Philadelphians; thousands of beautiful murals bringing new life to the walls of abandoned buildings; and tiny restaurants hiding in the middle of residential blocks. The country's first operating room is here, where surgery was performed by candlelight—without anesthesia! While you're cringing, how about a museum devoted entirely to gruesome medical deformities?

It's those odds and ends that this book explores. By all means, visit the Liberty Bell and Independence Hall. The historic district can still inspire even the most jaded Philadelphian. But be sure to explore some of these other

Phila-what?

The references to Philadelphia as the "City of Brotherly Love" are not just symbolic but a literal translation from Greek. William Penn likely borrowed the word from history, since an ancient city in Asia Minor was named Philadelphia in honor of an Egyptian of Greek descent, Ptolemy Philadelphua. The name also shows up in the Bible, Revelation 3:7, which reads: "And to the angel of the church in Philadelphia write, 'These things says He who is holy, He who is true, He who has the key of David, He who opens and no one shuts, and shuts and no one opens.'" The literal translation takes the Greek word *phylos,* which means "love," and attaches another Greek word, *adolphos*, which means "brother" (though some would argue that "sister" is also inherent in its meaning).

neighborhoods as well, and you'll be pleasantly surprised. Take time to go off the beaten path.

History

In November of 1682 William Penn sailed across the Atlantic carrying a deed from King Charles II for land west of the Delaware River. Charles called the area "Penn" in honor of William's father, and the son tacked on "-sylvania," meaning "woodlands." To William Penn this new adventure constituted a "holy experiment," and he set about building a community based on his Quaker values of pacifism, religious freedom, and tolerance. Penn chose Philadelphia as the capital of Pennsylvania, naming it after the Greek for "brotherly love," and began to plan what he called a "greene countrie towne." Having witnessed the dangers of narrow streets during London's Great Fire of 1666, Penn called for broad avenues and city blocks arranged in a grid and centered around a city square. Each quarter of the city was to have its own green square, for Penn intended his town to "never be burnt, and allways be wholsome." He composed a prayer that was displayed in City Hall: "And thou, Philadelphia, the Virgin settlement of this province named before thou wert born, what love, what care, what service and what travail have there been to bring thee forth and preserve thee from such as would abuse and defile thee."

As Philadelphia grew, so did opposition to British rule in the colonies, and it was in Philadelphia that colonial leaders hashed out the details of the Declaration of Independence and the Constitution. The city is inexorably linked to the American Revolution and the birth of a new nation.

The next one hundred years would see the city become a leader in the Industrial Revolution as well as a center of abolitionist activity. During the Civil War, Philadelphia became a major industrial supplier for the Union. After the war the city flourished as a shipping port, and its proximity to rivers and the eastern shore contributed to its rapid growth. Though the city's fortunes declined in the nineteenth century and the twentieth century saw many residents moving to the suburbs, the city's cultural and

thelivingdead

It is at least as possible for a Philadelphian to feel the presence of Penn and Franklin as for an Englishman to see the ghosts of Alfred or Becket. Tradition does not mean a dead town; it does not mean that the living are dead but that the dead are alive. It means that it still matters what Penn did two hundred years ago . . . I never could feel that in New York that it mattered what anybody did an hour ago.

— G. K. Chesterton
What I Saw in America, 1922

Don't Ask Where I–476 Is

You will likely travel on Interstate 476 getting to Philadelphia, but don't ask a local where it is. Many residents don't even know what it is. The highway that skirts the city, linking Interstate 95 to the Pennsylvania Turnpike, is known locally as the Blue Route. It got its name in the 1960s, when engineers used different colored markers to map out possible routes through the Philadelphia suburbs. The blue route won. Lawsuits and squabbles made constructing the road a nightmare. Some completed sections sat idle for fifteen years, and the whole thing wasn't finished until 1992.

educational institutions continued to thrive. The elaborate celebration planned for the nation's bicentennial in 1976 ushered in a period of renovation and revitalization that has continued to this day. Although some historic structures were lost to urban renewal, planners were cognizant of the city's historic treasures. Today the downtown area remains a fascinating mix of the old and the new, and Philadelphia is proud that it has been able to integrate its significant history while continuing to move forward.

Transportation

Most of the neighborhoods described in this book are best explored on foot, but Philadelphia has an extensive public transportation system to get you where you want to go. The Southeastern Pennsylvania Transportation Authority (SEPTA) oversees a large fleet of buses, subways, and trolleys throughout the city, as well as commuter rail service between the city, the suburbs, and the airport. Fares on most routes are $2.00 (exact change required); if you use tokens, the fare drops to $1.30. But the best bet for visitors may be the day pass, which provides unlimited trips. Day passes cost $5.50 and can be purchased at the visitor center and at other locations around the city. For current fares and more information, call SEPTA at (215) 580–7800 or visit www.septa.com.

The best bet for visitors during peak travel season is likely to be the Phlash trolleys. Operating between March and November from 10:00 A.M. to 6:00 P.M., the purple trolleys make frequent trips between eighteen of the city's key attractions and most downtown hotels. You can pay $1.00 each time you board, get an all-day individual pass for $4.00, or buy an all-day family pass for $10.00. Children under five and seniors sixty-five and older ride free. You can buy Phlash tickets at the visitor center or when boarding the trolley.

If you're venturing into New Jersey, the Port Authority Transit Corporation (PATCO) runs a high-speed line between Center City and suburban communities in southern New Jersey. For more information call (856) 772–6900 or visit www.drpa.org/patco.

Philadelphia has put a lot of energy into increasing its parking availability in Center City in the past few years, and most of the time you can find a place to park if you're willing to pay. It's usually worth it to pull into a lot or a garage, because even if you're lucky enough to find a meter, you have to keep a close eye on the time. The parking authority takes its ticketing duties quite seriously.

Fees, Prices, and Rates

Prices for restaurants, hotels, and entertainment in Philadelphia are comparable with most major American cities (though pleasantly less than for our neighbors in New York or Washington). Most museums and tourist sites have discounted fees for senior citizens, students, and children. Some visitors are surprised to find out that many attractions in the historic district are free (well, unless you count your taxes as admission). Many hotels offer packages that can get you discounts at museums and restaurants.

Prices at restaurants range across the board. This book attempts to provide options in several price ranges, with less than $10 per entree considered inexpensive, $11 to $29 considered moderate, and $30 or more per entree considered expensive. If these prices seem high, rest assured that statistics show the cost of living in Philadelphia is 37 percent lower than in New York. This despite the fact that in the Chinese language, the name *Philadelphia* apparently can be translated as "the city where you spend a lot of money." For hotel rooms, less than $125 is considered inexpensive, $125 to $200 is considered moderate, and more than $200 is considered expensive. Bed-and-breakfast options are included where available. You can find a more complete registry at the Bed & Breakfast Connection of Philadelphia by calling (610) 687–3565 or (800) 448–3619 or by visiting www.bnbphiladelphia.com.

One word of caution: When you're going off the beaten path, restaurants and stores aren't always surefire successes, so it's a good idea to call beforehand to make sure that hours haven't changed or even that the place is still open.

Area Codes

Kids growing up today in Philadelphia take it for granted that calling a friend means dialing a ten-digit number. Philadelphia and its suburbs currently share four area codes, but since this book covers only the city, you're likely to come across primarily two: the original 215 and the new 267. You have to dial all ten digits, however, even if you're just calling next door.

A City of Neighborhoods

They aren't kidding when they call Philadelphia a city of neighborhoods. The City Planning Commission points to at least 111 distinct neighborhoods within the city limits. That's why when you ask a Philadelphian where he or she lives, you won't get "Philadelphia" or "in the city" for an answer. You'll get "Olney" or "Oak Lane," "Fairmount" or "Fishtown," "Bridesburg" or "Bustleton." Neighborhood boundaries aren't drawn on any city maps, but rest assured, those who live there know where they are.

Sources of Information

You won't find any shortage of reading material when you're in Philadelphia. There are two free weekly newspapers—*Philadelphia Weekly* and the *City Paper*—that you'll see as you wander about town. The newspaper of record is the *Philadelphia Inquirer,* which publishes a detailed weekend section each Friday. The grittier *Philadelphia Daily News* is a tabloid-style paper that covers mostly local news and sports. Both are owned by the same company, which maintains a useful Web site—www.philly.com. The *Philadelphia Tribune* puts out four issues a week for the city's African-American community.

Assuming you're hooked up to the Internet, your best bet may well be the comprehensive Web site maintained by the Greater Philadelphia Tourism Marketing Corporation—www.gophila.com. You can find just about anything you need either there or by calling (215) 599–0776 or (888) 467–4452. The new Independence Visitor Center on Sixth Street between Market and Arch is also a good starting place. Call (215) 965–7676 or (800) 537–7676 or log on to www.independencevisitorcenter.com. Many districts also have their own Web sites; look for them at the end of each chapter.

Tour Groups and Organizers

There are many choices if you're looking for an organized tour of the city. Some of the best and most reliable organizations follow.

Philadelphia Trolley Works offers narrated tours on buses designed to put you in a historical frame of mind. The fare ($27.00 for adults and $10.00 for children) is for a twenty-four-hour pass with unlimited on and off privileges. Call (215) 925–TOUR or visit www.phillytour.com for more information.

One tour not to miss is the *Lights of Liberty,* an after-dark multimedia extravaganza that tells the story of the American Revolution. Each visitor gets a wireless headset—the kids hear Whoopi Goldberg and the grown-ups get Walter

A Metropolis of Murals

In one of the genius strokes of urban renewal, city leaders in the 1980s began an active **Mural Arts Program** that coincided with a new antigraffiti push. To say it took off is an understatement. Philadelphia is now a city of more than 2,100 murals, many beautifying neighborhoods where once there were graffiti-covered abandoned buildings. Some cover huge walls in very visible locations, while others peek out from alleys on residential streets. Professional artists have created their fair share, but most of the murals come about by the hard work of the staff of the Mural Arts Program, with assistance from community volunteers. In some cases the murals reflect unique qualities of the neighborhoods in which they're located. Some glorify local heroes, such as the wonderful mural of Jackie Robinson at Broad and Somerset Streets in North Philadelphia and that of Mario Lanza at Broad and Reed Streets in South Philadelphia. One of the most visible murals covers a wall on the Schuylkill Expressway near the Philadelphia Zoo. The Mural Arts Program offers trolley tours and provides maps. Call (215) 685–0750 or visit www.muralarts.org for more information.

Cronkite and Charlton Heston—that relates the narrative in 3-D surround sound. Visual images are projected onto buildings in the historic district where the events actually took place. This production combines the talents of the Philadelphia Orchestra with sound effects from Skywalker Sound. It's not cheap at $19.50 per adult ticket, but it's an experience you won't get anywhere else. Call (800) GO–2–1776, or visit www.lightsofliberty.org for more information.

There are a number of horse-drawn carriages more than willing to take you on a tour of the historic district. They line up on Chestnut Street near Independence Hall, but if you prefer to reserve in advance, call the '76 Carriage Company at (215) 923–8516 (www.phillytour.com) or the Philadelphia Carriage Company at (215) 922–6840 (www.philacarriage.com).

Recent years have seen an invasion of ducks around Philly's popular tourist sites. There are now no fewer than three companies offering so-called duck-boat tours in amphibious vehicles that go from land to water with the flick of a switch. You can look for them around the visitor center or just keep your ears open—some provide riders with noisy quackers to add to the experience and irritate those who live along the routes. For a more leisurely ride on the Delaware, your best bets are Liberty Belle Cruises at (215) 757–0800 (www.libertybelle.com) or the Spirit of Philadelphia at (215) 923–4993 (www.spiritcruises.com), both of which offer lunch and dinner outings.

Another new arrival to Philadelphia is London's Big Bus Company, which runs double-decker buses on ninety-minute tours. Visitors have the option of getting on and off at twenty sites; tickets are good for twenty-four hours. One advantage here is that the buses venture beyond the historic district to some of the city's other unique attractions. Tickets are $25 per adult and $10 per child. For more information call (866) 324–4287 or visit www.bigbustours.com.

Maybe the coolest way to see Philadelphia is by Segway—the two-wheeled human transporter. I–Glide Tours will give you a thirty-minute training session and then take you wheeling around Fairmount Park and the Art Museum area for two and a half hours of futuristic sightseeing. Several tours a day leave from Eakins Oval in front of the Art Museum, from March through November, at $69 a pop. Call (877) GLIDE–81 or visit www.iglidetours.com for more information.

If you're looking for something a little out of the ordinary, consider the Foundation for Architecture tours, which will take you to some different neighborhoods, (215) 569–3187; the Centipede Tour, where guides in period dress take you through Society Hill by candlelight, (215) 735–3123; or the spine-tingling Ghost Tour, (215) 413–1997.

theairportas artgallery

If you're flying in or out of Philly, don't just grab a coffee and rush to your gate. Take time to enjoy the art. Philadelphia is one of only a handful of airports that spotlights the fine arts. In addition to permanent installations, the airport has twelve exhibit spaces that house rotating displays of fine arts, crafts, and photography, primarily by artists from the region. Although most of the exhibits are in areas where only ticketholders can see them, if you're really serious, you can arrange for a group tour. See www.phl.org/art.html for more information.

There's no doubt that tours can be convenient if visitors are on a tight schedule, but they're not necessary to experience the history and charm of Philadelphia. Many people prefer to set out on their own. If that's your inclination, check out the Constitutional Walking Tour—a new, self-guided walking tour. The 3-mile journey hits all the hot spots and has one big advantage—it's free. You can download a map from www.theconstitutional.com.

The Independence Visitor Center has also started a program called Philadelphia Neighborhood Tours, which offers guided tours through some of the city's little-explored neighborhoods. Some are organized around themes, such as Philadelphia's role in the civil rights struggle, music and ethnic cuisine in the city's Latino community, or the hidden gardens of West Philadelphia. Costs and schedules vary, so it's best to inquire at the visitor center.

Finally, an upstart nonprofit group called Once Upon a Nation is adding a new dimension to the Philly tourism scene. It's the driving force behind the long overdue renovation of the city's fifth square, Franklin Square, catercorner to the National Constitution Center at Sixth and Race Streets. During the summer the group also sponsors so-called storytelling benches at thirteen locations throughout the historic district. Visitors can rest their feet while costumed storytellers regale them with little-known facts and characters from Philadelphia's history. The group also sponsors themed walking tours that run the gamut from exploring the city's spookier side to a "Tippler's Tour," which visits different taverns to taste traditional colonial drinks. For more information visit www.onceuponanation.org or call (215) 629–5801.

Enjoy!

Historic District and Old City

You may think there's nothing off the beaten path to see in the heavily traveled historic district. It's true there is plenty of information out there for tourists, because this is what most tourists come to Philadelphia to see. National Park Service statistics show that the vast majority of visitors tour Independence Hall and see the Liberty Bell, but that's it. Don't make the same mistake: There are many fascinating aspects of Philadelphia's history that most people miss.

First-time visitors are always struck that these historic buildings exist right in the middle of a busy city, and it sometimes seems like few people actually look up to see Independence Hall as they hurry by on their way to work. Some Philadelphians may take their history for granted, but others recognize that it has defined and shaped what the city has become. They call this area the Most Historic Mile in America, and with good reason. These are the cobblestoned paths walked by Benjamin Franklin and Thomas Jefferson as they worked out the fine points of forming a democracy.

There are a number of ways you can explore this area, including organized tours by trolley, amphibious vehicle, or horse-drawn carriage, but you'll experience it most if you're on foot. There are audio tours that can enhance your visit.

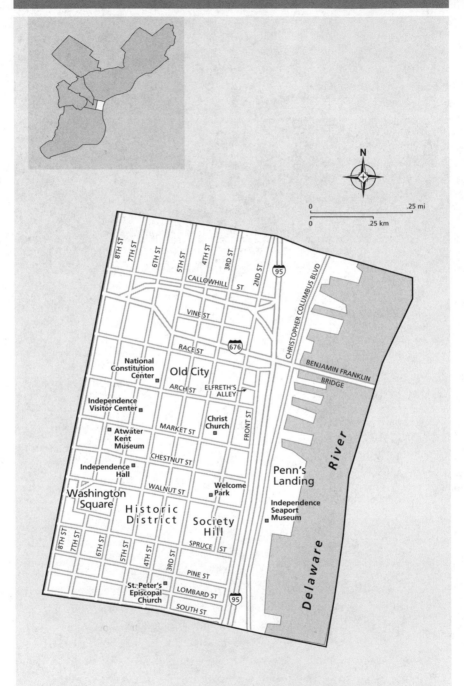

Take time to rest your feet on some of the thirteen storytelling benches scattered around the district. The area is easily accessible by public transportation or by the Phlash bus, and parking has improved significantly with the opening of the garages under the *National Constitution Center* and the *Independence Visitor Center* at Sixth and Market Streets. It makes sense to begin your tour here. In fact you have to if you want to see Independence Hall during peak times. Admission is free, but to get in you do need a timed ticket, which is available at the visitor center. You can get the tickets when you arrive or reserve them in advance by calling (800) 967–2283 or going to reservations .nps.gov. The new visitor center was the first part of the revitalization of Independence Mall. The staff has been impressively trained to answer virtually any question you could come up with about Philadelphia. You can plan an itinerary and they'll print it out for you. The visitor center also hosts rotating exhibits and you can see a thirty-minute introductory film. The visitor center is open from 8:30 A.M. to 6:00 P.M. during the summer and from 8:30 A.M. to 5:00 P.M. the rest of the year. Take advantage of the early opening to get a good start on your day. For more information call (215) 965–7676 or (800) 537–7676, or log on to www.independencevisitorcenter.com.

In today's world security restrictions are a sad reality, especially when you're dealing with symbols of America's freedom. Security requirements around the Liberty Bell and Independence Hall continue to evolve. For now, the security checkpoint for Independence Hall is in Old City Hall at Fifth and Chestnut Streets, and a separate security clearance is attached to the Liberty Bell Center. During peak times, the lines can back up at these checkpoints, so be sure to allow time when getting your tickets.

The *Liberty Bell Center,* which opened in 2003, is a huge improvement over the pavilion where the bell had hung since the nation's bicentennial in

AUTHOR'S FAVORITES IN HISTORIC DISTRICT AND OLD CITY

Atwater Kent Museum

Carpenter's Hall

Curtis Center mural

Franklin Court

La Locanda del Ghiottone

Old St. Joseph's Church

Pennsylvania Hospital surgical amphitheater

Philadelphia Contributionship

RiverLink Ferry to Camden attractions

St. Peter's Episcopal Church and graveyard

1976. The $12.6 million structure surrounds the bell in glass so visitors can see Independence Hall beyond, and greatly expanded exhibits help put the bell's symbolism in perspective. The project was slightly delayed by a controversy that had everything to do with liberty. The new complex is located at the southeast corner of Sixth and Chestnut Streets, which is the location of the house that served as the executive mansion for Presidents Washington and Adams during the 1790s, when Philadelphia was the nation's capital. Historians determined that the entrance to the new pavilion was precisely where Washington added slave quarters to the rear of the house. After protests that the issue of slavery should be more prominent in the planned facility, the park service agreed to include interpretive displays and exhibits on slavery.

theyhadn'tinvented spellcheck

"Pennsylvania" is spelled incorrectly on the Liberty Bell, where it appears as "Pensylvania." The founding fathers hadn't quite figured out how to spell the state's name yet; it's also misspelled on the original copy of the Constitution.

Cross Chestnut Street to get to *Independence Hall,* where park rangers lead comprehensive tours. Take time afterwards to wander around the park out back. Here the symmetry of the three buildings—Independence Hall, Congress Hall, and Old City Hall—is striking, as is the elegance of the spire, which some people don't know was actually added in an 1828 restoration. The west wing of Independence Hall is not part of the official tour, but you can go there to see an exhibit of the "real things": the final draft of the Constitution, a working copy of the Articles of Confederation, and the first printing of the Declaration of Independence.

TOP HITS IN HISTORIC DISTRICT AND OLD CITY

African American Museum	Liberty Bell Center
Betsy Ross House	National Constitution Center
Christ Church	National Museum of American Jewish History
City Tavern	
Elfreth's Alley	Penn's Landing
Independence Hall	Washington Square and Tomb of the Unknown Soldier

Just behind Old City Hall is *Philosophical Hall,* the only privately owned building on Independence Square. It is owned by the American Philosophical Society, an organization whose members have included some of the greatest minds of our time. Most of the building is not open to the public, but a first-floor exhibit hall features rotating displays from the society's archives, which include original journals from the Lewis and Clark expedition and Jefferson's handwritten copy of the Declaration of Independence. One bit of architectural trivia: The society added a third story to the building in 1890 to house its over-flowing library. Recognizing that the addition wasn't true to the building's archi-tectural style, the floor was removed in 1949 at a cost of about five times what it took to build it in the first place. The reconstructed *Library Hall* (105 South Fifth Street) across the street now houses the society's library. This building was originally built for the Library Company of Philadelphia, but it was torn down to make way for an office building. Seeing the error in this, the office building was

gonetothedogs

The basement of Independence Hall once served as the city's dog pound.

torn down in the 1950s, and Library Hall was rebuilt to its 1790 specifications. The library is primarily open for research purposes, but display cases in the lobby house original documents and manuscripts. The Philosophical Hall exhibits are open from 10:00 A.M. to 4:00 P.M. Thursday through Sunday from mid-February to Labor Day and the same hours Friday through Sunday from Labor Day through December. Call (215) 440–3400 or go to www.amphilsoc .org for more information.

With its strong Greek columns, the *Second Bank of the United States* is a hard building to miss. Modeled on the Parthenon, the building was designed by William Strickland in 1818 and served as a customs house until 1934. The Second Bank houses the park service's newly restored portrait gallery of Revolutionary heroes and colonial leaders. Many of the portraits were painted by Charles Willson Peale, the leading portraitist of the day. Admission is free, but hours vary by season, so it's best to check at the Inde-pendence Visitor Center.

Crossing Fourth Street you come to *Carpenter's Hall.* Tours stress the historic events that occurred inside the building, but it is worth noting that the building itself was originally built in the 1770s to house the Carpenters' Com-pany, a builders group that took advantage of its proximity to Independence Hall and rented out its space for the First Continental Congress. The company published a strictly guarded book of its articles and rules; even Thomas Jeffer-son, an amateur architect, was turned down when he requested a copy in 1817.

Carpenter's Hall

The Carpenter's Hall complex also includes the Military Museum at New Hall and a bookstore and gift shop in Pemberton House.

The history gets more personal as you head south on Fourth Street. At Walnut Street you come to the ***Todd House,*** built in 1775. Lawyer John Todd lived here with his wife, Dolley, who was to become far better known by marrying James Madison after Todd's death in the 1793 yellow fever epidemic. There's a charming eighteenth-century garden out back. Tours are available but must be arranged through the visitor center.

Continuing south you come to the fascinating yet long-winded ***Philadelphia Contributionship for the Insurance of Houses from Loss by Fire*** (212 South Fourth Street). Founded by Benjamin Franklin in 1752, this is the oldest fire insurance company in America. Since the beginning the company used the "hand-in-hand" symbol you see on the building's exterior. This firemark turns up on numerous buildings throughout historic Philadelphia. In the early days a firemark was a sign to firefighters that a building was insured, meaning they would be paid for putting out the flames. Inside you can see displays of old firefighting equipment and insurance policies. Open Monday through Friday from 10:00 A.M. to 3:00 P.M. Admission is free. Call (215) 627–1752 or visit www.contributionship.com.

Across the street down a tiny cobblestoned alley is ***Old St. Joseph's Church*** (321 Willing's Alley). This is a great off-the-beaten-path spot, and that's exactly the point. Wanting to maintain a low profile in Quaker Philadelphia, the oldest Catholic church in the city began in 1733 as a small chapel attached to the home of an English Jesuit. When time came to build a larger church in 1757, members still didn't want to call attention to themselves, so they chose a hidden location in the middle of a block. Philadelphia's Provincial Council wasn't too sure about these Catholics and set up an investigation, but because William Penn's original charter guaranteed religious freedom, the church was left in peace. A plaque in the charming interior courtyard pays tribute to Penn's vision. St. Joseph's remains an active Catholic parish. There's a Mass every day at noon, but visitors are invited to tour the church from about 1:00 to 4:00 P.M. Call (215) 923–1733 or visit www.oldstjoseph.org.

As you move into the heart of Society Hill, you pass another Catholic church, **Old St. Mary's** (252 South Fourth Street). Built thirty years after Old St. Joe's, this was the city's second Catholic church. Like St. Joe's, this church originally didn't want to call attention to itself. It was hidden by a row of houses until 1884, when the present brick facade was added. Visitors are welcome to explore the church and its historic graveyard Monday through Friday from 9:00 A.M. to 5:00 P.M. Sunday services are held at 9:00 and 10:30 A.M. Call (215) 923–7930.

Visitors usually assume that **Society Hill** got its name because this is where the upper crust lived. Not so. The name comes from the Free Society of Traders, a group of businessmen who invested in William Penn's new city. It's hard to believe as you walk the streets today, but just sixty years ago Society Hill was considered a slum. The houses were run down and commercial business was dying off. The push to revive Independence Park in the 1950s helped spur redevelopment here, and Society Hill is once again one of the city's most desirable areas.

You can see one of the finest residences in Society Hill at the **Physick House** (321 South Fourth Street). The Federal-style mansion was the home of Dr. Philip Syng Physick, who is said to be the father of surgery in America. He was one of the few doctors who stayed in the city to help treat the sick during the yellow fever epidemic. Tours of the house and its adjoining nineteenth-century garden are given on the hour Thursday through Saturday from 11:00 A.M. to 2:00 P.M. in the winter and from noon to 4:00 P.M. in the summer. Admission is $3.00 and reservations are recommended. Call (215) 925–7866.

An Important First

There is no shortage of historic churches in this part of Philadelphia. The **Mother Bethel African Methodist Episcopal (AME) Church** (419 South Sixth Street) sits on the oldest parcel of land continuously owned by African-Americans. Founded in 1797 by a former slave, the Reverend Richard Allen, this was the first AME church in the world and served as an important stop on the Underground Railroad. The first church building was a blacksmith's shop that Allen bought for $35 and had pulled to the site by a team of horses, an event recreated in a mural at the church. A basement crypt houses Allen's tomb and also displays historic artifacts from the church's history, including the original pulpit. Open from 10:00 A.M. to 3:00 P.M. Tuesday through Saturday and after services on Sundays. Call (215) 925–0616 or visit www.mother bethel.org for more information.

The Land of the Living

In laying out his city, William Penn and his planners followed the Quaker tradition of naming streets after living things, and in many cases they chose things that are native to Pennsylvania. In Center City, for example, it's trees. The large majority of east-west streets (except for Market) were named, and remain named, after trees: Chestnut, Walnut, Locust, Spruce, Pine, Cherry, and so forth. There are also species of flora, from Acorn Street to Verbena Avenue. Then there are animals, from Deer Lane to Sandpiper Place, and fish, from Bass Street to Salmon Street. And there are stones and minerals as well, from Agate Street to Rock Street. Penn didn't always get his way, however. He wanted the city's main east-west street to be called High Street. But that street was where all the marketing was done, and by 1750 it was known as Market Street.

If you have little ones, jog onto Delancey Street just past the Physick House, where you are sure to find a gaggle of strollers at one of the city's hidden oases known as **Three Bears Park** (Delancey between Third and Fourth Streets). The name refers to the beloved statue of—you guessed it—three lifelike bears, a favorite climbing spot for toddlers in the area. You'll frequently find the kids have used their sidewalk chalk to color in the bears' eyes and ears.

At Fourth and Pine Streets are two of the city's most historic churches. **Old Pine Presbyterian** (412 Pine Street) may not look very inviting with its stern wrought-iron fence, but you are welcome to wander around its atmospheric graveyard. David Rittenhouse, for whom Rittenhouse Square is named, is buried here, as is Eugene Ormandy, beloved musical director of the Philadelphia Orchestra from 1938 to 1980. During the Revolutionary War British troops used the church as a hospital, burning most of the interior on their way out. The striking Corinthian tiles weren't added until 1830. The church is open Monday through Friday from 10:00 A.M. to 5:00 P.M.; Sunday service is held at 10:30 A.M. (9:30 A.M. in the summer). Call (215) 925–8051 or go to www.oldpine.org.

Across Fourth Street you can go through the graveyard gate onto the grounds of **St. Peter's Episcopal Church** (313 Pine Street), where you're often incongruously met with the sounds of children playing at the church school next door. The Osage orange trees are descendants of seeds brought back by Lewis and Clark from their explorations of the Louisiana Purchase. St. Peter's opened in 1761 and has remained much the same since, except for the 1842 addition of the tower and spire. The church's interior is unusual because the altar is at one end and the pulpit is at the other. Note the high-backed pews: No. 41 is where George Washington sat when he worshipped here. The wooden angels flanking the organ were carved by William Rush. St. Peter's still houses an active parish. The church is open weekdays from 9:00 A.M. to 3:00 P.M. Guides are available to answer questions on Saturday from 11:00 A.M. to 3:00 P.M. and again on Sunday from 1:00 to 3:00 P.M. Services are held every Sunday at 9:00 and 11:00 A.M. Call (215) 925–5968 or visit www.stpetersphila.org.

Across from St. Peter's at Third and Pine Streets is one of the city's hidden historic sites; in fact, it may well be better known in Poland than it is in this country. Part of the U.S. Park Service, the **Kosciuszko National Memorial** honors the life of Thaddeus Kosciuszko. Born in Poland in 1746, Kosciuszko came to the colonies in 1776 and was one of the first foreign volunteers to join George Washington's cause. A military engineer, he was responsible for designing the Continental army's defenses in Philadelphia, West Point, and Saratoga. Thomas Jefferson called him "as pure a son of liberty as I have ever known," and Kosciuszko is also honored with a statue on the Benjamin Franklin Parkway. He returned to Poland in 1793 to help lead an uprising against the Russian czar, but he was imprisoned after being injured. After his release Kosciuszko returned to Philadelphia, where he lived in this double Georgian house during the winter of 1798. A bit of trivia: At just .02 of an acre, this is the smallest attraction in the National Park System. Hours vary, so call (215) 597–9618 or log on to www.nps.gov/thko for information.

Head now to Second and Pine, where you'll find **Head House Square** and a number of options for something to eat. Second Street was colonial Philadelphia's major north-south artery, and people put up sheds along the road to sell their wares. Head House was built in 1803 to give the marketers a place to gather: Butter and eggs were sold to the west side, meat under the overhang, vegetables to the east side, and those hawking fish were closest to the river. Now the street is lined with small shops, coffeehouses and restaurants, and one of the city's most tastefully designed drugstores. Craftspeople often spread out their wares under the shed on summer weekends.

For a fun break here, try the **Dark Horse** (421 South Second Street). The building dates from 1780 and is actually a rambling collection of four bars and a more upscale restaurant upstairs. The crowds gather on Saturday to watch rugby and English football televised from across the pond, and there's usually a dart game going on as well. The restaurant is more formal, and though the food is good, you'll have more fun and save some money if you order from the pub menu. The new owners have added standard American bar food—buffalo wings and bruschetta—but get into the English spirit and try the shepherd's pie or the bangers, creamy mashed potatoes topped with sausage. As an accompaniment, order a yard or a single malt from the bar. Open from 3:00 P.M. to 2:00 A.M. on Monday and from 11:30 A.M. to 2:00 A.M. Tuesday through Saturday. Open Sunday from 11:00 A.M. to 2:00 A.M. Call (215) 928–9307 or visit www.darkhorsepub.com. Moderate.

Back on Third Street, between Spruce and Locust, you can tour the *Powel House* (244 South Third Street) for a glimpse into the life of early Philadelphia's rich and powerful. Samuel Powel was the city's first mayor after the American Revolution, and he entertained often in this elegant home. The rooms are decorated in period furnishings and there's a formal eighteenth-century garden. Open Thursday through Saturday from noon to 5:00 P.M. and Sunday from 1:00 to 5:00 P.M.; tour reservations are recommended. Call (215) 627–0364.

At 308 Walnut Street is the *Polish American Cultural Center,* which houses a small museum highlighting Polish history, customs, and folk art. Open Monday through Friday from 10:00 A.M. to 4:00 P.M. from January through April and Monday through Saturday from 10:00 A.M. to 4:00 P.M. from May through December. There is no admission charge. Call (215) 922–1700 or visit www .polishamericancenter.org to find out more.

The *Bishop White House* (309 Walnut Street) was home to William White, rector of Christ Church and St. Peter's and chaplain of the Continental Congress. He chose this house because it was midway between the two churches he served. White became particularly beloved when he stayed in the city to minister to the ill and dying during the yellow fever epidemic of the 1790s. The home befits a respected citizen of the time, and it still contains many of his belongings. Particularly luxurious when the home was built in 1787 is the indoor commode. Tours of the house are given in conjunction with the Todd House down the street to contrast the differences between the upper and middle classes of the time. Free tickets are available at the visitor center. Call (215) 597–8974.

One of Philadelphia's most pleasant gardens adjoins the Bishop White House. Maintained by the Pennsylvania Horticultural Society, the corner garden illustrates many features of eighteenth-century formal gardens, from the arbors and gazebos to the geometric flower beds. The garden adjoins the *First Bank of the United States,* which was established so the government could pay off the debt from the Revolutionary War. Opposite Third Street is the park service's *Independence Living History Center,* which now occupies the old visitor center. Here you can observe archaeologists working to preserve some of the more than a million artifacts that were discovered during the construction of the National Constitution Center. Open daily from 9:00 A.M. to 5:00 P.M. During the summer, the center hosts interactive entertainment events in the evenings. For more information call (215) 965–7676.

I-95

The section of I-95 that travels through Philadelphia was one of the last links completed in the Florida-to-Maine highway. Completed in 1985, the highway took twenty-five years to complete in the Philadelphia area, largely because construction cut through crowded neighborhoods and skirted the historic district downtown. Many Philadelphians still rue the day that the superhighway cut off the city from its riverfront.

Turning the corner on Walnut, you come to the **Merchant's Exchange,** a striking Greek-Revival building designed by William Strickland in the early 1830s. This building is not open to the public. From the courtyard out front, you get a clear view of the **Society Hill Towers,** three huge apartment towers designed by I. M. Pei in the 1960s. The **Ritz 5** (214 Walnut Street) across the street is one of the city's premier venues for independent films.

Walk along the stone path paralleling the rear wall of the Custom's House to **City Tavern** (138 South Second Street). Though now largely a tourist trap, the tavern does have an interesting history as the social centerpiece of colonial Philadelphia. Washington and his cronies would gather here to eat, drink, and debate. Bishop White led the Philadelphia Dancing Assembly at the tavern, and Paul Revere came here to deliver the news that the British had closed Boston Harbor. The original building burned in 1854, so what you see is a faithful reconstruction, completed for the bicentennial in 1976. Diners today are offered an overpriced menu of early-American favorites, such as Martha Washington–Style Colonial Turkey Pot Pie. They swear the house ale is produced according to the exact formula preferred by Washington. Open from 11:30 A.M. to 10:00 P.M. daily, and reservations are recommended. Call (215) 413–1443 or visit www.citytavern.com. Expensive.

Across the street is **Welcome Park,** which serves as a logical approach to Penn's Landing and the riverfront. Named for William Penn's ship, The *Welcome,* the park is where Penn's house was located, now represented only by a small model. The park walls display a time line of Penn's life and accomplishments, and the statue of Penn in the middle is a miniature of the one that tops City Hall.

Walking by the Ritz East movie theater, you come to a park built over I-95. There are several walkways that cross the highway and take you to **Penn's Landing** (South, Spruce, Dock, Walnut, Chestnut, and Market Streets all have pedestrian access), though Philadelphians continue to grumble about how hard it is to get to the riverfront. If the city of Philadelphia has its way,

Worshipping on Water

Visitors to the Delaware riverfront in the mid-1800s must have done a double take, but that really was a floating church. The Floating Chapel of the Redeemer—steeple and everything—was built on a barge in 1849 to offer religious services to sailors. The church floated up and down the Delaware each Sunday, and even though it was moved to dry land after about thirty years, the organization remained known as the Seamen's Church Institute. It still operates today, serving the spiritual needs of overseas seamen while they're in Philadelphia.

you'll find construction going on when you visit Penn's Landing. Hope springs eternal that developers will finally figure out a way to make Philadelphia's waterfront a place where people want to be. It's not that there's nothing to do there, it's just that the area has never lived up to its potential, thanks in no small part to the decision long ago to construct a major interstate highway that cuts the riverfront off from the rest of the city. In the late 1960s the city began to renovate the dilapidated docks on the waterfront, plant trees, and fashion plans for turning the area into a recreation park. But that's pretty much where it stopped. City planners would love to see Penn's Landing renamed "Independence Harbor" and make it a major tourist destination, joining forces with the city of Camden, New Jersey, across the Delaware, which has successfully developed popular attractions on its riverfront. The latest plan calls for the construction of slot casinos north of the Benjamin Franklin Bridge. If you don't see bulldozers at work on the Philly side, it means the squabbling continues about what to put there and how to pay for it.

But don't let that stop you from exploring Penn's Landing as it exists, particularly the fascinating *Independence Seaport Museum* (211 South Columbus Boulevard), which tends to get lost in the shuffle of Philadelphia's more famous museums. Opened in 1995, the interactive museum is devoted to telling the story of Philadelphia's maritime history. Its central exhibit—Home Port: Philadelphia—details the role the city's river has played in commerce and trade, naval defense, shipbuilding, and immigration. You can try your hand at unloading cargo containers or ship welding or take a snooze on the hard bunks used by immigrants. The museum also displays thousands of artifacts, and hundreds of maps and ship plans are housed in the library. Open daily from 10:00 A.M. to 5:00 P.M. Admission is $9.00 for adults, $6.00 for children, and $8.00 for seniors, but you can get in free on Sunday mornings from 10:00 A.M. to noon. Call (215) 925–5439 or go to www.phillyseaport.org.

The city hopes someday to be connected to the Camden waterfront by an aerial tramway, but for now, the RiverLink Ferry is your best option to get across the river. The terminal for the **RiverLink Ferry** is next to the museum. The ferry operates daily from 9:00 A.M. to 6:30 P.M. between May and September and on weekends only during April and October, with boats leaving about every forty minutes. It's just a twelve-minute ride to the Camden waterfront, where you can visit the Adventure Aquarium, the Camden Children's Garden, the battleship *New Jersey,* and the Tweeter Entertainment Center, or take in a Camden Riversharks game in the new ball field, built in the shadow of the Ben Franklin Bridge. The fare is $6.00 for adults and $5.00 for seniors and children. There's also a River Taxi service that leaves from Spruce Street if you don't feel like waiting. Call (215) 925–LINK or go to www.riverlinkferry.org or www.camden waterfront.com.

Heading south past the Hyatt, you come to the **World Sculpture Garden,** which is dominated by an obelisk honoring Christopher Columbus. This is a favorite spot for picnickers. The marina at the end is home to the **USS Becuna** and the **USS Olympia.** Both are now part of the Seaport Museum, and admission is included with your museum ticket. Built in 1892, the *Olympia* was one of America's first steel ships and became the flagship of the country's fleet during the Spanish-American War's crucial battle at Manila Bay in 1898. It served as an escort ship in the Atlantic during World War I, and its final assignment, in 1921, was to carry the body of the Unknown Soldier from Europe to Arlington National Cemetery. Visitors to the ship today can see restored officers' cabins with surprisingly fine woodwork, the engine room below deck, and the ship's store, which is stocked as it was during WWI. Just a few feet away is the *Becuna,* a submarine commissioned in 1944 that was central to the Southwest Pacific Fleet under General MacArthur in World War II. The sub also served in the Atlantic and Mediterranean during the Korean and Vietnam Wars. Unless you're prone to claustrophobia, go on board. You can look around the torpedo room, the crew's sleeping berths and the much roomier officers' quarters, and

Cro$$ing to the Other Side

The Benjamin Franklin Bridge was built as a joint effort between Pennsylvania and New Jersey to handle the crowds expected for the sesquicentennial celebration in 1926. When it opened, the toll was 25 cents, over the objections of Philadelphians who wanted the crossing to be free. Today it will cost you $3.00 to get across, but you only pay coming into the city from New Jersey.

the control room. It's hard to believe the *Becuna* was once home to a crew of sixty-six. The ships are open daily from 10:00 A.M. to 4:30 P.M., (5:00 P.M. in the summer). Call (215) 413–8658 or log on to www.phillyseaport.org/historicships.

takeone

Oprah Winfrey's 1998 movie *Beloved,* based on the book by Toni Morrison, was filmed largely in Old City.

You'll save money and eat better if you find a restaurant in Old City, but for a riverfront dining experience, try the **Moshulu** (401 South Columbus Boulevard), the one-hundred-year-old, four-masted ship parked in the Penn's Landing Marina. Though once again entertaining visitors, the boat has had an unfortunate history in Philadelphia. In 1989 a fire gutted the interior, leading to an $11 million restoration, and in 2000 three people were killed when the dock at which the boat was moored collapsed. It reopened in its current location in 2003. That being said, the *Moshulu* is still a great place to eat. The ship was restored to an elegant turn-of-the-century restaurant, featuring a continental menu. Needless to say, seafood is a specialty. You can explore around the boat, and in warmer weather, they open the upper decks. Open daily for lunch from 11:30 A.M. to 3:00 P.M. and for dinner from 5:30 to 10:30 P.M. Sunday brunch is served from 11:00 A.M. to 3:00 P.M. Call (215) 923–2500 or visit www.moshulu.com. Expensive.

Retrace your steps heading north, and once you pass the Seaport Museum, you've come to the *Great Plaza,* the heart of the hopes for riverfront development. Currently you'll find a tiered amphitheater overlooking the Delaware River, site of many summertime music festivals (see Appendix: Annual Events). The area could use a pick-me-up, but it's still a safe bet that on any given weekend, you're likely to find some sort of entertainment going on here.

Time now to head back over I–95 via the Market Street Walkway to Old City. But before you leave the river, be sure to take in the *Benjamin Franklin Bridge.* Designed by architect Paul Philippe Cret, this was the longest suspension bridge in the world when it opened in 1926. You can walk over the bridge to Camden, and the bridge also carries commuter trains. The bridge is equipped with a computer-controlled lighting system that responds to the train, so at night, blinking lights follow the trains across the bridge.

The newest addition to the Penn's Landing area is the *Irish Memorial* (Front and Chestnut Streets), a 30-foot-long bronze monument by the sculptor Glenna Goodacre. Installed in 2003, the memorial depicts thirty-five life-size figures. It honors the million Irish people who died in the famine between 1845 and 1850 as well as the spirit of those who survived the harrowing journey across the ocean during the Great Migration to America. Find out more at www.irishmemorial.org.

On now to **Old City,** a neighborhood where history and hip intermingle. This area was the commercial center of colonial Philadelphia, a jumble of wharves, warehouses, taverns, and modest housing. Although the history remains, this area is now visited far more for its upscale restaurants, shops, and galleries than for what came before. The *National Geographic Traveler* article declaring Philadelphia the "next great city" called Old City "arguably the liveliest urban neighborhood between SoHo in New York and SoBe in Miami." Things get really lively here on what they call First Friday—5:00 to 9:00 P.M. on the first Friday of each month—when all the galleries open their doors and host receptions, and there's often live music added to the mix. The area is easily accessible by public transportation; both the El and New Jersey's PATCO commuter trains make stops here. Parking begins to open up a little, too.

There are so many restaurants and cool shops in Old City that you can pretty much take your pick. To get a feel for the neighborhood, head to the hottest block in Old City, Second Street between Market and Chestnut Streets, which is chock-full of hip restaurants and bars. Here you'll also find two of the mainstays of the Philly music scene—the indie rock club **Khyber** (56 South Second Street, www.thekhyber.com) and the acoustic-oriented **Tin Angel** (20 South Second Street, www.tinangel.com). A new addition to the block is **The Plough and the Stars** (123 Chestnut Street), a fine restaurant and Irish pub that happens to be in one of Old City's most beautiful buildings, the historic Corn Exchange Building. It's a perfect choice for lunch while you explore the historic district, with wonderful seasonal salads and traditional choices like shepherd's pie. Or you can just grab a pint and settle in by the fireplace on a cold winter's day. The dinner menu takes it up a notch, with such appetizer offerings as Goat Cheese Tartlet and mussels steamed in sherry, and entrees like rack of lamb and tasty seafood specials. The raised waffle station makes weekend brunches a hit. Brunch is served Saturday and Sunday from 9:30 A.M. to 3:30 P.M. Open for lunch weekdays from 11:45 A.M. to 2:30 P.M. and for dinner Monday through Thursday from 5:00 to 10:00 P.M., Friday and Saturday until 11:00 P.M. There's also live

Mum's the Word

One of Philadelphia's more unusual theater troupes is headquartered in Old City. The **Mum Puppettheatre** (115 Arch Street) has taken its unique puppet plays around the world, and its shows here in Philadelphia are a hit for adults and children alike. The annual production of *The Velveteen Rabbit* is a favorite for many families around the holidays. Phone (215) 925–7686 or visit www.mumpuppet.org.

traditional Irish music on Sundays from 4:00 P.M. to 8:00 P.M. You can bring your instrument and join the fun. For more information call (215) 733–0300 or visit www.ploughstars.com. Moderate.

Cross Market now on Second Street to get to **Christ Church.** Allow yourself to wander around the sanctuary and let the history seep in; these are pews where Washington, Jefferson, Franklin, and Betsy Ross worshipped. The font where William Penn was baptized was sent to the colonies from London, and the chandelier was brought from England in 1744. The pulpit was made by John Folwell in Philadelphia in 1770. The burial ground out back is a virtual Who's Who of the signers of the Declaration of Independence, including Benjamin Franklin, and, after being closed since the bicentennial, it is now open again for visitors. The church's 196-foot steeple was the first thing many immigrants saw as they approached Philadelphia after their long boat journey. Christ Church was declared a national shrine in 1950 and remains an active parish to this day. Open daily from 10:00 A.M. to 4:00 P.M. Services are held Sunday at 9:00 and 11:00 A.M. Call (215) 922–1695 or visit www.christchurchphila.org.

Just north of Christ Church is the **Arden Theatre** (40 North Second Street), one of the city's top regional theaters and one of several theater venues in Old City. The theater puts on five main-stage productions each year, helps develop and stage at least one new play a year, and runs an active children's theater program. Call (215) 922–1122 or visit www.ardentheatre.org.

The streets now become more characteristic of Old City—a mix of chic boutiques, galleries, and old-time restaurant supply stores; upscale restaurants next to old neighborhood pizza joints; and a dash of history thrown in here and there.

Just past the Arden you'll find the **Muse Gallery** (60 North Second Street), one of Old City's most respected galleries and one that originally served as the first cooperative for women artists in the city. Its members stage monthly shows in a variety of media. Open Wednesday through Sunday from noon to 5:00 P.M. Call (215) 627–5310 or visit www.musegalleryphiladelphia.com.

After you cross Arch Street, you'll come to **Elfreth's Alley,** which is pretty off the beaten path for being so well known. The words "oldest continuously inhabited street in America" roll off the tongues of local tour guides. The thirty-two homes here are charming, none more than 16 feet wide, and they do make it possible to imagine what it would have been like to live here in colonial days. Named for Jeremiah Elfreth, a land speculator who built and rented out many of the local homes, the street dates to 1702, when a blacksmith and other Colonial artisans settled there. They say Benjamin Franklin once lived here, but no one quite knows which house. The residents of Elfreth's Alley belong to an association that sponsors several events each year that open the homes to the public. During "Fete Days" each spring, there are house tours, craft demon-strations, and storytelling. The association is based at the ***Mantua Maker's Museum House*** (126 Elfreth's Alley), where you can see small exhibits and period rooms. The houses also put up colonial Christmas decorations each December. Don't miss the small cobblestoned pathway halfway down the alley that leads to Bladen's Court, a circular courtyard shared by several of the houses. The museum is open Monday through Saturday from 10:00 A.M. to 5:00 P.M., and from noon to 5:00 P.M. on Sunday from March through October, and from 10:00 A.M. to 5:00 P.M. Thursday through Saturday and noon to 5:00 P.M. Sunday from November through February. Suggested admission is $2.00 for adults, $1.00 for children six to eighteen, and free for children under six. Call (215) 574–0560 or go to www.elfrethsalley.org.

Ping-ponging between history and modern culture, you come next to the ***Clay Studio*** (139 North Second Street), a thirty-year-old educational arts organ-ization devoted to the ceramic arts. The gallery hosts a number of exhibits each year and offers classes, artist-in-residency programs, and outreach programs for schools. It's hard not to get enthused about the entryway, which was created by local mosaic artist Isaiah Zagar. Another major example of his work can be seen farther down the street at the Painted Bride Art Center (230 Vine Street), where the exterior is one huge mosaic. The gallery at the Clay Studio is open Tuesday through Sunday from noon to 6:00 P.M. A gift shop sells original cre- · ations. Call (215) 925–3453 or visit www.theclaystudio.org.

Two doors down, you come to the ***Fireman's Hall Museum*** (147 North Second Street), a restored turn-of-the-century firehouse that displays all sorts of firefighting memorabilia. There's a hand pump used by Ben Franklin, nineteenth-century fire wagons, leather water buckets, and displays on early fire horses. This is a must for every little boy who swears he wants to be a fireman when he grows up. The museum is open Tuesday through Saturday from 9:00 A.M. to 5:00 P.M. and stays open until 9:00 P.M. on First Friday. There is no admission, but donations are appreciated. Call (215) 923–1438.

Head now to Third and Race Streets. Here you have a choice. If your legs are tired, take a left and head back toward Market Street. If you still have energy, there are a few historic churches to see if you continue 1 block farther into Old City. On Fourth Street head right toward the underbelly of the Ben-jamin Franklin Bridge to ***Old St. George's Methodist Church*** (235 North Fourth Street), known as "The Cradle of American Methodism." The site of fanatic religious revival meetings in the early 1770s, the church complex now includes a historical society and a small museum, which features furniture, silver, and memorabilia from its past. St. George's was originally on the list of buildings that needed to be demolished to make way for the Benjamin Franklin Bridge.

However, angry protests convinced the designers to move the bridge slightly southward, where it misses the church by just 14 feet. Open daily from 10:00 A.M. to 3:00 P.M. Worship services are held Sunday at 11:00 A.M. Call (215) 925–7788.

Just across the street is **St. Augustine's Catholic Church** (Fourth and Vine Streets). The original church on this site was built in 1798 to serve the German and Irish Catholics who couldn't get to St. Joseph's. That building was destroyed in anti-Catholic riots in 1844. Rebuilt in 1847, this church was in the news in 1992, when a vicious storm blew the steeple onto the Benjamin Franklin Bridge, closing the bridge for three days and exposing many of the church's paintings and murals to water damage. Call (215) 627–1838 or go to www.st-augustinechurch.com.

At Fifth and Vine Streets, you'll find the **Wood Turning Center** (501 Vine Street), which houses a permanent collection as well as changing exhibits emphasizing woodworking as an art form. Now recognized internationally, the center also produces traveling exhibits. Its adjacent store sells a wide variety of wood gift items, from jewelry to boxes and bowls. Open Tuesday through Friday from 10:00 A.M. to 5:00 P.M. and Saturday from noon to 5:00 P.M. Call (215) 923–8000 or visit www.woodturningcenter.org to learn more.

At Third and Arch Streets you come to a block with some fun shops and a great place for dinner. Another of Old City's finest art spots is here. **The Wexler Gallery** (201 North Third Street) is an elegant, large space that highlights a wide spectrum of contemporary decorative arts, from furniture to jewelry. The gallery hosts bimonthly exhibitions of local and nationally known artists. For current exhibits call (215) 923–7030 or visit www.wexlergallery.com.

Indigo Arts (151 North Third Street) bills itself as a store and a gallery, and it is filled to the brim with objects from Asia, Africa, and South America. You're sure to find something with character and lots of color. The gallery upstairs houses regularly changing exhibitions of international folk and contemporary art. Open Monday through Saturday from 11:00 A.M. to 6:30 P.M. and Sunday from noon to 6:00 P.M.; open until 9:30 P.M. on First Friday. Call (215) 922–4041 or visit www.indigoarts.com.

You're probably not in Philadelphia hoping to buy furniture, but it's still worth stepping into **Flotsam + Jetsam** (149 North Third Street), a wildly decorated store that sells new and reconditioned furniture and crafts. Many of the items are created by local designers. Products can be quite pricey, but it's still fun to look. Open Tuesday through Friday and Sunday from noon to 6:00 P.M.; Saturday hours are 11:00 A.M. to 7:00 P.M. Call (215) 351–9914 or go to www.flotjet.com.

At Third and Cherry Streets you'll find a wonderful place to have dinner. *La Locanda del Ghiottone* (130 North Third Street) has survived the death several years ago of its beloved chef, Giuseppe Rosselli, a legend in the neighborhood who rebuilt his restaurant after a fire and billed it as "the only authentic Italian restaurant in the USA." Maybe that's a slight exaggeration, but it's a great place just the same. Locanda has atmosphere to spare, and come hungry—the name translates to "the place of the gluttons." It's a BYOB; the staff will open your bottle so you can have a glass of wine while you wait, which you will almost certainly have to do. Start with crepes stuffed with wild mushrooms or the mussels. An outstanding first course is the black fettuccini with fresh tuna, olives, and tomatoes. Second courses are heavier and include chicken, lamb, and beef offerings. Regulars swear by the osso buco, and even the rabbit stew is a favorite here. For dessert you can't beat the tiramisu. Two hitches: Locanda doesn't take reservations and it accepts only cash. Even so, it's worth it. Open Tuesday through Sunday from 5:00 to 11:00 P.M. Call (215) 829–1465. Moderate.

trivia

The Post Office on Market Street is the only active post office in the country that does not fly the U.S. flag. It hadn't yet been created in 1775.

A few doors down you come to *Fosters Urban Homeware* (124 North Third Street), one of those stores that's ready-made for browsing. It stocks lots of trendy kitchen and bath items; be sure to check out the fun toys and pet products in the back. Open Monday through Saturday from 10:00 A.M. to 8:00 P.M. and Sunday from noon to 5:00 P.M. Call (267) 671–0588 or go to www.shopfosters.com.

At Arch Street it's time to step back into history again. Make a quick left to the *Betsy Ross House* (239 Arch Street), which remains one of Philadelphia's most popular tourist attractions. Built in 1740, the house is charming, and plaques written from Ross's point of view. Though most people know the story of the making of the first flag, it is interesting to learn more about her. The eighth child of seventeen in a devout Quaker family, Ross was completely cut off from both her family and her religion when she married an Episcopalian man. John Ross was killed in an explosion just three years after they were married, and Betsy ultimately married three times. A committee from the Continental Congress, of which George Washington was a member, met with Ross in her house and chose her to make the first Stars and Stripes. Legend has it that after examining a sketch with six-pointed stars, she suggested that five-pointed stars would be more attractive. Open seven days a week during the summer from 10:00 A.M. to 5:00 P.M.; Tuesday through Sunday from 10:00 A.M.

to 5:00 P.M. October to March. Admission is $3.00 for adults and $2.00 for children. Call (215) 686–1252 or visit www.betsyrosshouse.org.

Right next to the Betsy Ross House is a building that will look familiar to the MTV crowd. It's a former bank building and headquarters of the Seaman's Church Institute, which served as home base for the Philadelphia cast of the network's *Real World* reality series in 2004. The building received $3 million worth of sprucing up for the show, including an atrium and hot tub, all closely observed by forty-two cameras mounted inside.

Heading north on Arch Street, you'll find the **Arch Street Friends Meeting House** between Third and Fourth Streets. Built in 1804, this simple brick building is still the largest Quaker meetinghouse in the country. Like all meetinghouses, this space is completely unadorned, which is very unlike the other religious buildings in the historic district. Rows of plain wooden pews face the center of the room. There is no pulpit, the floor is plain and the windows have no stained glass. Quaker worship services are conducted by the congregation as a whole, with no formal structure, and are often filled mostly with silence. Quakers believe that the light of God is in each and every person; thus anyone who feels moved to do so can stand up and speak during meeting. It is this belief in equality that led the Quakers to the forefront of the abolitionist and women's suffrage movements. Meeting is still held here twice a week, Sunday at 10:30 A.M. and Wednesday (what the Quakers refer to as Fourth Day) at 7:00 P.M. Visitors are welcome. The building is open from 10:00 A.M. to 4:00 P.M. Monday through Saturday. Call (215) 627–2667 or log on to www.archstreet friends.org.

If you're hungry, head back to Market and check out **Fork** (306 Market Street), one of the best restaurants in the city and an outstanding choice for Sunday brunch. The food manages to be creative and homespun at the same time, and the prices are surprisingly reasonable. The menu changes with the season. For a different dessert, try a bowl of coffee walnuts. If you go for the brunch, you've got to try the grits. Open Monday through Thursday from 11:30 A.M. to 10:30 P.M., Friday from 11:30 A.M. to 11:30 P.M., Saturday from 5:00 to 11:30 P.M., and Sunday from 11:00 A.M. to 10:30 P.M. A late-night bar menu is available on Thursday from 10:30 P.M. to midnight and on Friday and Saturday from 11:30 P.M. until 1:00 A.M. Fork is not large, so you'd be smart to call (215) 625–9425 for reservations or log on to www.forkrestaurant.com. Moderate.

A few doors up Market Street, look for the **Post Office** (316 Market Street). You may think it's a tourist trap, based on the fact that Ben Franklin was the first Postmaster General. But this is a working office of the U.S. Postal Service, and Franklin's postmark—B. Free Franklin—is still used to cancel postage.

Crossing through the archway next to the Post Office brings you to *Franklin Court,* not the easiest museum to find in the historic district, but one of the most creative. Located between two alleys off Market and Chestnut Streets, Franklin's original home is unfortunately long gone, and there are no accurate records about what the house actually looked like. The "ghost house" you see was created by Philadelphia architect Robert Venturi for the 1976 bicentennial. You can peek down and see part of the original foundation, the house's well, and even the privy pit. But most of the museum is underground, where you'll find artifacts and exhibits galore on Franklin and his inventions. There's also a brief film on Franklin's life and a phone bank where you can hear how other famous Americans described Philadelphia's most famous citizen. Several other small buildings on Market provide a close look at his printing career and a fascinating explanation of Franklin's interest in how to make buildings fire-resistant. Open daily from 9:00 A.M. to 5:00 P.M. Admission is free. Call (215) 597–8974 or visit www.nps.gov/inde/Franklin_Court.

If you need a break from history and are one of those people who fondly remembers high school chemistry, drop into the *Chemical Heritage Foundation* (315 Chestnut Street). Located in the historic First Bank building, this little-known organization spotlights artifacts, artwork, and books that trace the history of chemistry and molecular science from the days of alchemy. In addition to publishing its own manuscripts, the foundation has a growing collection of historic and rare books, including a copy of *De Re Metallica,* by Georgii Agricola, which dates to 1561. Rotating exhibits are on display in the foundation's galleries, which are open from 10:00 A.M. to 4:00 P.M. Monday through Friday. Admission is free. For more information call (215) 925–2222 or visit www.chemheritage.org.

You come now to one of the city's newest museums. The *National Liberty Museum* (321 Chestnut Street) can seem a little tough to figure out at first, but it's all about the concept of freedom. Dozens of exhibits and more than

The Mint's Mascot

The flying eagle inside the entrance to the U.S. Mint has nothing to do with our nation's symbol. It's more of a tribute to a pet. Apparently, an eagle nicknamed Peter took up residence inside the Mint in the early 1800s. The bird became a favorite character in the Philadelphia skies, and when Peter passed away, his carcass was lovingly preserved and put on display.

one hundred works of art illustrate the struggle for freedom. From profiles of people who have fought the good fight to a room where children can feed hateful words into a paper shredder, the museum strives to offer alternatives to violence and bigotry. The museum is built around a 20-foot-tall, red glass sculpture by artist Dale Chihuly. Open daily from 10:00 A.M. to 5:00 P.M. during the summer; closed Monday the rest of the year. Admission is $5.00 for adults, $4.00 for seniors, and $3.00 for children. Call (215) 925–2800 or visit www.libertymuseum.org.

Next door to the Liberty Museum is a restaurant that's managed to stay on the city's "hot spot" list for years. ***Buddakan*** (325 Chestnut Street) is one of Stephen Starr's restaurants, which give diners an experience to remember as well as great food. Walking in you are greeted by a 10-foot-high Buddha and a wall of water. There are those who say the prices are way too high for what you get, so this could be the perfect place to have a drink before eating dinner someplace else. If you do stay, foodies rave about the wasabi-crusted filet mignon and the fish of the day, which comes coated in a sweet, black bean–chili sauce. Desserts are something to behold as well. Open for lunch Monday through Friday from 11:30 A.M. to 2:30 P.M.; dinner is served Sunday through Thursday from 5:00 to 11:00 P.M. and Friday and Saturday from 5:00 P.M. to midnight. Reservations are a must. Call (215) 574–9440 or go to www.buddakan.com. Expensive.

If you want to eat something simpler and far more reasonably priced, head for the ***Bourse*** (111 South Independence Mall East), which you can also enter off of Fourth Street at Ranstead. This is the place to go if you want a quick bite to eat or to find that Philadelphia souvenir. The building was state of the art when it was built in the late 1800s to serve as the business center for Philadelphia. Natural light streams in from a skylight three stories above the great hall, where there are tables surrounded by a number of fast-food options. When the building underwent a $20 million renovation in the early 1980s, the hope was that the Bourse would attract high-end shops. That didn't pan out, but there's a place in every city for a place like the Bourse—fast, cheap food; T-shirts; and souvenirs galore. Open year-round Monday through Saturday from 10:00 A.M. to 6:00 P.M.; from March through November also open on Sunday from 11:00 A.M. to 5:00 P.M. Call (215) 625–0300 or visit www.bourse-pa.com.

As you come out the front entrance, you are once again facing Independence Mall. Head back across Market Street to the ***National Museum of American Jewish History*** (55 North Fifth Street). Depending on when you're visiting, this may or may not still be there. The museum is in the process of raising $100 million to build a new facility on the southeast corner

Famous Feet

If your feet start to hurt from walking around the historic district, you'll feel better after a visit to the bizarre **Shoe Museum** at the Temple University School of Podiatric Medicine (Eighth and Race Streets). Tucked away on the sixth floor of the building, the museum displays hundreds of shoes, everything from burial sandals to Eskimo snowshoes. Some of the shoes look like torture devices, such as the tiny, so-called "lily shoes" some Chinese women were forced to wear to bind their feet and stunt their growth. Numerous celebrities, presidents, and sports stars have also donated their shoes to the museum. Admission is free but you've got to call ahead. Call (215) 625–5243.

of Fifth and Market Streets, which it hopes to occupy in the fall of 2009. Sidney Kimmel, the philanthropist for whom the Kimmel Center is named, got the fund-raising ball rolling with a $25 million contribution. The museum's collection focuses on the Jewish experience in America and highlights the contributions of the Jewish people in the growth of the country and in its cultural and political development. Open Monday through Thursday from 10:00 A.M. to 5:00 P.M., Friday from 10:00 A.M. to 3:00 P.M., and Sunday from noon to 5:00 P.M.; closed Saturday and major Jewish holidays. Admission is $4.00 for adults and $3.00 for seniors and children. Call (215) 923–3811 or go to www .nmajh.org.

As you continue north toward Arch Street, you pass the brick wall of the **Christ Church Burial Ground.** You can't enter the church from here, but those people you see peeking into the graveyard just south of Arch are looking at Benjamin Franklin's grave, which can be seen through the grating (as can that of Mrs. Franklin, who tends to get lost in the shuffle). There's no doubt someone will be pitching a penny onto the grave for good luck. (The church earns about $750 a year from people *not* saving their pennies.) When Franklin died in 1790, more than 20,000 Philadelphians escorted his cortege here.

Crossing over Arch, you come to the **United States Mint** (151 North Independence Mall East). The Mint has once more opened its doors for tours, after several years of a closed-to-the-public policy following the September 11th terrorist attacks. It's good to have the Mint back in the circuit, because you don't get many opportunities to watch money being made. A self-guided tour takes you along a gallery that overlooks the entire process, as huge presses pump out hundreds of coins per minute. In any given year, the Mint produces, for example, 1,443,600,000 quarters. It's fun just to imagine running your fingers through

Can You Say "Gross Gibbet"?

If you're visiting the Atwater Kent Museum, don't miss its most macabre artifact. It has the only complete gibbet in the country. A gibbet was a human form made of iron bands and was used to display the bodies of criminals executed for particularly heinous crimes. Bodies were sometimes left in a gibbet for weeks, a particularly effective deterrent to others considering a life of crime.

one of the huge bins full of coins. There's also a museum with cases of historic medals and coins, and a lobby mural with Tiffany mosaics that tell the story of how coins were made in ancient times. The mint is open for tours Monday through Friday from 9:00 A.M. to 3:00 P.M. Call (215) 408–0114 or log on to www.usmint.gov.

Catercorner to the Mint at Fifth and Arch Streets is the *Free Quaker Meeting House,* built in 1783 to house a splinter group of Quakers that broke away during the Revolutionary War. Because Quakers abide by the tenet of pacifism, they will not swear oaths or take part in armed conflicts. About 200 Free Quakers—or "Fighting Quakers"—were forced to leave the Arch Street meeting down the street because they were willing to fight during the Revolutionary War. Betsy Ross was a member here. The building is now maintained by the U.S. Park Service and is open to the public during the summer. There is no admission charge.

Across the street is the *National Constitution Center* (525 Arch Street), a museum whose mission is to increase awareness and understanding of the U.S. Constitution. Opened on July 4, 2003, the center features interactive displays and exhibits, above which the full text of the Constitution, the Bill of Rights, and the Constitution's amendments are etched in illuminated glass. It has a little show business, too—a live multimedia show in a star-shaped theater incorporating film, live actors, and a 360-degree video projection screen. You can also see life-size bronze statues of the thirty-nine men who signed the Constitution, as well as three who dissented (George Mason from Virginia, Elbridge Jerry from Massachusetts, and Edmund Randolph from Virginia, in case you are curious). The facility includes a restaurant that overlooks Independence Mall. Open weekdays from 9:30 A.M. to 5:00 P.M., and until 6:00 P.M. on Saturday. Admission is $9.00 for adults and $7.00 for children and seniors. Call (215) 409–6600 or (866) 917–1787 (get it? It's the day the Constitution was signed.) or visit www.constitutioncenter.org.

Heading west, duck into the lobby of the **Federal Reserve** (100 North Sixth Street) for an interactive exhibit entitled Money in Motion. They've done their best to make the country's money system interesting, with videos and displays that show exactly how it all works. You can find out how to tell if a bill is counterfeit or play a money game called "Match Wits with Ben." It's hard not to sigh when you see the tower of money—$100 million of shredded bills. And visitors don't leave empty handed—you get your own bag holding $100, shredded as well, unfortunately. Open Monday through Friday from 9:30 A.M. to 4:30 P.M., except in January and February, when it's open from 10:00 A.M. to 2:00 P.M. To find out more call (215) 574–6257 or visit www.phil.frb.org.

Summer 2006 saw the opening of the renovated **Franklin Square** (Sixth and Race Streets), at the foot of the Ben Franklin Bridge and across the street from the Philadelphia Police Department headquarters. One of Philadelphia's original squares, this public space had been all but forgotten and was in poor condition. Then along came the cleaning crews of the nonprofit Once Upon a Nation, and the square has new life, with a Liberty Carousel, Philly-themed miniature golf, two playground areas, storytellers, and a renovated Franklin Square Fountain.

One block west on Arch you come to the **African American Museum** (701 Arch Street). Founded in 1976 for the bicentennial, this museum highlights African-American history and culture in Pennsylvania. The site of the museum itself was once part of a historic black community. The emphasis is on African-American contributions since the beginning of the twentieth century, particularly in fine arts and photography. An affiliate of the Smithsonian, the museum's exhibits are drawn from its collection of 450,000 objects. It also hosts a jazz series each summer. Open Tuesday through Saturday from 10:00 A.M. to 5:00 P.M. and Sunday from noon to 5:00 P.M. Admission is $8.00 for adults and $6.00 for children and seniors. Call (215) 574–0380 or go to www .aampmuseum.org.

An Honored Tree

While wandering Washington Square, keep your eyes open for a monument honoring the Treaty Elm, which was memorialized in Benjamin West's famous painting. It was on this spot in 1682 that William Penn signed a treaty with the Indians, though historians have since pointed out that many details of this event likely came entirely from West's imagination. Still, the legend makes for a better story. So feel free to imagine Penn and a group of Indians making solemn promises of mutual friendship under the elm's graceful branches.

Flights of Fancy

Washington Square is home to a sycamore tree born of a seed that was carried to the moon by astronaut Stuart Roosa on *Apollo XIV.* Planted for the bicentennial, the so-called "moon tree" grows near where the first "spaceflight" in America occurred. It was on January 9, 1793, that Frenchman Jean Blanchard lifted off in a balloon from Washington Square and floated across the Delaware River, landing near Gloucester, New Jersey. George Washington was on hand for the event.

As you head back to Market Street, you'll pass the **Lit Brothers Building.** The city almost tore this beauty down in the 1980s, but clearer heads prevailed and its cast-iron facade was restored. The former store now houses shops and offices. At the corner of Seventh and Market Streets, Philadelphia's past and present come crashing together. Across the street from a hulking parking garage and a Dunkin' Donuts and next to a large, urban clothing store stands a re-creation of the 1775 **Jacob Graff House** (Seventh and Market Streets), the place where Thomas Jefferson wrote the Declaration of Independence. Charged with writing a declaration to make the case for breaking ties with England, Jefferson, then thirty-three, retreated from the crowded city to the home of bricklayer Jacob Graff. Graff had built his house the year before on the outskirts of town, where his home was surrounded by fields and open space. It was here Jefferson cranked out the Declaration of Independence in just over two weeks. In 1883 the Graff house was torn down and went the way of many of the city's other historic buildings. But in honor of the bicentennial in 1976, the National Park Service used photographs of the original site to carefully reconstruct the structure. The house includes re-creations of the two rooms Jefferson rented on the second floor. Hours vary. For more information call (215) 965–2305 or visit www.nps.gov/inde.

Across Seventh Street is one of Philadelphia's small museum treasures, the **Atwater Kent** (15 South Seventh Street), which tells the story of Philadelphia's history. There are major artifacts here—the wampum belt the Lenni-Lenape Indians gave William Penn in 1682 and some of Benjamin Franklin's personal belongings—but perhaps more interesting are the common household items used by early Philadelphians. You can see undergarments, toys, and even a cockroach trap from the eighteenth century. In the museum's permanent exhibit Experience Philadelphia, visitors walk on a 40-by-40-foot map of the region, the largest map ever made by Rand McNally. Finished in 1827, this building was the original home of the Franklin Institute, now firmly settled in much larger digs on the Benjamin Franklin Parkway. When the institute moved out, the building was almost torn down, but it was saved by A. Atwater Kent, a pioneering radio manufacturer. The museum also houses a collection of Norman Rockwell's work, including all 321 covers he created for *The Saturday Evening Post.* Open Wednesday through Sunday from 1:00 P.M. to 5:00 P.M., though group tours are available at other times. Admission is $5.00 for adults and $3.00 for teens and seniors. Children under twelve are free. Call (215) 685–4830 or visit www.philadelphiahistory.org.

When you've just got to have comfort food, ***Jones*** (700 Chestnut Street) is the place to go. This former stationery store has been gussied up beyond recognition, but the food is as simple—and in most cases as delicious—as mom used to make. Here you can get macaroni and cheese, tomato soup, and grilled cheese. For something a little more adventurous, try the chicken and waffles, a favorite from coal country in central Pennsylvania. On a cold fall day, you can sit by the fireplace in the middle and order a complete Thanksgiving dinner—all for just $12. Need dessert? How about a piece of chocolate cake and a glass of cold milk? Open Monday through Friday from 11:30 A.M. to midnight (1:00 A.M. on Friday night). On the weekends brunch is served from 10:30 A.M. to 3:00 P.M. Jones is open for dinner from 5:00 P.M. to 1:00 A.M. on Saturday and from 4:00 to 11:00 P.M. on Sunday. Call (215) 223–5663 or visit www.jones-restaurant.com—it's a great Web site. Moderate.

Across the street from Jones is one of the most impressive projects of the city's Mural Arts Program. The ***Lincoln Legacy Mural*** (707 Chestnut Street), a short distance from Independence Hall, honors Abraham Lincoln where he spoke in 1861 on the way to his inauguration. Made of 750,000 Venetian-glass tiles, the mural was assembled in 2005 largely by students from five Philadelphia schools, under the careful guidance of muralist Joshua Sarantitis.

At Seventh and Sansom, you come to ***Jewelers Row,*** the oldest diamond district in the country and second only to New York in size. Unless you're shopping for gems, there's not much to see, but if you are, you've arrived at the right place. There are more than 150 jewelry stores in this compact area.

Cross Seventh Street here and duck into the ***Curtis Center*** (601 Walnut Street), now an office building, but the one-time home of the Curtis Publishing Company and such titles as *The Saturday Evening Post, The Ladies Home Journal,* and *Jack and Jill.* The building itself is a beaux arts beauty, but what's really worth seeing is inside. Cross the marbled atrium, taking in its terraced waterfall, and head to the lobby that fronts Sixth Street. There you will find an extraordinary work of art, made more extraordinary due to its corporate setting. A mosaic re-creation of *The Dream Garden* by Maxfield Parrish, 15 feet high and almost 50 feet long, fills the space. Created by the Tiffany Studios in 1916, this mural contains more than 100,000 pieces of hand-fired glass in colors fired especially to match Parrish's painting. The city gave a collective gasp in 1998 when descendants of the Curtis family sold the mosaic to casino owner Steve Wynn, who planned to move it to Las Vegas. The day was saved by the Pew Charitable Trusts, which gave the Pennsylvania Academy of Fine Arts $3.5 million to purchase Dream Garden and keep it right where it has always been.

Exiting onto Sixth Street, you're back at Independence Hall. But wait, there's still more to see here. Turn right into **Washington Square,** one of William Penn's original squares that has recently been spruced up to the tune of $4 million. Though this square lacks the energy of Rittenhouse Square, its history is far more notable. Shortly after Penn laid out his city plan, Washington Square began to be used as a burial ground for the unknown. During the Revolutionary War, workers dug 20-by-30-foot pits and piled the dead on top of each other. When the British occupied Philadelphia, they used the Walnut Street Jail that faced the square to hold prisoners of war, and the horrible conditions there caused many deaths. Understandably, the square was not a pleasant place to be for many years. Things started to change in 1815, when the city planted trees and tried to make the square more pleasant. It was renamed in honor of George Washington in 1825 and became the center of the city's thriving publishing industry. The **Tomb of the Unknown Soldier** from the Revolutionary War dominates the center of the square.

There are several buildings of special interest on the square. The Penn Mutual building at Sixth and Walnut was built on the site of the Walnut Street Jail. Next door is the **Athenaeum** (219 South Sixth Street), a private library that in colonial days attracted the city's brightest minds. The building is also architecturally significant. Built in 1845 by architect John Notman, it was the first Italianate building in America. It currently serves as headquarters for the Victorian Society of America, whose archives contain a large collection of Victorian interior designs. The Athenaeum continues to draw thousands of visitors each year. You are welcome to look at the galleries on the first floor; the research library is open to scholars for research purposes, but you have to arrange a visit ahead of time. Call (215) 925–2688 or log on to www.philaathenaeum.org.

It's worth a close look at the colonial-looking house tucked in between the Athenaeum and the Lippincott Publishing building, assuming it's still there. It's a complete fake, built by then-mayor Richardson Dilworth in 1957 in an effort to maintain the historic character of the square. The building at the southeast corner of the square once housed Lea & Febiger, the oldest publishing house in the country. It's now home to the **Locks Gallery** (600 Washington Square South), which specializes in contemporary art. Call (215) 629–1000 or go to www.locks gallery.com. The townhouses surrounding the square's southwest corner—one of which belonged to writer Christopher Morley—give a sense of Philadelphia's more elegant nineteenth century.

You'll leave Washington Square on Locust Street, next to the building housing the **Farm Journal,** which was founded in 1827 and has been published from this building since 1912. Today it's the largest farming magazine in the country, though when it was founded it was aimed at "farmers living within a day's buggy ride of Philadelphia." Note the bountiful cornucopia overhanging the door. Before you go, take a look at the other buildings facing the park on the west. The W. B. Saunders Publishing Company was built in 1910. The art deco building next to it was designed by Ralph Bencker for N. W. Ayer & Son, the country's oldest advertising company; the building now houses a Stephen Starr restaurant, aptly named Washington Square. On the corner of Seventh and Walnut is a beauty of an Italianate bank building that sat vacant for years and was finally renovated and incorporated into a luxury apartment building.

If you're looking for someplace to eat, your best bet is **Ristorante La Buca** (711 Locust Street), whose name translates to "cave" and refers to its location down a long flight of brick stairs. Despite the basement location, the space is cheery, with walls decorated with bold Italian frescoes and other Florentine touches, including olive oil carafes that are replicas of the Leaning Tower of Pisa on each table. Chef Giuseppi Giulini hails from Tuscany, which is reflected in the menu. To start try the lobster cannelloni or the pasta crepes stuffed with spinach and cheese. La Buca is known for its seafood, and you can't go wrong with the catch of the day. You choose your selection from a seafood cart as you enter. If you have room for dessert, you've got to try the rum cake. Open for lunch Monday through Friday from 11:30 A.M. to 3:00 P.M. and for dinner Monday through Saturday from 5:00 to 10:00 P.M. Call (215) 928–0556 or visit www.ristlabuca.com. Expensive.

Make a left onto Eighth Street at Locust, walking by the Greek Orthodox cathedral to **Pennsylvania Hospital.** Though patients and doctors in operating scrubs bustle around like they do in any modern hospital, there is much that is historically fascinating about the nation's first hospital. Founded in 1751, Pennsylvania Hospital included Benjamin Franklin among its founders. The hospital is used to visitors peeking around in its halls, and it even provides a tour brochure at the welcome desk in the historic Pine Building on Eighth between Spruce and Pine. A classic example of colonial and federal architecture, the Pine Building is worth exploring. A large painting by Benjamin West, *Christ Healing* *the Sick in the Temple,* was a gift to the hospital from the artist. Upstairs the building's central entrance is framed by sweeping staircases that rise from a nineteenth-century Portuguese tile floor. The hospital had its own fire engine, now displayed under the staircase, since in the early years candles and fireplaces provided the only light and heat. On the second floor, the ornate, wood-paneled historic medical library contains more than 13,000 volumes, some dating back to the fifteenth century, and a set of nineteenth-century plaster casts that were used to teach anatomy to medical students. On the third floor is the hospital's original operating amphitheater, which opened in 1804. The country's first surgeries were performed here before audiences

Pennsylvania Hospital

of physicians and medical students, who watched from the gallery encircling the room. Procedures were performed only on sunny days between 11:00 A.M. and 2:00 P.M., to make the most out of available sunlight. Patients at the time had three anesthesia options: rum, opium, or a tap on the head with a mallet. Outside the original entrance is a statue of William Penn, which was given to the hospital by Penn's family in 1804. Turning right you can visit the unusual Physic Garden, originally planned in 1774 to grow medicinal plants for the doctors. There was no money for the project at the time, but 200 years later, as part of the bicentennial celebration, the plants finally went in. Although it's mostly just

An Insane Admittance Policy

In creating Pennsylvania Hospital the Quakers insisted that part of the building be designated for the insane. Though the Institute of Pennsylvania Hospital would grow to be highly regarded, in its early years mentally ill patients were housed in rooms in the basement, and in 1762 the hospital instituted a fee for curious onlookers who wanted to watch the inmates. The minutes from the hospital board read, "Persons who come out of curiosity to visit the house should pay a sum of money, a groat at least, for admittance."

Merry Christmas, Mr. Hayes

Surely one of the most bizarre Christmas observances of 1805 occurred in the circular operating theater at Pennsylvania Hospital. It was there, before an audience of almost one hundred awestruck medical students, that America's most renowned surgeon removed an enormous tumor from the neck and cheek of a Pennsylvania man. The poor man—James Hayes of Dauphin County—had been living with the tumor for twenty years, and it had grown to be 25½ inches in circumference and weighed seven pounds. Dr. Philip Syng Physick removed the tumor, proclaimed it to be a "wen," a harmless cyst, and placed it in a jar of alcohol. That's where it remains to this day, and—if you are so inclined—you can view James Hayes's tumor in the hospital's library.

a beautiful garden today, in the eighteenth century these plants would have been used to boost heart performance, treat toothaches, ease indigestion, and cleanse wounds. Guided or self-guided tours of the Pine Building are available Monday through Friday from 8:30 A.M. to 4:30 P.M. Call (215) 829–8092, visit the welcome desk at the entrance on Eighth Street, or log on to www.pennhealth.com/pahosp.

Places to Stay in the Historic District and Old City

Best Western Independence Park Inn, 235 Chestnut Street; (215) 922–4443 or (800) 624–2988, www.independencepark inn.com This is a charming small hotel in Old City that is much more like a B&B than a Best Western. Its thirty-six rooms are housed in a recently renovated 1856 building that for a long time was a dry-goods store. Rooms are standard size, but have nice, high ceilings. Continental breakfast is served in a glass-enclosed garden courtyard. There is no restaurant in the hotel, but ask about discounts to eateries in the neighborhood. Moderate.

Comfort Inn, 100 North Christopher Columbus Boulevard; (215) 627–7900, www.comfortinnphila.com The Comfort Inn is right on the riverfront and very convenient to the historic district and attractions in the area, as well as to the city's major highways. It is tucked into a corner between I–95 and the Benjamin Franklin Bridge, but it was built with the traffic in mind, and insulated windows keep the rooms fairly quiet. The rooms are basic Comfort Inn, but the view of the river is great, and there's no better seat to watch the lights on the bridge at night. Ask for a room on the upper floors, where it's quieter and the view is better. A continental breakfast is included, but there is no restaurant. You'll want to eat at some of the many great restaurants in Old City anyway. Inexpensive.

Omni Hotel at Independence Park, 401 Chestnut Street; (215) 925–0000 or (800) THE–OMNI, www.omnihotels.com The nicest hotel in this part of town, the Omni adds a touch of luxury to the history right outside its door. Horse-drawn carriages clip-clop past the front lobby, flowers abound, and there's music in the bar every night. Most of the rooms have outstanding views overlooking Independence Park, so you can slip on your terry cloth robe and have coffee while the historic district wakes up. The Azalea restaurant is a step above most hotel offerings. Expensive.

Sheraton Society Hill, 1 Dock Street; (215) 238–6000 or (800) 325–3535, www.sheraton.com/societyhilll Conveniently located at Second and Walnut, this is a nice option for staying just blocks from Independence Hall but still in the heart of the more quiet, pleasant Society Hill area. The brick, low-rise hotel was built to fit into the neighborhood. There's a pleasant skylit atrium, and the hotel displays some of the historic artifacts found during an archaeological dig before it was built. The rooms are small but pleasant and are furnished in colonial reproductions. Your only views are from the fourth floor facing the river. Two restaurants and a bar. There's free shuttle service to the City Hall area. Expensive.

Thomas Bond House, 129 South Second Street, Society Hill; (215) 923–8523 or (800) 845–2663, www.winston-salem-inn .com/philadelphia If you want colonial atmosphere to go along with your Philly stay, this is your place. This B&B occupies a brick Georgian-revival house built in 1769 for physician Thomas Bond. It's right in the heart of the historic district, overlooking Welcome Park and the City Tavern (though unfortunately they squeezed in a large parking garage next door). The ten rooms and two suites have faithful reproductions, featuring four-poster beds. The house, however, has many amenities that Dr. Bond was not so lucky to have: it's air-conditioned, and all the rooms have private baths. There are muffins and coffee for breakfast during the week and a more elaborate spread on weekends. Moderate.

Places to Eat in the Historic District and Old City

Amada,
217–219 Chestnut Street,
Old City;
(215) 625–2450,
www.amadarestaurant.com
One of the hottest—and busiest—new restaurants in Old City, Amada jumps on the tapas bandwagon with a sophisticated spin. Cured hams hang from the ceiling and on some nights there's flamenco dancing, but people are packing this place for the food. Servers recommend three or four tapas per person, but of course the fun is in the sharing. Among the favorites on the menu are the artichoke flat breads, Spanish octopus, and the piquillos rellenos, peppers stuffed with lump crabmeat. Save room for the goat's milk cheesecake with braised pears. Although there's an extensive wine list, you can't beat the home-made sangria. Open Monday to Wednesday from 5:00 P.M. to 11:00 P.M., Thursday through Saturday from 5:00 P.M. to midnight, and Sunday from 5:00 P.M.to 10:00 P.M. Moderate.

Chloe,
232 Arch Street,
Old City;
(215) 629–2337
A great BYOB option in Old City, this is a perennial in the list of Philadelphia's most romantic restaurants. It's small and cozy, and it doesn't take reservations, so

AUTHORS' FAVORITE PLACES TO EAT IN THE HISTORIC DISTRICT AND OLD CITY

The Bourse
111 South Independence Mall East;
(215) 625–0300,
www.bourse-pa.com

Buddakan
325 Chestnut Street;
(215) 574–9440,
www.buddakan.citysearch.com

City Tavern
138 South Second Street;
(215) 413–1443,
www.citytavern.com

Dark Horse
421 South Second Street;
(215) 928–9307,
www.darkhorsepub.com

Fork
306 Market Street;
(215) 625–9425,
www.forkrestaurant.com

Jones
700 Chestnut Street;
(215) 223–5663,
www.jones-restaurant.com

La Locanda del Ghiottone
130 North Third Street;
(215) 829–1465

Moshulu
401 South Columbus Boulevard;
(215) 923–2500,
www.moshulu.com

The Plough and the Stars
123 Chestnut Street;
(215) 733–0300,
www.ploughstars.com

Ristorante La Buca
711 Locust Street;
(215) 928–0556,
www.ristlabuca.com

HELPFUL WEB SITES

www.ushistory.org

www.independencevisitorcenter.com

www.historicphiladelphia.org

www.pennslandingcorp.com

www.oldcity.org

try to get there early. Chloe is known for its signature salad, topped with warm goat cheese, and its out-of-this-world banana bread pudding. Open Tuesday through Saturday from 5:00 to 9:45 P.M. Moderate.

El Azteca II Mexican,
714 Chestnut Street,
Washington Square;
(215) 733–0895
Here's some of the best Mexican food in the city. This restaurant is a particular standout because it's on the same block as some of the biggest-name eateries in town and does itself proud. It's a BYOB, but if you need a margarita, the servers will add your tequila to their concoction. You can't beat the fried ice cream. Open daily from 11:30 A.M. to 10:00 P.M. Inexpensive.

Farmicia
15 South Third Street,
Old City;
(215) 627–6274
www.farmiciarestaurant.com
Specializing in organic, locally grown produce and meats, Farmicia has quickly become an Old City favorite. The menu is well rounded and hearty, but you may

have trouble getting past the salads. Try the crispy-fried corn-crusted squid salad or the beet and fennel salad with orange rosemary citronett. The eggplant cannelloni is one of the city's great vegetarian dishes. Its Metro Cafe offers breakfast and light fare daily from 8:00 A.M. to 4:00 P.M. Lunch is served Tuesday through Friday from 11:30 A.M. to 2:30 P.M., with weekend brunch from 11:00 A.M. to 3:00 P.M. Dinner is available Sunday from 5:00 P.M. to 9:00 P.M. and Tuesday through Saturday from 5:30 P.M. to 9:00 P.M. Moderate.

La Famiglia,
8 South Front Street,
Old City;
(215) 922–2803,
www.la-famiglia.com
You don't have to go to South Philly for old-world Italian dining. This family-run restaurant has occupied a former colonial tea warehouse since 1976 and is a longtime favorite for many Philadelphians. Owner "Papa" Sena brought his Italian secrets from Naples. The food is great and the wine list is outstanding. Open for

lunch Tuesday through Friday from noon to 2:30 P.M. and dinner Tuesday through Sunday from 5:30 to 10:00 P.M. Very expensive.

Society Hill Hotel,
301 Chestnut Street,
Old City;
(215) 925–1919,
www.societyhillhotel.com
The tiny bar and restaurant of this small hotel is a great place to grab a bite when you're in the historic district. The food is a cut above standard bar fare. Live piano music adds to the atmosphere most nights. When the weather is warm, grab a table outside overlooking Independence Park. Open Sunday through Wednesday from 11:00 A.M. to midnight, Thursday from 11:00 A.M. to 1:00 A.M., and Friday and Saturday from 11:00 A.M. to 2:00 A.M. Inexpensive.

Center City

People who move to the Philadelphia area sometimes spend a lot of time looking at maps searching for "Center City." It's not there. Most major cities have "downtown" areas: Philly has Center City. It makes sense that this part of town would emanate from *City Hall,* which sits in the middle of the metropolis envisioned by William Penn. Thus, your tour of Center City begins here at Broad and Market Streets, with the one building in Philadelphia that you really can't miss.

This "center square" was the largest in Penn's original layout, and he always intended it to be used for public buildings. It took a while for the city's development to work its way west, but by the 1870s it was time to build a city hall. And what a city hall they built. The elaborate Second Empire–style building took thirty years to complete. The studio of local sculptor Alexander Milne Calder, whose son and grandson would also go on to fame as sculptors, created more than 250 architectural sculptures to adorn the building, most notably the figure of William Penn that sits atop the building, keeping watch over his "greene countrie towne." Standing 500 feet above the street, Penn's statue is 37 feet high and weighs twenty-six tons—the largest sculpture on a building anywhere. Until 1986 a "gentlemen's agreement" between city planners and developers

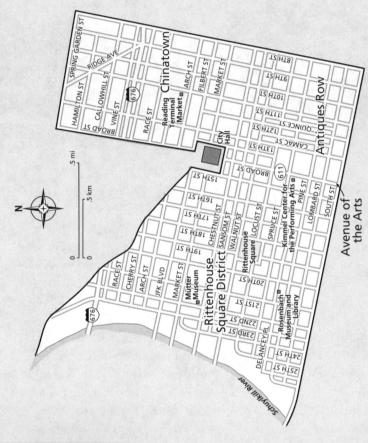

Color Confusion

When the scaffolding came off after an extensive renovation of the City Hall tower in the 1980s, you could almost hear a collective "oops." What was with the color? It didn't match the rest of the building at all, and some said the dull gray color looked like a primer coat. It turns out the tower was originally designed to be painted a lighter color so that the statue of William Penn would stand out more. Over the years, the tower had faded, but the renovators decided to remain true to the original color scheme and go with the lighter gray.

ensured that Penn's hat would be the highest point on the city's skyline. That's obviously not the case anymore, but William Penn and City Hall remain the literal and figurative center of Philadelphia.

It's a big, imposing building, but it hasn't always been universally adored. Famed Philadelphia architect Louis Kahn once called it "the most disreputable and disrespected building in Philadelphia." In the early 1950s city leaders even proposed tearing it down, until they found out the demolition would cost more than it did to build the thing. So the city decided to embrace its city center instead. An ongoing renovation is spiffing up the exterior of what the American Institute of Architects has called "perhaps the greatest single effort of late nineteenth-century architecture." Guides conduct free tours of City Hall Monday through Friday at 12:30 P.M. The tower is also open for tours Monday through Friday from 9:30 A.M. to 4:15 P.M. but is usually reserved for school groups in the mornings. You can get timed tickets at the tour information center in Room 121. Call (215) 686–2840 or visit www.phila.gov/property/virtual cityhall for more information.

AUTHOR'S FAVORITES IN CENTER CITY

Academy of Music

Bag lunch in Rittenhouse Square

Camac Street

Fabric Workshop and Museum

Joseph Fox Bookshop

Lee How Fook Tea House

Mask and Wig Club

Pennsylvania Academy of the Fine Arts

Reading Terminal Market

Rosenbach Museum and Library

Another of Philadelphia's most striking buildings sits directly across Market Street to the north of City Hall. The opulent *Masonic Temple* (1 North Broad Street) was designed in 1868 by a twenty-seven-year-old member of the secret society, the Free and Accepted Masons, which flourished in colonial times. Each of the temple's seven lodge halls was designed in a different architectural style. A Grand Lodge Museum includes George Washington's Masonic apron. Forty-five-minute tours are available weekdays at 11:00 A.M., 2:00 P.M. and 3:00 P.M. and on Saturday at 10:00 A.M. and 11:00 A.M. Closed Saturdays during July and August. There is a $3.00 suggested donation. Call (215) 988–1917 or go to www.pagrandlodge.org.

Some visitors miss one of the city's real treasures by visiting only the museums on the Benjamin Franklin Parkway. Two blocks north of City Hall on Broad Street is the *Pennsylvania Academy of the Fine Arts* (Broad and Cherry Streets), worth seeing for both the building and the collection it houses. Designed by Frank Furness, the stately building was completed in 1876, drawing primarily from French Gothic and Renaissance-Revival styles. Furness was Philadelphia's premier architect of the time, and many consider the academy his finest work. Be sure to cross Broad Street to take in the full glory of the building. Inside, the elegant interior complements the collection of the academy, which includes more than 1,700 paintings and 300 sculptures. When it was founded in 1805, the academy was the first art school in the country, as well as the first public art museum. Open Tuesday through Saturday from 10:00 A.M. to 5:00 P.M. and Sunday from 11:00 A.M. to 5:00 P.M. Admission is $5.00 for adults, $4.00 for students and seniors, and $3.00 for children. Call (215) 972–7600 or visit www.pafa.org.

Pennsylvania Academy of the Fine Arts

Art School No-No

Today the Pennsylvania Academy of the Fine Arts boasts that famed painter Thomas Eakins taught at the school from 1876 to 1886. Among his accomplishments, he was responsible for bringing the study of human anatomy to an artist's education. What the school doesn't always tell you is that Eakins was fired from the faculty for permitting male models to pose nude in front of female students. Eakins actually studied anatomy at the medical school of Thomas Jefferson University. One of his greatest paintings—*The Gross Clinic*—was originally shocking for the realism with which it portrayed Dr. Samuel Gross performing an operation. That painting and several others by Eakins can be seen in a gallery at Jefferson's Alumni Hall (1020 Locust Street).

One of Philadelphia's best-kept secrets—the *Fabric Workshop and Museum* (1315 Cherry Street)—is located near the Academy, on the fifth and sixth floors of the Gilbert Building just west of Thirteenth Street. This is the only organization in the country dedicated to creating and exhibiting new works in fabric. The museum has a collection of more than 5,500 objects and changes its exhibitions six to eight times a year; many are organized in conjunction with an active artist-in-residence program.

theclothespin

For the site of his giant clothespin, the sculpture installed just west of City Hall in 1976, Claes Oldenburg originally proposed a 45-foot-long screw. He is said to have been playing with a wooden clothespin on an airplane one day, and realized that the buildings below appeared to be the same size as the clothespin.

Over the past thirty years, the museum has developed an international reputation, but many people in Philadelphia still don't know it's there. And it won't be in this location for long. The Fabric Workshop and several other arts organizations in the Gilbert Building are being forced to find new homes because the building lies in the path of plans for an expanded convention center. Hours in this location are Monday through Friday from 10:00 A.M to 6:00 P.M. and Saturday from noon to 4:00 P.M. There is a suggested donation of $5.00 for adults and $2.00 for children. Call (215) 568–1111 or log on to www.fabricworkshop.org for updates about its future location.

If you're hungry, or even if you're not, frankly, it's time to head to the *Reading Terminal Market,* at Twelfth and Arch Streets. You'll see the *Pennsylvania Convention Center* on the north side of Arch, but unless you're headed to an event there or are in town for a convention, there's not much to

Measure Twice

Center Square, site of City Hall, is not where William Penn's surveyor, Thomas Holme, intended it to be. Hampered by dense woods and swampy terrain, Holme thought he placed the square at the watershed dividing the two rivers. Later surveyors corrected the error and moved the square. What occupies Holme's original square today? The Pennsylvania Convention Center.

see. The real fun awaits inside the market. This is one of the places that locals think of as being the "real" Philadelphia.

Reading Terminal Market has been around since 1892, when the Reading Railroad purchased the site of two street markets to build its new, huge train shed. The vendors were given space beneath the elevated tracks, enough for up to 800 merchants to have 6-foot stalls, arranged in a grid system much like the city's streets. As long as the railroads flourished, so did the market, but in the 1970s the Reading Railroad went out of business, and it looked like the market would go with it. But in the 1980s public support and the construction of the Convention Center saved the day. The train shed was converted into a grand hall and ballroom for the Convention Center, and over the past decade, the market has been given new life and spruced up—well, as spruced up as a bustling farmers' market can be. Eighty-six merchants operate from the market floor; three of them descend from original stall owners.

There are shops that sell imported gift items, books, and crafts, but people come for the food. If you want it, you can get it here: piles of fresh produce, meat, fish, poultry, cheeses, baked goods, candies, breads, and fresh-cut flowers. Counter restaurants serve up cheesesteaks and pizza, while Amish merchants sell prepared foods made in their Lancaster County kitchens. There are tables and chairs if you're lucky enough to grab one around lunchtime, and locals take turns at the piano. Among the must-visit merchants are: **DiNic's** for the pork sandwich, **Delilah's** for the ribs, **Salumeria** for the hoagies, **Rocco's** for the chicken sandwich, **Pearl's Oyster Bar** for fried seafood, **Fisher's** for soft pretzels, and the **Down Home Diner** for breakfast. The Down Home Diner is also said to be the best place in the city to sample a uniquely Philadelphia delicacy—scrapple. Don't ask what it's made of—trust us on this one—just taste it on a leap of faith.

The only problem with the market is that it's not exactly easy to shop there. You pay each merchant separately and you lug around too many bags that you then have to figure out how to get home. To Philadelphians, that's part of the charm. But everyone—even Philadelphians—agrees parking is a hassle. If you get your ticket stamped, discounted parking in the garage at Twelfth and Filbert helps ease the pain. The market is open every day except Sunday. The debate about whether to open on Sunday has gone on for years and been quite heated at times. Most of these merchants are their own bosses and think they deserve a day off. Who can argue with that? So for the time being, the market is open Monday through Saturday from 8:00 A.M. to 6:00 P.M. A few things to keep in mind, though: The Amish merchants are not there on Monday and Tuesday, and many of the merchants start to close up shop at about 3:00 P.M. Go early in the morning if you want the best produce; go at lunch for the best people-watching in town. Call (215) 922–2317 or visit www .readingterminalmarket.org.

You're now on the cusp of **Chinatown,** a compact neighborhood bordered roughly by Arch Street to the south, Thirteenth Street to the west, Vine Street to the north, and Eighth Street to the east. Though most people come to Chinatown to eat, there are other things worth seeing, so if you've just filled up at the Reading Market, a walk around the neighborhood may be in order. Most visitors enjoy seeing the Friendship Gate, with its fire-breathing dragons, at Tenth and Arch Streets. The gate was built in the 1980s as a joint project between Philadelphia and a sister city, Tianjin, in China. The **Trocadero Theatre** at Tenth and Arch is a reminder of the days when this was the city's red-light district. A former burlesque house featuring such performers as W. C. Fields and Mae West, the Troc, as it is known, is now primarily a midsize music venue. Wander through the area taking in the street scene. Along with the restaurants, you'll find gift shops with their windows full of Buddhas, Chinese video stores, a fortune-cookie factory, and a Chinese-Christian church. You may have to look hard to find the **Chinatown Mall** (Eleventh Street between Race and Cherry), but this underground

Gateway to the Delaware

One of Center City's only east-west streets *not* bearing the name of a tree, Arch Street did start out with one: Mulberry. But then came "the great arch," called an engineering wonder at the time. It seems that when Mulberry Street reached the riverfront, one side of the street was higher than the other, necessitating an arch to carry traffic to the river. Built in 1690 the arch was 66 feet long, and even though it was torn down in 1721, the name stuck.

market is where locals shop or grab a quick bite. It's also fun to wander up some of the small side streets, such as Spring Street, where Chinese touches have been added to Philadelphia's urban architecture.

As far as the food goes, there's lots of it, most of it is reasonably priced, and there's something for every taste. You can choose between Szechuan, Mandarin, Hunan, and Cantonese, and there are now a few Vietnamese, Burmese, Japanese, and Thai restaurants as well.

Two of the best restaurants in Chinatown are right next door to each other. They may not look like much, but step inside. *Lee How Fook Tea House* (219 North Eleventh Street) has been around for a long time, but every once in a while, it seems to be discovered again. There's nothing fancy here, it's small and plain and can get noisy, but the food is great and the round tables have lazy Susans so you can share. What more do you need in a Chinese restaurant? The menu goes on forever, but try one of the hot pots it's known for or the salt-baked shrimp. Many people swear Lee How Fook has the best hot-and-sour soup in town. Even an old standby like fried rice is great here; it's got lots of ingredients and it's not greasy. Lee How Fook is also a BYOB, which helps with the bill. Open daily from 11:30 A.M. to 10:00 P.M. If you stop in on a Saturday afternoon, you can watch them make dumplings in the dining room. Call (215) 925–7266. Moderate.

The reporters and editors from the nearby *Philadelphia Inquirer* hang out next door at *Vietnam* (221 North Eleventh Street), and with good reason. Since a recent renovation, the atmosphere is a step up from most of the restaurants in Chinatown—it has polished wood tables—but it remains casual and comfortable and the prices are right. You may want to make a meal out of the appetizers once you taste the spring rolls, and you could if you toss in the green papaya salad with shrimp and pork. For an entree, consider the lime chicken. If you have room for dessert, try the sweet rice pudding with corn and coconut milk. Open Sunday through Thursday from 11:00 A.M. to 9:30 P.M. and Friday and Saturday from 11:00 A.M. to 10:30 P.M. Call (215) 592–1163 or log on to www.eatatvietnam .com. Moderate.

athanksgivingfirst

Gimbel Brothers Department Store sponsored the first Thanksgiving Day parade in Philadelphia in 1920. Santa climbed up the outside of the building (at Eighth and Market) to the toy department. Philadelphia's Thanksgiving Day Parade continues, but it has since been outdone by its competitor, Macy's, in New York.

Heading south back toward Market Street, you'll pass *The Gallery at Market East,* Center City's answer to the suburban mall. Nothing special here, but

Is, Was, and Always Will Be Wanamaker's

The name has changed several times in the last decade, but most Philadelphians still refer to the department store at Thirteenth and Market as Wanamaker's. Founded by Philadelphian John Wanamaker in 1876, the store was the first to combine many different departments under one roof. Wanamaker is credited with introducing many innovative ideas to retailing, including the use of price tags, money-back guarantees, and "white sales." Wanamaker was also the first retailer to use newspaper advertising for his store. He was once quoted as saying, "Half the money I spend on advertising is wasted; the trouble is I don't know which half."

it's the place to go if you need socks or soap. At Twelfth and Market Streets is the former **P S F S** building, considered a classic of modern architecture. Now a sparkling and swanky Loews Hotel, this skyscraper is classic international style with a good deal of art deco thrown in. Architects George Howe and William Lescaze went so far as to design the doorknobs, coat hooks, hinges, and furniture that outfitted the building when it opened in 1932. And Philadelphians love the letters "P S F S" atop the building. Twenty-seven feet high, they stand for the Philadelphia Savings Fund Society, which was the country's first savings bank when it was founded in 1814. When this historic building was transformed into the hotel, management listened to the cries of Philadelphians who just couldn't imagine their nighttime skyline without those big red letters and let them stand.

The next block brings you to what is now **Macy's,** but what old-timers still think of as Wanamaker's, the country's first department store. In many ways it's now a modern department store, but it has retained some of its original touches. A bronze statue of an eagle, purchased at the 1904 World's Fair, still keeps watch over the first floor. Generations of Philadelphians made plans to "meet at the eagle" when in Center City. The store still stages its annual Christmas light and music show, another favorite for the generations, and a 30,000-pipe organ still looms over a four-story central court. The store still hosts daily organ concerts at noon and 5:00 P.M. (7:00 P.M. on Wednesday). Much of the building has now been converted into office space, but the memories remain.

If you leave Macy's on the Chestnut Street side, you can find your way to one of the city's oldest taverns. It's way off the beaten path though, so it's probably best not to try to find it after dark, which may sound strange given that it's a bar. Still, it's worth a visit to **McGillin's Olde Ale House** at 1310

Drury Lane. (Drury is just a small alley between Thirteenth and Juniper that parallels Chestnut Street.) Established in 1860, McGillin's boasts that it's the oldest continuously operating tavern in the city, and it's decorated with more than a century's worth of tavern licenses to prove it. Bar food is standard fare, but you're there more for the atmosphere, and that can't be beat. Open Monday through Saturday from 11:00 A.M. to 2:00 A.M. Call (215) 735–5562 or go to www.mcgillins.com. Moderate.

If you're out for a more serious meal, look for the lions at the **Capital Grille** (1338 Chestnut Street), which is, plain and simple, just a great steak house. Housed in a former bank, the restaurant is huge, but surprisingly it keeps the noise in check. Start with the pan-fried calamari with hot cherry peppers— a specialty of the house. If you're feeling carnivorous, you're at the right place; it brags most about its porterhouse steak. Open Monday through Thursday from 11:30 A.M. to 3:00 P.M., then from 5:00 to 10:00 P.M.; Friday from 11:30 A.M. to 3:00 P.M., then from 5:00 to 11:00 P.M.; Saturday from 5:00 to 11:00 P.M.; and Sunday from 4:00 to 10:00 P.M. Call (215) 545–9588 or visit www.thecapitalgrille.com. Very expensive.

Now that you're fortified, it's time to take on Broad Street, or, as this stretch of Broad is now called, the **Avenue of the Arts.** At one time South Broad was known mostly as the place where the mummers marched on New Year's Day. Now a stroll down South Broad takes you past some of Philadelphia's most esteemed cultural institutions and some of the city's hottest restaurants. The Avenue of the Arts is also Philadelphia's nod to Hollywood, as the sidewalks of South Broad contain bronze plaques commemorating Philadelphia's music legends in a "Walk of Fame." You'll find stars honoring everyone from Marian Anderson to Fabian. As city planners dreamed, this has finally become one of Philly's most-beaten paths, so there's not much detail here. Each institution has a comprehensive Web site and phone numbers are listed for information.

Here you'll also find some of Philadelphia's most luxurious hotels, starting with the **Ritz Carlton** (10 Avenue of the Arts), which occupies the neoclassical former Mellon Bank building. You should wander in just to take a look, and perhaps have a drink at the Paris Bar and Grill.

The Prince Music Theater (1412 Chestnut Street) was founded in 1984 and it now houses the city's second-largest theater company. In 1999 the Prince moved into its permanent spaces in a renovated theater and now brags that none of its 450 seats are farther than 60 feet from the stage. Named after legendary director Harold Prince, the company devotes itself to musical theater and shows movies on the biggest screen in town. Call (215) 569–9700 or visit www.princemusictheater.org.

The **Union League** (140 South Broad Street) is one of the city's poshest and most private clubs. Don't bother knocking because they won't let you in, but do take time to admire the Second-Empire building, built in 1865. The league was founded a few years before that as a patriotic society to support the policies of President Abraham Lincoln, but it is now known mostly for its conservatism. Women were finally allowed to join in the 1980s, and it's now a tony place in town for the "in crowd" to lunch. Call (215) 563–6500 or log on to www.unionleague.org.

The next block brings you to what Philadelphians still refer to as the Bellevue Stratford Hotel, though it's now technically called the **Park Hyatt Philadelphia at the Bellevue.** This hotel has been through several incarnations since it became infamously associated with the 1979 breakout of Legionnaires' disease that killed twenty-nine people. Only seven floors are now devoted to hotel space; the rest is composed of offices, a five-level health club, and upscale shops. If you need a quick bite, the city's best food court is on the lower level. Philadelphia power brokers still populate the Palm restaurant, and many of the city's fanciest functions are held in its 14,000-square-foot ballroom. Adjacent to the Bellevue is the Sporting Club at The Bellevue, a large athletic facility most noted for its design, which architect Michael Graves configured on top of a parking garage.

The Academy of Music (1420 Locust Street) is home to the Opera Company of Philadelphia and the Pennsylvania Ballet. Though its acoustics are well suited to opera, they weren't up to today's standards for orchestral music, leading to the construction of a new home for the Philadelphia Orchestra at the Kimmel Center down the street. This, despite the fact that when the building was being built, its roof was intentionally left off for an entire year to allow the walls and the floors to become seasoned. With opulent interiors modeled on La Scala in Milan, the Academy of Music opened in 1857. The exterior of the building was never finished according to plan, since money ran

And You Thought Windows Were Bad

Certainly the most striking thing about the Academy of Music is the chandelier. When the building was constructed, a separate iron structure was built above the ceiling just to support the five-ton chandelier, which once hung in the old Crystal Palace in New York. Every year at the end of the summer, workers carefully lower the chandelier and wash and dry each of the thousands of crystals.

out, so architects settled on the dark brick that Philadelphians came to love. Notice the gaslights that still flicker out front. With the opening of the Kimmel Center, the academy was able to complete a $40 million renovation to attract Broadway shows, touring dance companies, and even single-night music acts. Call (215) 893–1999 or visit www.academyofmusic.org.

Take a break from Broad Street for a bit, and head east on Locust to the *Library Company of Philadelphia* (1314 Locust Street). This is the library founded by Benjamin Franklin and forty-nine of his friends, each putting in forty shillings and promising to pay ten shillings a year. That gave them access to books, which were a rarity in the 1730s but were fuel for curious intellects. Today the collection has grown to include about 500,000 printed volumes, 160,000 manuscripts, and a small but distinguished collection of early American art and artifacts. Open Monday through Friday from 9:00 A.M. to 4:45 P.M. Call (215) 546–3181 or go to www.librarycompany.org.

The landmark building across the street at 1319 Locust was once the headquarters of the Poor Richard Club, the distinguished advertising club. It now houses the district headquarters of the National Union of Hospital and Health Care Employees. Another historic landmark is the New Century Guild Building (1307 Locust), once a settlement house for working women. At Thirteenth and Locust is the *Historical Society of Pennsylvania* (1300 Locust Street). If you're seriously interested in the history of Philadelphia, this is the place to be. The society merged with the Balch Institute for Ethnic Studies in 2002, so now the resources are even greater. Of particular note is the manuscript collection, which includes some of the nation's most important historical documents. Call (215) 732–6200 or visit www.hsp.org.

Continuing east on Locust you come to a quiet, often unexplored part of town with historic row houses and gardens tucked in alleys and courtyards. Sometimes called Philadelphia's *Littlest Streets,* these narrow alleys were once home to the servants who worked in the nineteenth-century mansions along the main streets. Many are barely wide enough to fit a cart through. Camac Street and Quince, its small counterpart in charm on the block between Eleventh and Twelfth Streets, stretch from Walnut to Lombard. Many of these small houses date to the 1840s. This is also the heart of Philadelphia's gay community, roughly bounded by Walnut and South Streets from Eleventh to Broad. The area has always appealed to alternative lifestyles, and a number of private clubs for artists and actresses set up shop here. Some still exist on Camac Street between Twelfth and Thirteenth, which has now officially been declared "The Avenue of the Artists." You come first to *The Philadelphia Sketch Club* (235 South Camac Street), the country's oldest professional artists' club, founded in

1860 by students at the Pennsylvania Academy of the Fine Arts. It is open to the public during exhibitions (215–545–9298; www.sketchclub.org). The ***Plastic Club*** (247 South Camac Street) was founded in 1897 by a group of women artists, making it the oldest women's art club in the country. Members agreed to start accepting men in 1991, and the club still hosts exhibitions several times a year in its gallery space. It's open to the public during those shows (215–545–9324; www.plasticc.libertynet.org).

Heading back to the Avenue of the Arts, you'll find the ***Merriam Theater*** (250 South Broad Street) at Spruce Street, which was known as the Shubert Theater when it opened in 1918. Over the years such performers as Al Jolson, John Barrymore, Helen Hayes, and Laurence Olivier have graced its stage. The University of the Arts took over the theater in 1972 to stage its productions as well as those of traveling and regional companies. Call (215) 732–5446.

Much of the Avenue of the Arts is overshadowed by the glistening ***Kimmel Center for the Performing Arts*** (260 South Broad Street), a $265 million state-of-the-art center that opened in December 2001. The building, with its signature 150-foot, vaulted glass ceiling, was designed by Rafael Viñoly and features a 2,500-seat, cello-shaped concert hall designed especially for the Philadelphia Orchestra. In addition, a 650-seat theater has a rotating stage to accommodate chamber music, recitals, and dance. The two freestanding performance spaces are surrounded by a public plaza that includes a gift shop and a rooftop garden. The glass end walls are supported by steel cables and are designed to move up to 2 feet in high wind, much like a suspension bridge. The Kimmel's $6.5 million, 7,000-pipe organ, the centerpiece of the concert hall and one of the largest of its kind in the world, had its debut in 2006. Along with the Philadelphia Orchestra, the Kimmel Center is home to Peter Nero and the Philly Pops, the Chamber Orchestra of Philadelphia, American Theater Arts

Romanian Treasures

A small museum in the Rittenhouse Square area houses the largest collection of Romanian artifacts in the country. The ***Romanian Folk Art Museum*** (1606 Spruce Street) features costumes, rugs, pottery, weavings, and furniture dating from the turn of the twentieth century and representing most of the regions of Romania. Originally founded in Chicago, the collection has been based in Philadelphia since the 1990s. For more information call (215) 732–6780 or go to www.romanianculture.us.

TOP HITS IN CENTER CITY

Antiques Row	Pennsylvania Academy of the Fine Arts
Chinatown	
City Hall	Reading Terminal Market
Kimmel Center for the Performing Arts	Restaurant Row
	Rittenhouse Row shopping

for Youth, the Philadelphia Dance Company (PHILADANCO), and the Philadelphia Chamber Music Society. The complex is named for Sidney Kimmel, a businessman who grew up in West Philadelphia and donated $30 million to the project. Call (215) 790–5800 or visit www.kimmelcenter.org for more information. If you're curious about the building but music isn't your thing, you can take a free tour of the facility at 1:00 P.M. on Tuesday through Sunday. While you're there, be sure to check out the ***Intermission Gift Shop,*** an outpost of a famous Chestnut Hill store that stocks all things musical and theatrical. The shop is open from noon to 6:00 P.M. Tuesday through Sunday, or until thirty minutes after a performance ends. Enter through the lobby. Call (215) 54MUSIC.

A new building for the ***Philadelphia Theatre Company*** is scheduled to open in fall 2007 next to the Kimmel Center. The Suzanne Roberts Theater at Broad and Lombard Streets will feature a traditional proscenium auditorium as well as a studio space. The thirty-year-old company is known as an innovator in presenting emerging American playwrights, but up until now, it has never had a permanent home to call its own.

Along with new life on the Avenue of the Arts have come new restaurants and nightspots. The Kimmel itself offers three dining options, or you can choose from a number of upscale restaurants that line Broad Street. One of those is ***Bliss*** (224 South Broad Street), the latest creation of chef Francesco Martorella, who has worked his way through some of Philadelphia's finest restaurants. Martorella has fashioned his menu from his Italian roots and French training, with some Asian flair thrown in. Popular lunch entrees include porcini -dusted salmon and a great Philly chopped salad, with the rock shrimp tempura and asian duck getting high marks for dinner. Bliss serves lunch Monday through Friday from 11:30 A.M. to 2:30 P.M. and is open for dinner Monday through Thursday from 5:00 to 10:00 P.M. and Friday and

Saturday from 5:00 to 11:00 P.M. For more information call (215) 731–1100 or visit www.bliss-restaurant.com.

Across the street is the **Wilma Theater** (265 South Broad Street), with its cascading neon. Founded in 1980 by two Czechoslovakian natives who are still at the helm, the Wilma's mission is to present theater as an art form. Known for its bold and innovative productions, the Wilma settled into its current digs in 1996. The popular Student Sunday program allows high school or college students to attend discounted productions. Call (215) 893–9456 or go to www.wilmatheater.org.

The University of the Arts (333 South Broad Street) is housed in a Greek-Revival building designed in 1825 as the Asylum for the Deaf and Dumb. Its Rosenwald-Wolf Gallery on the first floor shows changing exhibits throughout the year. The University of the Arts is the result of the 1987 merger of the Philadelphia College of Art and Design and the Philadelphia College of Performing Arts. Call (800) 616–ARTS or log on to www.uarts.edu.

On the southeast corner at Broad and Pine Streets is the **Gershman Y** (401 South Broad Street), a branch of the Jewish Community Centers for Greater Philadelphia. The Gershman hosts a number of cultural events during the year, including a Jewish film festival, an Israeli film festival, concerts, and a Jewish book festival. The facility also includes the Borowsky and Open Lens Galleries, which display art exhibits of interest to Jewish audiences and the wider cultural community. Call (215) 545–4400 or go to www.phillyjcc.com/branches/gershman.html. In addition, the Gershman is home to the **Philadelphia Jewish Sports Hall of Fame,** which honors local Jewish teams and athletes, some of whom started their careers there. The Hall of Fame is free to visitors and is open Monday through Friday from 9:00 A.M. to 7:00 P.M. Call (215) 446–3016 or go to www.pjshf.com for further information.

If you cut west a block to Fifteenth and South, you'll come to one of Philly's favorite eating joints, which had a starring role in the 2005 movie *In Her Shoes.* The **Jamaican Jerk Hut** (1436 South Street) may look like just a storefront, but it has great island food. In the winter you'll do best to take out, but spring through fall the spirit of the place comes alive in its hidden garden. There's a bandstand with frequent live calypso music and an atmospheric vegetable and herb plot that supplies the kitchen. Owner Nicola Shirley's signature jerk chicken is always a favorite, as are the Jamaican curry shrimp and the oxtail stew. Don't miss the fried plantains. It's a BYOB, so bring some rum to mix with the wide selection of tropical juices. Open Monday through Thursday from 11:00 A.M. to 10:00 P.M., Friday and Saturday until 11:00 P.M., and Sunday from 5:00 P.M. to 10:00 P.M. Call (215) 545–8644. Inexpensive.

Back on Broad, the Avenue of the Arts reaches slightly into South Philadelphia for its final venues.

Though not quite as elegant, you're getting more off the beaten path here, which can hold some surprises. Note the wonderful mural at Lombard Street, then just south of South Street is the **Philadelphia Arts Bank** (601 South Broad Street). Owned and operated by the University of the Arts, this 230-seat theater is housed in a renovated bank building, now capped in bright neon-red letters. This was the first new theater to open on the Avenue of the Arts. Performances include theater, dance, music, and film festivals. Call (215) 569–9700.

On the next block you'll find the **Brandywine Workshop/Firehouse Arts Center** (730 South Broad Street), a historic firehouse that's been renovated into two floors of gallery space. The workshop promotes the art of printmaking, and many of the rotating exhibits in the gallery focus on printmaking as well. Limited edition prints are for sale in the small gift shop. Call (215) 546–3675 or go to www.brandywineworkshop.com.

Right next door is the **Philadelphia Clef Club of Jazz and Performing Arts** (738 South Broad Street), the southern outpost on the Avenue of the Arts. Often called "The House that Jazz Built," the Clef Club grew out of the former Black Musician's Union, and the club's mission is simple: "To perform, preserve, perpetuate, and promote the art of jazz." The club sponsors concerts throughout the year, has an active artist-in-residence program, and runs workshops and ensemble classes. Call (215) 893–9912 or log on to www.clefclubofjazz.com.

After all of this culture, you might be in the mood for some shopping. If you head down Pine Street from Broad, you'll find **Antiques Row.** Most of the better-known stores are between Ninth and Twelfth Streets, but the action has begun to spread, and some trendy new nonantiques stores and galleries are popping up as well. You'll have to look hard to find **Halloween** (1329 Pine Street) because nothing identifies this funky jewelry shop except a small orange business card in the front window. You descend into a richly decorated dungeonlike space that is stuffed with all types of jewelry. There are several other unusual stores not to miss along this stretch. **Spirit of the Artist** (1022 Pine Street) is a family-run shop featuring arts and crafts made by American artists. A few doors down at **Blendo** (1002 Pine Street) you'll find a small shop packed to the gills with an interesting blend of past and present. Unusual contemporary crafts and jewelry are also featured at **Show of Hands** (1006 Pine Street), which sponsors monthly craft exhibits, too. Add those stores to a few new galleries and dozens of varied antiques shops, and you can have a fun afternoon of shopping. You can find a complete list of shops and restaurants in the area at www.antique-row.org.

If you're looking for someplace along Pine to eat, you have two great choices. **Mixto** (1141 Pine Street) is an outpost of Tierra Colombiana, a very popular Cuban restaurant in North Philly. Its flavor is south of the border, and lots of it. Plus, they open at 9:00 A.M., so you can even get some adventurous breakfast dishes here. Open Sunday through Wednesday until 11:00 P.M. and Thursday through Saturday until 12:30 A.M. Call (215) 592–0363 or go to www .mixtophilly.com. Moderate.

If you're hungry for dinner, try **Effie's** (1127 Pine Street). It's a tiny BYOB with great Greek food, a garden and carriage house out back, and very reasonable prices. Start with the grilled feta and go with one of the special fish entrees. Effie's doesn't take reservations for parties under six, but if it's too crowded, on a summer night you can get your food to go and grab one of the tables in **Louis Kahn Park** at Eleventh and Pine. Open Sunday through Thursday from 5:00 to 10:00 P.M. and Friday and Saturday from 5:00 to 11:00 P.M. Call (215) 592–8333. Moderate.

Be sure to wander down Quince Street, where it reappears here along Pine Street. Hidden midblock is the **Mask and Wig Club** (310 Quince Street), an incongruous chateaulike building that has housed a University of Pennsylvania theatrical troupe for more than one hundred years. Architect Wilson Eyre, better known for much more prominent jobs in the city, was hired to convert the building into a small theater. Eyre then hired artist Maxfield Parrish to decorate the interior. The club still puts on one production a year and rents out its historic space when not in use. Call (215) 923–4229 or log on to www.maskandwig.org.

Heading west again on Pine, after you cross Broad Street, you'll pass by the brick buildings of Pierce College, one of the country's first business schools and one of the first to offer all of its courses online. You're now in the Rittenhouse Square district, best known as the epicenter of the city's high-end shopping and dining, but put that off for a bit and enjoy the neighborhood's hidden treasures first. At Seventeenth and Delancey you'll find **Plays and Players** (1714 Delancey Place), the city's oldest small theater group. Cross the street and take in the theater's terra-cotta frieze and the old carriage house next door at 1718 Delancey. Call (215) 735–0630 or visit www.playsand players.org.

Jogging back onto Pine, you come to the **Civil War and Underground Railroad Museum of Philadelphia** (1805 Pine Street), a small museum that for a time turns your attention away from Philadelphia's Revolutionary War–era history. Founded in 1888, shortly after the end of the war, this museum pays tribute to Philadelphia's role in the Civil War. The state gave the museum a much-needed infusion of funds to help inventory and care for its vast collection of artifacts, and plans are in the works to build a new facility to house it. For now, it remains tucked away in a town house. Here you will find rooms devoted to General Ulysses S. Grant and General George Gordon Meade, both of whom lived in this neighborhood during the war. You'll see the uniform Meade wore while commanding the Union army at Gettysburg. The Lincoln Room displays interesting artifacts, including a mask of the president made just before his death and a lock of his hair. There's even a paisley dressing gown worn by Jefferson Davis when he fled from the Union army, which subjected him to no small amount of ridicule. Perhaps more interesting are the belongings of ordinary soldiers: the uniforms, rifles and swords, journals and diaries, even a soldier's sewing kit. A 10,000-volume library is open to scholars and others conducting Civil War research. The museum has expanded its mission to incorporate the issues of slavery and the Underground Railroad, and its growing collection includes memoirs of abolitionists and copies of the *Liberator,* a nineteenth-century antislavery newspaper. Open Thursday through Sunday from 11:00 A.M. to 4:30 P.M. Admission is $5.00 for adults, $4.00 for students and seniors, and $3.00 for children under twelve. For more information call (215) 735–8196 or log on to www.cwurmuseum.org.

Take the time to wander up and down Delancey Place. Like many Philadelphia streets, Delancey runs for a few blocks, disappears, then reappears a few blocks away. The stretch between Eighteenth and Twentieth Streets is one of the nicest. Most of the houses here date to the mid-1800s and have been lovingly kept up. You'll see beautiful ironwork, stained-glass windows, and well-

Beloved "Old Baldy"

That's not just any horse head hanging on the wall of the Civil War and Underground Railroad Museum. That's "Old Baldy," the beloved steed of General George Meade, Philadelphia's greatest Civil War hero. As commander of northern forces at the Battle of Gettysburg, Meade relied heavily on his stoic steed, who was apparently the Civil War version of the Energizer Bunny. Records indicate that Baldy was wounded in battle fourteen times but always made a quick recovery and returned to the battlefield, the names of which read like a history of the war: Bull Run, Antietam, Fredericksburg, Chancellorsville, and Weldon Railroad. At Gettysburg, legend has it that Baldy took a shot in the ribs that missed Meade by an inch. The loyal stallion outlived Meade by ten years, passing away on Christmas Day 1882. Once word of Old Baldy's demise reached some of Meade's veterans, they quickly dug up his carcass from the farm where he had been buried and had the historic head mounted for all posterity.

tended small gardens. One building of particular note is the **Horace Jayne Mansion** (1900 Delancey), considered to be one of Frank Furness's townhouse masterpieces.

The next block of Delancey brings you to the **Rosenbach Museum and Library** (2010 Delancey Place), another of the city's hidden treasures. Once the elegant home of two brothers, Dr. A. S. W. and Philip Rosenbach, the museum now houses their amazing collection of rare books, manuscripts, fine arts, furniture, silver, and antiques. The brothers lived in the mansion, built in the 1860s, from 1926 until 1950. During that time they built what was said to be the most successful book business in the world. The Rosenbach boasts such priceless manuscripts as James Joyce's *Ulysses,* Charles Dickens's *Pickwick Papers,* many works by Joseph Conrad, and drawings and manuscripts by Maurice Sendak, including the original artwork for his much-loved *Where the Wild Things Are.* It also holds the only known copy of the first issue of Benjamin Franklin's *Poor Richard's Almanack.* The Rosenbach augments these collections with regular exhibits drawn from its voluminous archives. The museum is also hailed for its huge collection of portrait miniatures. There are more than 1,000 in the collection, including a portrait of King James I of England. Open Tuesday through Sunday from 10:00 A.M. to 5:00 P.M. (Wednesday until 8:00 P.M.). Guided tours are available on the hour from 11:00 A.M. to 3:00 P.M. and at 6:30 P.M. on Wednesdays. Closed from August 7 until mid-September. Admission is $8.00 for adults and $5.00 for students and seniors. Call (215) 732–1600 or log on to www.rosenbach.org.

If you're looking for something to eat, you have two great neighborhood eateries to choose from. **Audrey Claire** (276 South Twentieth Street) is a plain-and-simple BYOB with great Mediterranean food. You'll have to search hard to find the name anywhere, but just look for the striking flowers and the big bowl

Why Rittenhouse?

Rittenhouse Square is named in honor of David Rittenhouse (1732–1796), a noted Philadelphian known as the finest American astronomer of his time and as a maker of clocks and mathematical instruments. A friend of Ben Franklin's, Rittenhouse also served as a legislator, administrator, financier, state treasurer, and the first director of the U.S. Mint. The square that bears his name was first known simply as the Southwest Square or—as one legend has it—Governor's Woods, the result of an early eighteenth-century law that set a five-shilling fine for shooting fowl on the streets of Philadelphia, which sent hunters scurrying to "the governor's woods."

Rittenhouse Square Guardhouse

of apples in the window. This was the first restaurant of Audrey Taichman, one of the city's few female restaurateurs, who later opened 20 Manning Street across the street. Audrey Claire isn't as noisy and it's not as expensive, which are two big pluses. If the weather is nice, huge windows are opened wide and the energy of the city contributes to the mood inside. Make sure you try the flat bread; for many people it's the highlight of a meal here. Two downsides: It does not take credit cards, and it doesn't take reservations on weekends. Open Tuesday through Thursday from 5:45 to 10:00 P.M., Friday and Saturday from 5:45 P.M. to 10:30 P.M., and Sunday from 5:15 to 9:30 P.M. Call (215) 731–1222 or visit www.twentymanning.com. Expensive.

Just a block away is ***Friday Saturday Sunday*** (261 South Twenty-first Street). This place has been around since the mid-1970s, largely because the atmosphere is great, the food is consistently good, and the owners don't gouge the price of the wine. Plus there's a fun story that goes along with how the restaurant came to be. The founders were overeducated restaurant neophytes who basically started the restaurant on a string, a prayer, and a dare. They insist that their earliest refrigeration system was a bunch of secondhand refrigerators lined up in a row, that one of the partners was a carpenter who put the space together himself, and that another made the desserts in her apartment up the street and carried them to the restaurant. Within six months, lines to get in were stretching around the block. Luckily it's easier to get in now, and the restaurant does take reservations. The food is basically new American; the crab cakes and roast duck are perennial favorites. Be sure to start with cream of mushroom soup—what it's known for, along with the cozy upstairs bar. Lit by tiny white lights with draped walls and a large aquarium filled with tropical fish, the Tank Bar shows up frequently as one of the most romantic spots in the city. Open for dinner Monday through Saturday from 5:30 to 10:30 P.M. and Sunday from 5:00 to 10:00 P.M. Call (215) 546–4232 or visit www.frisatsun.com. Moderate.

The ***Thomas Hockley House*** (235 South Twenty-first Street) is just across the street from Friday Saturday Sunday. This is another classic example of the residential architecture of Frank Furness.

Time now to walk down Locust and head to **Rittenhouse Square.** One of William Penn's original five squares, this urban park is largely what has made this neighborhood so desirable; it has been a prestigious address since the first house went up in the 1840s. The construction you're likely to see going on in the area is thanks to condominium projects that have popped up around the square in response to a rapid rise in empty-nest baby boomers who want to leave their homes in the suburbs and move to where the action is. Today there's always something going on in the square; there are concerts and art shows in the spring and summer, and on a nice day at lunchtime, it can be hard to find a spot on one of the many benches. A Philadelphia newspaper once quoted a local architect as saying Rittenhouse Square was "the very fabric of Philadelphia." The central plaza, with its pool and fountain and entrances, was designed by Paul Cret, the architect responsible for many buildings on the Benjamin Franklin Parkway. Among the statues in the park, the billy goat has always been a favorite climbing place for kids. The best way to experience Rittenhouse Square is to grab a sandwich from one of the take-out eateries nearby (Le Bus and Paninoteca at 135 and 120 South Eighteenth Street, respectively, are particularly good), sit on a bench, and take it all in. This is Philadelphia's favorite urban oasis.

Several buildings around the square are worth noticing. The two-story Italianate building on the southwest corner houses the **Philadelphia Ethical Society** (1906 South Rittenhouse Square). On the northwest corner is the **Church of the Holy Trinity** (1904 Walnut Street), designed by John Notman in the 1850s; its rector, Phillip Brooks, penned the words to "O Little Town of Bethlehem." On the northeast corner are three wonderful buildings: The building at 1811 Walnut once housed the exclusive Rittenhouse Club; the **Alison Building** next door is home to the offices of the Presbyterian Ministers' Fund, the oldest life insurance company in the world; and the exquisite building at the corner of Eighteenth and Walnut Streets houses **Anthropologie** (1801 Walnut Street), a hip clothing and accessories store that's a local success story gone national. The 1898 beaux arts building, with its grand winding staircase, was once home to Sara Drexel Fell and financier Alexander Van Rensselaer. In another past life it housed the Pennsylvania Athletic Club. Now its floors are filled with flimsy lingerie and evening dresses, as well as retro door hardware and delicate linens. Open Monday through Saturday from 10:00 A.M. to 8:00 P.M. and Sunday from 11:00 A.M. to 6:00 P.M. Call (215) 568–2114 or visit www.anthropologie.com.

At the corner of Eighteenth and Locust is the **Curtis Institute of Music** (1726 Locust Street), the renowned conservatory housed in what were once four turn-of-the-century houses. Founded in 1924, Curtis trained some of the twentieth century's greatest musicians, including Samuel Barber, Leonard

Bernstein, Gian Carlo Menotti, and Anna Moffo. The institute provides full-tuition scholarships to ensure that talent is the only consideration in admitting students. Among the best bargains in the city are the free student recitals given by Curtis students during the school year on Monday, Wednesday, and Friday evenings at 8:00 P.M. Call (215) 893–5252 or visit www.curtis.edu.

One of Philadelphia's grandest old hotels, the **Barclay** (237 South Eighteenth Street) is across the street from the Curtis Institute. Though it still maintains opulent rooms and suites as a hotel, much of the elegant building has been converted into luxury condominiums. Tucked inside on the third floor is the **Center for Emerging Visual Artists** (Suite 3A). Here's where you can see works by artists who haven't hit it big yet. Founded in 1984, this organization helps promising Philadelphia artists whose work is not yet represented by a gallery. The center claims quite an impressive track record. Exhibitions in the center's gallery turn over frequently, so call (215) 546–7775 or visit www.cfeva.org for more information.

The **Philadelphia Art Alliance** (251 South Eighteenth Street), is a multidisciplinary art center headquartered in a historic Italian Renaissance mansion built in 1906. The Art Alliance sponsors art exhibits, dramatic and poetry readings, dance and musical events, architectural displays, and a variety of lectures throughout the year, many of them free. A sculpture garden is open in warm weather. The gallery is open Tuesday through Sunday from 11:00 A.M. to 5:00 P.M. Call (215) 545–4302 or log on to www.philartalliance.org.

The Art Alliance building is also home to a romantic restaurant, **Le Jardin** (251 South Eighteenth Street). Here's something you don't find very often, particularly in the Rittenhouse area—an elegant restaurant with good food that is actually quiet and peaceful. In nice weather you can grab a table in the hidden garden, but leather banquettes inside make for a more intimate meal. Modeled on a Parisian bistro, Le Jardin has taken a while to find its culinary feet, but the food is consistently good now and you can't beat the setting. Open Tuesday through Friday from 11:00 A.M. to 2:30 P.M. and again from 5:00 to 10:00 P.M. Open for Saturday dinner from 5:00 to 11:00 P.M. and for Sunday brunch from 11:00 A.M. to 3:00 P.M. Open Mondays during the summer. For more information call (215) 545–0821 or visit www.le jardinsquare.com.

Head 1 block east to Latimer Street, a quiet enclave in the heart of the city and a street with some wonderful private gardens. A renovated carriage house is home to a gem of Philadelphia's art community. Though not widely known locally, the **Philadelphia Print Center** (1614 Latimer Street) has an international reputation. Founded in 1915 as the Print Club, it's now the oldest organization in the country devoted to promoting printmaking as an art form, with an enormous collection of prints and photographs. In 1942 the Print Center established a permanent collection at the Philadelphia Museum of Art, and the two organizations have worked closely together ever since. The center hosts solo and group exhibitions throughout the year, with an emphasis on emerging artists. Its annual competition draws the attention of artists from around the world. Original prints and quality reproductions are for sale in the gallery store. The Print Center is free and open to the public Tuesday through Saturday from 11:00 A.M. to 5:30 P.M. Call (215) 735–6090 or go to www.printcenter.org.

Locust Street between Sixteenth and Seventeenth is a particularly elegant block, dominated by **St. Mark's Episcopal Church** (1625 Locust Street). This church was designed in 1848 by John Notman, who also designed the Church

ahappycapacity

"There is enough of interest in the friends one makes in a day's idling among the floating population of this quaint corner to leave a lasting impression of the Philadelphian's happy capacity for an intelligent appreciation of an infinite number of things apart from the mechanical daily routine."

—Charles Henry White,
Philadelphia, 1906

More than Just *Rocky*

Well, you may think that *Rocky I, II, III,* etc., etc., etc., are the only movies ever filmed in Philadelphia, but not so. There have actually been more than fifty feature films shot here since the city hit the big screen with the first *Rocky* flick. Philly continues to run a successful campaign to convince Hollywood that its neighborhoods can be cinematic and cost-effective movie sets. Some recent movies shot here are *Annapolis; In Her Shoes,* which was based on the novel by Philadelphia writer Jennifer Weiner; *National Treasure,* a thriller starring Nicolas Cage; *Philadelphia* (surprise, surprise); and native son M. Night Shyamalan's *The Sixth Sense.* Remember *Trading Places* with Dan Aykroyd and Eddie Murphy? The opening was filmed in Rittenhouse Square, and the law firm's offices in the movie were in the First Fidelity Bank, now Wachovia, on South Broad Street. Not surprisingly, City Hall has popped up in a film or two. Its courtyard was featured in a scene in *Fallen,* and City Hall was an important setting in the futuristic *12 Monkeys,* starring Bruce Willis and Brad Pitt, which also utilized Eastern State Penitentiary as an insane asylum. In *Blow Out,* John Travolta drives his jeep through the City Hall courtyard, crashing it into the window of Lord & Taylor, which at the time was Philadelphia's beloved store John Wanamaker. Wanamaker's was also the setting for the forgettable *Mannequin* and *Mannequin Two.*

Philadelphia's Talking Skyline

PECO Energy's building at Twenty-third and Market Streets doesn't look like much during the day, but it's an integral part of Philadelphia's nighttime skyline. Wrapped around the top two floors are almost 3,000 lightbulbs displaying messages that encircle the building. The messages vary each night, but every morning the sign tells the time and wishes Philadelphia a good morning. It's all run by computer now, but it wasn't always that way. When the sign debuted in 1976, the messages were in red, white, and blue, and anytime they changed, someone had to climb up there and screw or unscrew hundreds of lightbulbs to spell out the message. Understandably, messages stayed up for weeks at a time.

of the Holy Trinity you saw right off Rittenhouse Square, as well as the Athenaeum in the historic district. Notman is also believed to have designed several of the brownstones that line the street, most of which date to the Civil War. Call (215) 735–1416 or visit www.saintmarksphiladelphia.org.

At Seventeenth and Walnut Streets you're ready to explore what they call either **Rittenhouse Row** or **Restaurant Row,** depending on whether you feel like shopping or eating. The block between Seventeenth and Eighteenth has long been considered the ultimate shopping experience. The strip recently went through a major reorganization and renovation spree, causing some to grumble that the national chains and their big box stores are taking over. Many of the original small, independent shop owners have been forced to less prime spots, but the Philadelphia flair is still there to be discovered. Heading east on Walnut, you're surrounded by the city's hottest dining spots. Philadelphia's reputation as a mecca for fine dining has only increased in recent years. Led by restaurateur Stephen Starr, trendy high-end eateries have popped up all over town. But this is where the standards are, and they line up like bottles of fine wine along this stretch of Walnut Street: Le Bec Fin (1523 Walnut), Susanna Foo (1512 Walnut), Striped Bass (1500 Walnut). Yes, they're wonderful, but also wonderfully expensive. If you're bound and determined to eat at one of these renowned restaurants, consider **Le Bar Lyonnaise,** which is downstairs from Le Bec Fin and which also features the handiwork of Le Bec Fin's master chef, Georges Perrier. It won't cost you a fortune and you don't have to get so dressed up to eat there. The mood is French bistro, and the menu ranges from Perrier's signature soups and salads to a few hearty entrees, but many diners are content with a glass of wine and the outstanding cheese plate. Open for lunch Monday through Saturday from 11:30 A.M. to 2:30 P.M. Dinner is served from 6:00 to 10:00

P.M. Monday through Thursday, until 10:30 P.M. on Friday and Saturday, and until 9:30 P.M. on Sunday. You can order from the lunch menu in the lounge area until 4:00 P.M. Monday through Saturday. Call (215) 567–1000 or go to www.georges perriergroup.com. Expensive.

If you want something less formal—and if you're a seafood lover—head around the corner to the **Sansom Street Oyster House** (1516 Sansom Street), a Philly favorite for years. The oyster bar is in front, with the dining room in back. The oyster stew and chicken salad with fried oysters are consistent favorites. Take time to appreciate the collection of oyster plates. Open Monday through Saturday from 11:00 A.M. to 10:00 P.M. and Sunday from 3:00 to 10:00 P.M. Call (215) 567–7683 or visit www.sansomoysters.com. Moderate.

Continue west on Sansom to Seventeenth Street, where you'll find the **AIA Bookstore** (117 South Seventeenth Street), many people's favorite place to browse or shop for unique gifts. Run by the American Institute of Architects, whose local offices are in the same building, this store keeps a close eye on design and stocks striking jewelry, gifts, and toys, as well as a wide selection of art and architecture books. Open Monday through Saturday from 10:00 A.M. to 6:00 P.M. (Wednesday until 8:00 P.M.). Call (215) 569–3188 or go to www.aiabookstore.com.

Halfway up the next block, tucked away below street level, is the **Joseph Fox Bookshop** (1724 Sansom Street), a charming independent bookstore that always tops Philadelphia's "best of" lists. This is your classic bookstore—a little musty and stuffed from floor to ceiling with books on any subject you could want. It's a testament to the warm staff, service, and selection here that Joseph Fox has held its own—despite the presence of several book superstores nearby. It's particularly well known for its selection of architecture books. Open Monday through Saturday from 9:30 A.M. to 6:00 P.M. Call (215) 563–4184 or visit www.foxbookshop.com.

The twentieth block of Sansom Street is experiencing something of a renaissance, with trendy restaurants and coffee shops popping up. If you're in the mood for a movie, the **Roxy Cinema** (2023 Sansom Street; 215–923–6699) is one of the city's best independent movie houses.

Right across the street you'll find the **Adrienne** (2030 Sansom Street), a small cooperative venue named after Adrienne Neye that's home to a number of cultural organizations. This was the original home of the Wilma Theater, and it now houses three performance spaces and two dance studios. The InterAct Theatre Company performs on the main stage, which, at only 103 seats, provides an intimate theatrical experience. This company develops and performs new dramatic works focusing on political and social issues. Sharing this space is 1812 Productions, a comedy troupe. The building also has a cabaret space and a smaller theater upstairs that is used by other theater groups and dance companies. Call (215) 568–8077 for schedules or visit www.interacttheatre.org.

The *First Unitarian Church of Philadelphia* (2125 Chestnut Street) was the only church designed by famed Philadelphia architect Frank Furness, and the reason is obvious: His father, the Reverend William Henry Furness, was pastor here for fifty years. The lectern in the pulpit was an original Furness design. The stained-glass window on the north wall is Tiffany. Parodoxically, First Unitarian has become something of a draw for Philadelphia's punk rock crowd. The local music promotions company R5 Productions regularly uses the space for its inexpensive punk and indie concerts. Call (215) 563–3980 for church information or go to www.firstuu-philly.org.

On Twenty-second Street between Chestnut and Market, you'll find what is surely the most bizarre place in Philadelphia. You really have to visit the *Mütter Museum* (19 South Twenty-second Street) to believe it, but one word of caution—don't go before lunch. The museum is actually a scholarly archive of "oddities and diseases," established by Thomas Dent Mütter in 1865. But to the uneducated eye, it's wall after wall of the weirdest of the weird. (The uneducated eye can wander over the Eye Wall of Shame, a display of assorted eye injuries, including a burned eye and one with a toothpick protruding from its retina.) The highlights, so to speak, of the museum are the remains of a man whose skeleton began to develop outside his body and the huge human colon—27 feet long and 8 feet in circumference. You can also view a cast of Siamese twins Chang and Eng Bunker, who fathered twenty-one children

Hahnemann's Harriet

Not all of Philadelphia's oddities are at the Mütter Museum. In the first-floor library of Hahnemann Hospital's New College Building (245 North Fifteenth Street), you'll find Harriet. She may look like a human form made of string, but that's actually the entire human nervous system. It seems Harriet Cole, an African-American cleaning lady at the medical school, willed her body to the school when she died in 1888. Anatomy professor Dr. Rufus Weaver worked overtime for five months, meticulously picking out bone and flesh from the cadaver until all that was left was the nervous system and eyes. Weaver preserved each strand in gauze soaked in alcohol, then coated every one with paint and shellac. Several hundred tiny pins later—voilà—a display of every nerve in the body. Harriet even traveled to the 1893 Columbian Exposition in Chicago, where she was awarded a gold medal. Visitors are welcome but must be cleared through security. Call (215) 762–7631 or visit www.hahnemannhospital.com.

between them and lived to be sixty-three years of age; the liver they shared has been preserved in a jar. But don't forget the exhumed body of an obese woman whose fat condensed down to soap—99.7 percent pure. There's a large collection of bizarre objects that one doctor pulled from his patients' throats. And for the politically inclined, there are the bladder stones of Chief Justice John Marshall, the thorax of John Wilkes Booth, and the so-called Secret Tumor of Grover Cleveland, which was clandestinely removed from his cheek while he was in office. Open daily from 10:00 A.M. to 5:00 P.M. Admission is $10.00 for adults and $7.00 for children and seniors. Your admission also gets you into the College Gallery, where you can see such changing exhibitions as Emerging Infectious Diseases: Ancient Scourge and Modern Menace. Call (215) 563–3737 or log on to www.collphyphil.org.

Places to Stay in Center City

Clarion Suites,
1010 Race Street,
Chinatown;
(215) 922–1730
This is your best budget bet in Center City, if a suite setup makes sense for you. It's actually right in the middle of Chinatown, so you get atmosphere as well as economy. Continental breakfast included. If you're using a car, look into the discount rates, because parking is scarce around Chinatown. Inexpensive.

Latham Hotel,
135 South Seventeenth Street,
Rittenhouse Square;
(215) 563–7474,
www.lathamhotel.com
Built in 1907 as an apartment building, this registered landmark was converted into a hotel in the 1970s. It's more on the romantic side,
with most rooms decorated in Victorian style, and has a reputation for personalized service. Moderate.

Marriott Philadelphia,
1201 Market Street,
Center City;
(215) 625–2900
If there's a convention in town, this may be too busy for your liking, but you can't beat the location. It's convenient to the historic district as well as Center City and Rittenhouse Square. Best of all, it's close enough to the Reading Terminal Market that you can eat breakfast and lunch there if you want—you'll save a fortune! A lush, five-story lobby adds to the atmosphere. Moderate.

Rittenhouse Hotel,
210 West Rittenhouse Square,
Rittenhouse Square;
(325) 546–9000,
www.rittenhousehotel.com
The rooms are large and the views are outstanding from this hotel right on Rittenhouse Square. An indoor
garden provides a nice breather, as do the room's luxurious marble bathrooms. The concierge service is a standout. You can also have high tea in the Mary Cassatt Tearoom every afternoon, and chef Jean-Marie Lacroix presides over Lacroix at the Rittenhouse, a deluxe eatery to match the best in town. Expensive.

Sofitel Philadelphia,
120 South Seventeenth Street,
Rittenhouse Square;
(215) 569–8300
The ultimate in French luxury, this is one of Philadelphia's newer hotels. It's tucked between Rittenhouse Square and the Avenue of the Arts in the former Philadelphia Stock Exchange Building. Its 306 rooms and fifty-five suites are decorated in modern but elegant French decor, with a cut rose in every room. The staff is particularly friendly. The bar is a favorite late-night destination offering live music. Expensive.

AUTHOR'S FAVORITE PLACES TO EAT IN CENTER CITY

Audrey Claire
276 South Twentieth Street;
(215) 731–1222

Bliss
224 South Broad Street;
(215) 731–1100,
www.bliss-restaurant.com

Capital Grille
1338 Chestnut Street;
(215) 545–9588

Effie's
1227 Pine Street;
(215) 592–8333

Friday Saturday Sunday
261 South Twenty-first Street;
(215) 546–4232,
www.frisatsun.com

Jamaican Jerk Hut
1436 South Street;
(215) 545–8644

Le Bar Lyonnaise
1523 Walnut;
(215) 567–1000,
www.georgesperriergroup.com

Lee How Fook Tea House
219 North Eleventh Street;
(215) 925–7266

McGillin's Olde Ale House
1310 Drury Lane;
(215) 735–5562

Mixto
1141 Pine Street;
(215) 592–0363,
www.mixtophilly.com

Sansom Street Oyster House
1516 Sansom Street;
(215) 567–7683,
www.sansomoysters.com

Vietnam
221 North Eleventh Street;
(215) 592–1163,
www.eatatvietnam.com

Places to Eat in Center City

Astral Plane,
1708 Lombard Street;
(215) 546–6230,
www.theastralplane.com
An out-of-the-way, off-the-wall alternative to Rittenhouse Square dining. It can be crowded and noisy, but that's part of the scene. The decor is delightful, if a little crazy, but the food is down-to-earth good. You can't go wrong with one of their generous salads or the daily special. They're also not shy about telling you all the famous people who've eaten there. Open Sunday through Thursday from 5:00 to 10:00 P.M., Friday and Saturday from 5:00 P.M. to midnight, and Sunday from 11:00 A.M. to 4:00 P.M. Moderate.

Ludwig's Garten,
1315 Sansom Street;
(215) 985–1525
Bavaria at its best. You're greeted in German by waitresses in dirndls and can start with a sampler of beers. There are sauerbraten, schnitzel, spaetzle, and strudel, and those in the know say you can't find better sauerkraut in Philadelphia. Open daily from noon to 2:00 A.M. Moderate.

Monk's Cafe,
264 South Sixteenth Street;
(215) 545–7005,
www.monkscafe.com
This casual, affordable restaurant has a European bistro feel. Some come just for the beer—they claim to

HELPFUL WEB SITES

www.centercityphila.org

www.phillychinatown.com

www.rittenhouserow.org

www.antique-row.org

have more than 200 varieties to choose from—but the food is surprisingly good. For lunch try the chicken and apple sausage, served with a tangy raspberry mustard. Regulars rave about the mussels. Open daily from 11:30 A.M. to 2:00 A.M. Moderate.

¡Pasión!,
211 South Fifteenth Street; (215) 875–9895, www.pasionrestaurant.com Just around the corner from Restaurant Row, this restaurant serves up nuevo Latino

food that may well be unlike anything you've ever eaten. Grab a seat at the ceviche bar, where chef Guillermo Pernot works his magic in plain view. Pernot wrote the book on ceviche—literally— and you won't find better. Open Monday through Thursday from 5:00 to 10:00 P.M., Friday and Saturday from 5:00 to 11:00 P.M., and Sunday from 5:00 to 9:00 P.M. Very expensive.

Porcini,
2048 Sansom Street; (215) 751–1175

Often named as one of the city's best Italian restaurants, this small BYOB is one of the top neighborhood hangouts. It doesn't take reservations, so you may have to wait, but once you get in, the waiters make you feel like family. If you're a regular, you often get a kiss on the cheek from the owner. For the quality of the food, the prices are quite reasonable. Open Monday through Thursday from 11:30 A.M. to 10:00 P.M. and Friday and Saturday from 11:30 A.M. to 11:00 P.M. Moderate.

South Street and South Philadelphia

South Street serves as a geographic dividing line between Center City and South Philadelphia, the land of *Rocky* and rigatoni, but it is absolutely no indication of what you see when you get to South Philly. South Street is a world unto itself. If you're a teenager and you want to go someplace your parents don't want you to be, you go to South Street. It is as hip and counterculture as Philadelphia gets. Funky shops, restaurants, and bars line the street, but one of the main activities here is watching the street life. There are lots of leather, tons of tattoos, and plenty of piercings to be seen.

Most of the action takes place at the east end of the street, between Front and Tenth Streets, where you'll find dozens of restaurants and stores, many with brightly painted facades to add to the colorful street life. Though the chain stores have tried to tag onto South Street's aura, you can still find shopping here you won't find anywhere else. Ironically, one of the street's first funky enterprises has now been pushed around the corner to lower rents, but you can still stock up on whatever spikes, studs, or rock t-shirts you need at ***Zipperhead*** (528 South 4th Street). It long ago set the punk standard for South Street. Zipperhead's original storefront on South has

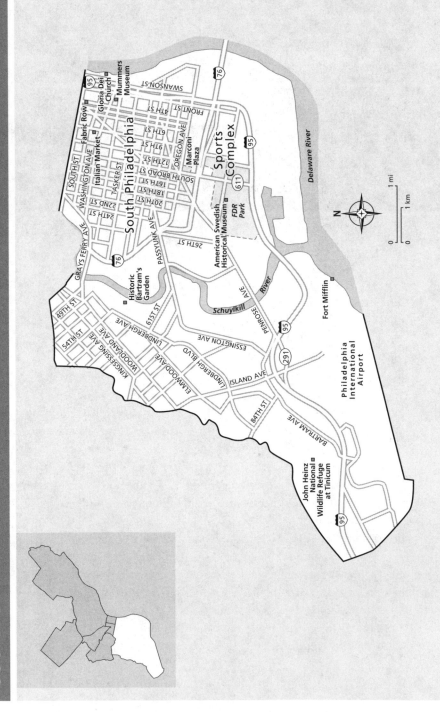

Name That Tune

If you're starting to hum as you walk down South Street, you may be showing your age. Remember The Orlons? They forever memorialized this drag as "the hippest street in town," in their 1963 song "South Street." A predominately female group of Philadelphia R&B singers, the Orlons were also responsible for such hits as "Wah-Watusi," "Don't Hang Up," and "Shimmy Shimmy." But "South Street" was their claim to fame, rising to the number-three spot on the *Billboard* music charts. The group disbanded in 1968. The music lingers on.

been taken over by a women's boutique, but it still displays the signature zipper and huge ants. Up the block is the ever-popular ***Condom Kingdom*** (437 South Street), where the window displays are always a highlight. Say no more (215–829–1668). And by now you're ready for ***Erogenous Zone*** (525 South Street), which specializes in erotic wear and adult novelty items (215–592–7302).

South Street likes to sell its bad-boy image, but you can also find some great gifts, crafts, and clothing here. One of the South Street originals is ***Eye's Gallery*** (402 South Street), owned by mosaic artist Isaiah Zagar and his wife, Julia. The storefront is one of Zagar's signature mosaics; what lies inside is an extravaganza of folk art and crafts from around the world (215–925–0193; www.eyesgallery.com). ***Benjamin Lovell Shoes*** (318 South Street) is a favorite, where you can find fashionable European shoes and comfortable clogs, many at discounted prices (215–238–1969). Across the street at ***Mineralistic*** (319 South Street), you're sure to find something you never knew you needed. As the name suggests, there's a large variety of minerals, crystal, and fossils, but there are also gargoyles, fountains, and figurines to choose from (215–922–7199). Not all of the action on South Street is cutting edge. Some authentic old-time Philadelphia classics remain, so you end up with electric supply stores next to tattoo parlors.

AUTHOR'S FAVORITES ON SOUTH STREET AND IN SOUTH PHILADELPHIA

Gloria Dei Church	Pink Rose Pastry
Italian Market	Tre Scalini

When it comes to eating, the establishments on South Street run the gamut. You can get everything from a cheesesteak to a gourmet meal. Don't shirk off that cheesesteak, though. There are those who swear *Jim's Steaks* (400 South Street) makes the best in town.

It's not all about eating, drinking, and shopping on South Street. Along with the nightclub scene, there are a few other places to check out. Comedian David Brenner continues to make his presence felt in his hometown with *David Brenner's Laff House* (221 South Street), a South Street comedy club of which he is co-owner. Acts range from big-name talent to local wannabes. The club's size (it accommodates about 250) makes the laughter infectious. Shows are at 8:30 P.M. on Wednesday and Thursday; 8:30 P.M. and 10:45 P.M. on Friday; and 8:00 P.M., 10:00 P.M., and midnight on Saturday. Call (215) 440–4242 or visit www.laffhouse.com to get more information. On the next block west you'll find the *Theater of the Living Arts* (334 South Street), an intimate venue for musical performances. This is the perfect place to catch a show from one of your favorite singer-songwriters or an up-and-coming local band; even Bob Dylan has graced the stage. Call (215) 922–1011 for a concert schedule or go to www.the ateroflivingarts.net.

After the buzz of South Street, there are also a few wonderful, lower-key places to check out just a block south on Bainbridge. For a cup of coffee and a treat, you can't beat *Pink Rose Pastry* (630 South Fourth Street). People drive here from the suburbs just to get their desserts, and the atmosphere is delightful (800–ROSE–383, www.pinkrosepastry.com). If tea is more your thing, you'll be in heaven in *The House of Tea* (720 South Fourth Street). It offers more than 300 fresh teas from all over the world. Buy it by the cup or by the pound. Articles hanging on the walls, one of them a cover story from *Life* magazine, tell about the founder of this unusual shop, Nathaniel Litt, who was an architect

Antiques Row No.2

If you enjoy antiquing, head to Sixth and Bainbridge. Though not officially Philly's antiques district (that's a little farther west), *Antiquarian's Delight* (615 South Sixth Street) is a great place to browse. A former synagogue was converted into space for more than twenty antiques dealers, which cater to South Street's hip crowd with an emphasis on vintage clothing and kitsch. Don't tell the folks on Pine Street, but some think this is the best antiquing in town. Open Wednesday through Sunday from noon to 7:00 P.M. (Saturday until 8:00 P.M.). Call (215) 592–0256.

TOP HITS ON SOUTH STREET AND IN SOUTH PHILADELPHIA

The American Swedish
Historical Museum

Geno's and Pat's

Italian Market

Mummers Museum

South Street scene

turned circus clown turned magician turned gourmet chef turned jam maker turned tea shop owner. Call (215) 923–8327 or go to www.houseoftea.com.

Catercorner to the Pink Rose is **Southwark** (701 South Fourth Street), one of the area's more popular new restaurants. It's the best white-tablecloth offering in the area. The front room houses an impressive mahogany bar that offers a high-end bar menu; no burgers or wings here. Next, there's a narrow dining room that overlooks a secluded courtyard, perfect for warmer weather. The menu offers seasonal specials using mostly local organic ingredients, accompanied by homemade crunchy parmesan bread. Open Tuesday through Thursday from 5:30 to 10:30 P.M., Friday and Saturday from 5:30 to 11:00 P.M., and Sunday for brunch from 11:00 AM. to 5:00 P.M. The bar is open Tuesday through Saturday until 2:00 A.M. (215–238–1888). Moderate.

Time now to move south—*really* south—into the heart of South Philadelphia, a widely diverse area of people and places that's known to the outside world as the Philadelphia of the *Rocky* movies. Many of the scenes for the original movie were filmed here, and they captured the feel of the narrow streets and street corners, as well as the character of the people. Food and family reign supreme here. If you asked Philadelphians where you should go if you wanted to go off the beaten path, most would likely say the Italian Market. It's where the area's commerce and characters come together, and if you want to shop for the freshest produce around or grab a cup of coffee and sit and watch the street life, this is the place to do it. But first, a tour of some of the sites near the Delaware will help you work up an appetite. Attractions here become further apart, so it's best to give your feet a rest and get behind a wheel. The area's one-way streets can make navigation frustrating, but the parking crunch eases considerably.

The transition from the South Street scene to South Philly is easiest and most interesting if you stay on Fourth Street, which from Bainbridge south to Catharine Street is known as **Fabric Row.** This is the real thing—Philadelphia's

Mosaic Magic

Philadelphia may be well known for its murals, but you'll also find numerous mosaic walls sprinkled around town, many gracing buildings on South Street. That's largely thanks to artist Isaiah Zagar, who has been plastering pieces of broken mirrors, tiles, bottles, bricks, and just about anything else he can find in designs throughout the city for decades. His masterpiece is the *Magic Garden* (1020 South Street). This was a derelict vacant lot in 1994 when Zagar moved into an adjacent building. He began to use the lot as his canvas, and soon it took on a life of its own. "I make art voluminously," Zagar has said. That's an understatement. The only problem is Zagar doesn't own the lot, and panic spread several years ago when the Boston owner threatened to sell it. An anonymous patron bought him some time and is covering the monthly payments while Zagar works to raise the money. Donations are coming in from many places, including through the front fence of the garden, where passersby drop about $100 a month into a swing-top trash can. See www.philadelphiasmagicgardens.org for more.

version of the garment district—and some of these businesses have been handed down through generations. You'll find portraits of the founders hanging in back rooms. Even if you're not in the market for material, it's a pleasant walk (www.fabricrow.com).

For an interesting historical detour, head to Pemberton Street between Second and Front Streets. Midway on the block you come to two brick houses facing each other across a walkway. If you stand across the street, you can see built into the brick walls the initials "G. M." on one house and the date "1748" on the other. That's the year these houses were built by George Mifflin, grandfather of General Thomas Mifflin, who built Fort Mifflin and was governor of Pennsylvania from 1790 to 1799.

Just a few blocks away is a favorite neighborhood restaurant, **Dmitri's** (795 South Third Street at Catharine). There's not much to see at this funky Mediterranean-style grill, but there's plenty to eat. Start with the avocado citrus-style and the hummus, which everyone raves about. The grilled octopus is also a favorite. It can be crowded, they don't take reservations, and it's a cash-only BYOB, but it's still worth it. The New Wave Cafe is right across the street; you can get a beer and the hostess will come get you when your table is ready. Open Monday through Saturday from 5:30 to 11:00 P.M. and Sunday from 5:00 to 10:00 P.M. Call (215) 625–0556. Moderate.

On Queen Street, between Second and Third Streets, is **St. Philip Neri Church** (218 Queen Street), a Greek-Revival church designed by architect Napoleon LeBrun when he was just nineteen. He would go on to design

A Fulladulfya Primer

"The dialect of the citizens of Philadelphia, particularly of the children . . . is very defective."

—Anne Royall, 1826

"Yo! Youse in Fulladulfya now." If you want to talk like a local, there are a few adjustments you're going to have to make. First you think it's a stereotype, then you hear it everywhere you go. So to help in the translation of Philadel-phese:

"jeez take" = cheesesteak;
"dah Fills" = the Phils (as in baseball);
"iggles" = Eagles (as in football);
"pavement" = sidewalk;
"ack-a-me" = Acme (a local grocery store);
"thirsty" = Thursday;
"addytood" = attitude;
"youse" = more than one of you;
"down the shore" = where you go on weekends (absolutely, positively, never "down to the shore");
"Wall Women" = the Walt Whitman Bridge you take to get down the shore; and
"segal" = the birds you see when youse down the shore.

Philadelphia's Cathedral Basilica of Saints Peter and Paul. Built in 1840, St. Philip Neri has a simple facade, but inside is a beautiful fresco of the Resurrection and an altarpiece created by Italian painter Nicola Monachesi. This church was the site of anti-Irish riots in 1844, in which several people were killed. Masses are celebrated daily at 8:00 A.M. and on Sunday at 8:00 and 11:00 A.M. Call (215) 468–1922. Or visit www.churchofstphilipneri.org.

Directly across the street from the church is *Mario Lanza Park* (200 Queen Street), a small park honoring a beloved South Philadelphia native. The famous tenor grew up on nearby Christian Street, and the park was dedicated in his memory in 1967. The nearby *Mario Lanza Museum* (712 Montrose Street) is chock-full of memorabilia and exhibits that tell the story of Lanza's life. Open Monday through Saturday from 10:00 A.M. to 3:00 P.M. Admission is free. Call (215) 238–9691 or log on to www.mario-lanza-institute.org.

Off the beaten path but very historic is the *Gloria Dei Church* (916 Swanson Street), which can be reached by taking Christian Street under Interstate 95. Also known as Old Swede's, this is the oldest church in Pennsylvania. Gloria Dei was finished in 1700, replacing the log structure that had served the church since the 1640s. Originally the congregation was Swedish Lutheran, but it joined the Episcopal Church in 1845. It is maintained as a historic site, and it's worth a close look. There's a bible from 1608 that once belonged to Sweden's Queen Christina. The carvings on the lectern and balcony were saved from the log church after a fire. Models of the ships that brought the settlers from Sweden hang from the ceiling. The church is surrounded by a courtyard that contains a caretaker's house, a guild house built in the eighteenth century, Parish Hall, and a historic cemetery in which several of George Washington's officers are buried. The highlight of every year is the festival of Santa Lucia, which is held during Advent. Open from 9:00 A.M. to 5:00 P.M. daily. Services on Sunday at 9:00 and 11:00 A.M. Call (215) 389–1513 or go to www.nps.gov/glde.

Just across Front Street from Gloria Dei, you'll see **Sparks Shot Tower** (Front Street between Christian and Carpenter) looming overhead. The centerpiece of what is now a playground and recreation center, this was the first shot tower of its kind in the United States when it was constructed in 1808. For almost one hundred years this was an ammunition plant. It was built by plumber Thomas Sparks and a partner, who developed a new method of making musket balls based on the principle that molten lead forms perfectly round balls when dropped from a high place. They would pour molten lead into molds, then drop them from the top of the tower into cooling water below. This tower produced tons of ammunition used during the War of 1812 and the Civil War, and it remained in the Sparks family for four generations before closing in 1903.

One of the most fun and least-known museums in Philadelphia is the **Mummers Museum** (1100 South Second Street at Washington Avenue). You won't get the refined cultural experience you'll have at some of the museums on Benjamin Franklin Parkway, but you'll sure get a feel for this city's unique mummers tradition. The celebration of mummery is practiced here in Philadelphia like nowhere else. This museum charts the history of the parade here, and exhibits

What's a Mummer, Anyway?

The roots of Philadelphia's famed New Year's parade can be traced back to ancient Greece. The word "mummer" derives from *Momus,* the Greek god of ridicule and blame. Not one of your better-known gods, understandably, but the story goes that Momus made the big mistake of complaining that Aphrodite's golden slippers squeaked when she walked. He was banished from Olympus in shame. His followers took to wearing golden slippers to protest his treatment. Thus the parade's anthem, "Oh, Dem Golden Slippers," which was written by African-American songwriter James Bland in 1879.

The Return of Rocky

While the world may have had enough of Rocky, they still love him in some quarters of Philly, so there was naturally great excitement in the air in early 2006 when Sylvester Stallone came back to town to film *Rocky Balboa,* the sixth and final chapter of his epic story. On the streets of Kensington, South Philly, and of course on the steps of the Art Museum, the film crews were back in action. There was Rocky again in the Italian Market—only this time he was buying produce for the restaurant he owns, thirty years after running these same streets as a struggling boxer. In Northern Liberties Rocky runs up a huge dirt mound in the vacant lot that once held the Schmidt's brewery. The Irish Pub at Twentieth and Walnut Streets gets air time, as does the Laurel Hill Cemetery in Fairmount Park, where Rocky grieves for his beloved Adrian. There was a certain nostalgia in the air as well, because Stallone insisted this was the end of the road for Rocky. And this time, he swore he really meant it.

give you an appreciation of how much work goes into making the elaborate, feathered costumes the performers wear. The Broad Street Room gives you a feel for what the parade is like, without having to shiver through the New Year's Day temperatures. There are video performances of past parades, and mannequins show off award-winning costumes of years past. You can even pretend to be a mummer yourself, following along with the steps to the mummers strut, of course accompanied by the requisite "Oh Dem Golden Slippers," the mummers theme song. Open Tuesday through Saturday from 9:30 A.M. to 4:30 P.M. and Sunday from noon to 4:30 P.M. You can catch a string-band concert during the summer on Tuesday night at 8:00 P.M. in the parking lot at the museum, weather permitting. Admission is $3.50 for adults and $2.50 for children and seniors. Call (215) 336–3050 or visit www.riverfrontmummers.com/museum.html.

Here you have a choice. You can head west toward the Italian Market or take off on the first leg of the South Philly Cheesesteak Tour (with some roast pork thrown in for good measure). Two of the best joints in town for real Philly food are buried deep in South Philadelphia near the riverfront. That's because they largely cater to the dock worker and construction crowd. You'll have to grab your sandwich and sit on a sidewalk picnic table, but it's a classic Philly experience. The cook taking your order may be gruff, but the food is great. You can reach ***John's Roast Pork*** (14 Snyder Avenue, 215–463–1951) and ***Tony Luke's*** (39 East Oregon Avenue, 215–551–5725) by heading south on Columbus Boulevard. Both have their cheering sections who swear these are the best cheesesteaks in town, much better than the other South Philly cheesesteak rivalry at Pat's and Geno's. (For the record, the *Philadelphia*

Inquirer's food critic sided with John's, a shack between a train track and factory.) You have to have a cheesesteak if you're visiting Philly, so your decision may be moot, but don't pass up the roast pork at either place. Drenched in juice and topped with garlicky broccoli rabe and sharp provolone, these sandwiches make converts of even the most diehard cheesesteak fans. The timing of your visit may also make your decision for you. The catch with John's is that it's only open weekdays until 2:30 P.M.—they're serious about catering to the working crowd. Tony Luke's—a little farther south but no more atmospheric, tucked under an I–95 overpass—is open Monday through Thursday from 6:00 A.M. to midnight and Friday and Saturday from 6:00 A.M. to 2:00 A.M. Although it is still an industrial stronghold, this area of South Philadelphia has undergone a retail transformation in the past few years, with the invasion of the big box stores.

If you're not quite up for such a curbside dining experience, have no fear—there's plenty of food fun if you head up Washington Avenue to the Italian Market. Ironically, it's probably a good idea to get something to eat before you explore the market, because your stomach won't appreciate all of that delectable food if it can't consume any of it.

You can pick up a piece of pizza or a hoagie from one of the storefronts in the market, but for something more refined, there are two South Philly landmarks near the market. ***Dante & Luigi's*** (762 South Tenth Street at Catharine) has a family feel to it, despite the linen tablecloths. This is classic Italian food, and lots of it. Try the osso buco or the cioppino for something a little different. Along with your food come the legends of Philadelphia's mob wars, since this is the restaurant where mob boss Nicky Scarfo was gunned down in the 1980s. But don't worry—things have calmed down considerably since then. Open Tuesday through Thursday from 11:30 A.M. to 9:30 P.M., Friday from 11:30 A.M. to 10:30 P.M., Saturday from 3:00 to 10:30 P.M., and Sunday from 3:00 to 9:30 P.M. Call (215) 922–9501. Moderate.

From a more down-to-earth lunch, 2 blocks south is ***Shank and Evelyn's Luncheonette*** (932 South Tenth Street), a small, quintessential luncheonette tucked into a residential block between Christian and Catharine Streets. This family-run spot has drawn some bigwigs over the years. Even Bill Clinton stopped by on a presidential visit to town. It's best known for its roast beef sandwiches, accompanied by pickled peppers and green tomatoes, but breakfast satisfies as well. Look for the RC sign. Open Tuesday through Saturday from 8:00 A.M. to 5:00 P.M. Call (215) 629–1093. Inexpensive.

Now you're well fed and ready for the ***Italian Market,*** which encompasses Ninth between Christian and Federal Streets. When tourists come to Philadelphia, they often want to see the Italian Market because they remember vividly the scenes in *Rocky,* when Sylvester Stallone jogs among the vegetable stalls and chases a chicken through the streets. Those tourists are often surprised because this is far from a movie set. This is the real thing, with almost one hundred vendors plying their goods in an open-air environment that doesn't always smell great and sometimes looks downright grimy. Every once in a while, the city jumps on a bandwagon to spruce up the market to make it more attractive to visitors and suburbanites, such as a recent replacement of rusted corrugated metal awnings with specially designed canopies. Some businesses have renovated, and there's an odd upscale coffee bar or crafts store here and there, but change comes slowly at the market, particularly considering that many of these businesses have been passed down through generations.

The Italian Market remains what it has been longer than any other outdoor market in the country: curbside stalls selling the freshest produce you can get, butchers wrapping up the special cuts, and boxes of ice topped with an amazing variety of fish. It can be a little overwhelming: There are four cheese stores; seven meat markets; four fish merchants; two pasta manufacturers; four poultry stores, including one with live chickens in pens out front; three spice markets; and four coffee and tea merchants. The list goes on, and you can even pick up some underwear, cleaning products, or a cheap pair of shoes. You'll also find the local gun shop. This is a bizarre bazaar, and while still largely Italian, there's been an influx of Asian merchants and other cultures as well, so there are often several languages flying around. In cold weather flames flare up from oil drums, and the tarps come down when it rains. Appropriately, at Ninth and Montrose Streets, a large mural of former mayor Frank Rizzo, beloved in this part of South Philly, watches over it all. You don't come here to eat, you come to shop, and you'll frequently see people packing up coolers for the trip back home. The market is open six days a week, every day except Monday, though not all stores observe the same hours. Most close early on Sunday. Come on a Saturday morning to have the real experience.

A few standouts not to miss include ***D'Angelo Brothers Products*** (909 South Ninth), where you can buy not only fresh game meat, but the hides and furs of some of them as well. (It can be a little disconcerting to order your emu fillets with an elk head watching over your shoulder.) At ***Dibruno Brothers*** (930 South Ninth), who knew cheese could come this big? This store stocks more than 400 cheeses—just try to find one they don't have. With food on your mind, it might make sense to drop into ***Fante's Cookware*** (1006 South Ninth Street), a shopping mecca for kitchen supplies. You want it, they've got it. Founded in 1906, this store sits right in the heart of the market, so you're in

A Hidden Art Treasure

The *Samuel S. Fleisher Art Memorial* (719 Catharine Street) is the largest tuition-free art school in the country. Founded in 1898, the school was set up to fulfill Fleisher's desire that "the world come and learn art." He took over first an abandoned school building at St. Martin's College for Indigent Boys, then the adjoining Romanesque-Revival Church of the Evangelist, both designed by Frank Furness. Most striking is the sanctuary of the church, which houses Fleisher's collection of ecclesiastical art, which the Philadelphia Museum of Art has supplemented with works from its own collections. There are medieval statues, stained-glass windows by John LaFarge, and beautiful wrought-iron gates. The gallery is open Monday through Friday from 11:00 A.M. to 5:00 P.M., Monday through Thursday from 6:30 to 9:30 P.M., and Saturday from 10:00 A.M. to 3:00 P.M. Call (215) 922–3456 or visit www.fleisher.org.

luck if you need supplies to cook all the food you just bought. Get the lineup of all the merchants and more information about the market at www.philly italianmarket.com.

If you want to experience the height of South Philly's scene, head to the dueling cheesesteaks. Everybody will tell you there are better cheesesteaks in town, and there are (there's even a Web site to address this pressing issue: www .bestcheesesteaks.com). But the classics square off catercorner at the intersection of Ninth and Passyunk Avenue: *Geno's* (1219 East Ninth Street, 215–389–0659) and *Pat's* (1237 East Passyunk Avenue, 215–468–1546). Both are open seven days a week, twenty-four hours a day when you've absolutely got to have a grease fix. Both have their loyalists, but for one-timers, it usually comes down to which line is shorter. For the record, Pat's claims to have invented the cheesesteak in the 1930s, though it was originally topped with pizza sauce. When President Clinton came to town, he diplomatically bought cheesesteaks at both places, though in failing to master the so-called "Philly lean," he did manage to drip grease down the front of his shirt.

There is an art to ordering a cheesesteak. Outsiders can be spotted a mile away; they're the ones asking for their "cheesesteak with onions." It's simply "with" or "without"—or, if you want to be really authentic, "wid" or "widout." If you want it the way it was originally invented, that's now called a "pizza steak." "With sauce" will get you a simple tomato sauce topping. There are subtleties in ordering peppers; you can choose hot, sweet, or cooked. And whatever you do, don't ask for a steak hoagie. That will get you a steak sandwich, with the standard hoagie accompaniments: lettuce, tomatoes, onions, and the like—nowhere near the real thing.

The heart of the commercial district on East Passyunk Avenue, from Broad Street to Tasker, is showing increasing signs of renewal, with more upscale restaurants and rehabbed apartments. They've even got an upscale Web site (www.passyunkrevitalization.org) aimed at bringing a more affluent crowd in to fill those newly fixed-up apartments. There's a restored Roman fountain at Tasker Street, with piped-in mellow music, and a nearby espresso bar where a furniture store used to be.

Despite the influx of trendier restaurants, many in the neighborhood still insist that South Philly's best dining spot is in a midstreet converted row house that is home to **Tre Scalini** (1533 South Eleventh Street). When you climb the three steps (the *tre scalini*) into this family-owned BYOB, there's no indication you're in for a superb meal. The dining room is tiny and cramped, and the walls alternate mirrored and wood panels. But as soon as they bring out the food, you stop looking around. Each meal begins with bruschetta, but go easy because you shouldn't miss the appetizers, especially the bouillabaisse. They offer a number of daily specials, and if they have it, go for the squid-ink pappardelle and shrimp in a tomato crabmeat sauce. The servings are hearty, so you'll leave with leftovers for lunch the next day. With that in mind, save a little room for a light sorbet for dessert. You'll spend more than you think you would for a BYOB, but it's worth it. Because Tre Scalini is so small, make reservations as soon as you can. Open Tuesday through Saturday from 5:00 to 10:00 P.M. and Sunday from 3:30 to 9:00 P.M. Call (215) 551–3870. Expensive.

Time now to continue even farther south, but if you've been walking up until now, get back in the car or head to Broad Street and hop on the Broad Street subway. (Any Philadelphia sports fan will tell you to leave the car at home: The subway is the best way to get to the sports complex.) If you do

Add Onions and Stir

It will never be the same as standing in South Philly with cheese dripping down your arms, but you can indeed make a cheesesteak at home. This is not brain surgery. Proceed as follows: Use fresh, good beef. (No Steak-ums!) Shave the beef very thin, so it cooks fast. If you want yours "with," sauté the onions as the meat cooks; whether to mix at this point or not is your choice. Use a fresh Italian roll—Amoroso's if you want to be authentic. Your key question is the cheese. To be the real thing, you should smear some Cheez Whiz right on the roll, but if you want "real" cheese, melt a slice of American or provolone on the meat until it slightly melts. Put the roll over your concoction and scoop it into the sandwich. Garnish with hot or sweet peppers. Enjoy.

Paying Tribute to Marian Anderson

Tucked away on a small cross-street in South Philadelphia is the *Marian Anderson Historical Residence and Museum* (762 South Martin Street). In 1924 the great contralto purchased this row house, just across the street from the Union Baptist Church where she sang as a child. Born in 1897 in Philadelphia, Anderson became the first African–American concert artist to sign with a major recording company. The home has now been restored by the Marian Anderson Historical Society and houses memorabilia, books, rare photos, and films relating to Anderson's life. Various rooms in the house are also used for lectures and musical programs. Tours can be scheduled by appointment; there is a $10 suggested donation. For more information call (215) 732–9505 or go to www.mariananderson.org.

drive down South Broad, you'll encounter one of South Philly's oddities: On wider streets, there's usually a line of cars parked right smack in the middle of the street. Only in Philadelphia.

At Broad and Oregon is *Marconi Plaza,* a center of neighborhood activities and celebrations. In 1926 this entire area was home to the sesquicentennial celebration of the signing of the Declaration of Independence. Though not quite the success of the 1876 centennial celebration in Fairmount Park—largely because it rained 107 out of the 184 days—the sesquicentennial did leave its mark on South Philadelphia. Right where Marconi Plaza now stands was the gateway to the exhibition, which was marked by an 80-foot-tall Liberty Bell, covered with 26,000 lights, that spanned Broad Street.

For an essential summer South Philly treat, stop in at *Pop's Water Ice* (1337 Oregon Avenue), a perennial winner of the "best water ice" contests around town. Pop's has been around since 1932, when Philippo Italiano—the original "Pop"—started selling frozen treats from a pushcart. These treats were popular in his native Italy, where they were called "water ice." Known by most people now as Italian ice, it's still "water ice" in Philly, where the third generation of Pop's family still scoops out generous portions. Open seven days a week March through September. Call (215) 551–7677 or log on to www.popsice.com.

Most of the sesquicentennial exhibition took place in the area now occupied by the city's sprawling *sports complex.* The Sesquicentennial Stadium, one of two permanent structures built for the fair, was later renamed JFK Stadium and stood at Broad and Pattison until the late 1980s. (The second permanent structure was the Ben Franklin Bridge, built to handle the traffic the fair was expected to bring.) The sports complex has recently undergone a major transformation, with two new venues replacing the old Veteran's Stadium. The NFL Philadelphia Eagles now call the 66,000-seat Lincoln Financial Field home, while Major League Baseball's Philadelphia Phillies inaugurated their digs with the 2004 season. The 43,500-seat, state-of-the-art Citizens Bank Park features natural grass and a dirt field, a view of the city skyline, and entertainment and food options that sometimes seem more exciting than the play on the field.

The Wachovia Center opened in 1996 and houses the NHL's Philadelphia Flyers and the NBA's Philadelphia 76ers. It is also a popular venue for big-ticket concerts and hosted the 2000 Republican National Convention. Right next door is the Wachovia Spectrum, which is now home to two minor-league hockey teams and the Kixx, the city's professional soccer team.

Across Broad Street are a few hidden treasures offering a different dimension to this sports-oriented neighborhood. ***The American Swedish Historical Museum*** (1900 Pattison Avenue) is located in FDR Park just west of Broad. Housed in a beautiful seventeenth-century Swedish manor house, the museum highlights the contributions of Sweden and its American settlers. You enter a two-story hall painted with colorful murals depicting scenes of the early life of Swedes in America. Twelve permanent galleries created by Swedish craftsmen take you through a history of Swedish interior design. Photographs and artifacts throughout trace the history of Swedes in Philadelphia. There's a re-creation of a *stuga,* a Swedish farmhouse, with its traditional corner fireplace and painted ceiling. An 11,000-volume library is open to the public, and the museum also hosts Swedish cooking lessons, lectures, and special workshops throughout the year. Open Tuesday through Friday from 10:00 A.M. to 4:00 P.M. and on weekends from noon to 4:00 P.M. Admission is $6.00 for adults and $5.00 for children and seniors. Call (215) 389–1776 or visit www.americanswedish.org.

FDR Park is also home to the city's premier ***Skate Park,*** since the police cracked down on the skateboarders who had taken over LOVE Park in Center

You'd Better Watch Out . . .

There's nothing like Philadelphia sports fans, who seem to love to hate their teams. In fact, Eagles fans have come to be known affectionately as "boo birds." The low point in Philly fandom came in December 1968, when a bunch of rowdy guys in the cheap seats at an Eagles game started pelting Santa Claus with snowballs during a half-time show. The city thinks it's found a solution to the problem and has opened an "Eagles Court" right at the stadium, allowing fans to be arrested, tried, and convicted on the spot. Philly sports fans have also become the fans other fans love to hate. Bob Uecker has said that when games are rained out in Philadelphia, fans go to the airport and "boo" landings. And Pete Rose once observed, "Some of these people would boo the crack in the Liberty Bell." Play on!

City. Here, tucked away under I–95, are 16,000 square feet of heaven for skate-boarders. This park, featuring pyramids, ramps, moguls, and a 12-foot half pipe, is not for beginners, and it's all concrete, so bring your protective gear.

Much farther off the beaten path, **_Historic Bartram's Garden_** (Fifty-fourth Street and Lindbergh Boulevard) is the country's oldest botanical garden and was home to the famed eighteenth-century botanist John Bartram. You won't believe you're on your way to someplace beautiful as you wind around the streets of southwest Philadelphia, but have faith and persevere. This is a place like no other. Overlooking the banks of the Schuylkill River, where you now gaze upon Philadelphia's skyline and an oil tank or two, it is fascinating to try to put yourself back in Bartram's time and see the beautiful, wild spot that must have spoken to him when he settled here in 1728. What remains is a forty-five-acre National Historic Landmark that includes Bartram's house; a barn and farm outbuildings; a few amazing historic trees, among them the oldest gingko in the country; and several gardens.

An American-born Quaker, Bartram was a self-taught botanist whose humble goal was to document all of the native flora of the New World. Toward that end, he traveled the uncharted land of the new colonies, bringing back seeds and plants to his farm. He was often accompanied on these journeys by his son William, who became a famous botanical illustrator. Bartram was responsible for one of the most important collections of North American plant life in the world. He forged a partnership and a deep friendship with Benjamin Franklin, who published several of Bartram's pieces in his almanacs. The two also

Rodin It Isn't

It is perhaps the most famous Philadelphia scene in modern memory—Rocky Balboa, a.k.a. Sylvester Stallone, raising his fists in victory atop the steps of the Art Museum. Well, you should have seen what happened when Sylvester Stallone commissioned a 9-foot-tall bronze sculpture of Rocky and put it at the top of the Art Museum steps for 1982's _Rocky III_. He thought he'd leave it there as a gift to the city. The art community begged to differ, calling the statue an ugly "movie prop." The debate raged in the city's newspapers, with suggestions ranging from "Put it near the Liberty Bell" to "Dump it in the Schuylkill." No one could argue that tourists loved the photo op, but _really_—the hallowed Philadelphia Museum of Art?! The Art Commission came up with a compromise that actually made sense: For several years, the half-ton statue stood outside the Spectrum sports arena in South Philly, Rocky's home turf. Recently the Art Commission and the city came up with a new compromise that lets _Rocky_ return to the Art Museum, although this time the statue stands at the bottom of the famous steps, rather than at the top.

Bartram's Home at Historic Bartram's Garden

exchanged seeds and together established the American Philosophical Society. In fact, Bartram's son would later name a tree he and his father discovered along the banks of Georgia's Altamaha River after Franklin—the *Franklinia altamaha*. The tree has never since been found growing in Georgia or any other native habitat, and the Bartram family is credited with saving it from extinction. Every *Franklinia altamaha* that exists today is the result of the propagation and cultivation of two plants that William Bartram grew from seeds brought back from the South. One looks out lovingly on the grounds of Bartram's Garden. Bartram also was fascinated by the medicinal use of plants and was said to have offered treatment to neighbors who could not afford medical care. His garden includes a thriving prickly ash, also known as the toothache tree. Chewing the bark was said to work wonders in easing the pain of tooth decay. Thomas Jefferson visited Bartram and purchased plants for Monticello, though it is said that George Washington found Bartram's garden a bit "tasteless."

Bartram regularly shipped seeds and plants from the New World to botanists in England, and he is credited with introducing 200 species of plants to Europe, which prompted King George III to name him the Royal Botanist in America in 1765. Bartram and his descendants lived in the stone house for 125 years, and the garden continued to flourish. The family published the world's first catalog of American plants in 1783. The city of Philadelphia bought the property in 1891 and has maintained it as a public park and historic site.

Visitors today can walk through the grounds, enjoying a wildflower meadow, a water garden, a kitchen garden with herbs and vegetables grown for culinary and medicinal purposes, and flower gardens. A wooded river trail winds through the floodplain. And don't miss the cider press, which was carved in bedrock on the banks of the Schuylkill.

The grounds are open from 10:00 A.M. to 5:00 P.M. throughout the year at no charge. Bartram's house and the museum shop are open Tuesday through Sunday from noon to 4:00 P.M. from March to December; tours are $5.00 for adults and $4.00 for children. A popular new series of Schuylkill River summer cruises from Bartram's Garden through Center City to the Water Works complex and back was inaugurated in 2004. Call (215) 729–5281 or visit www.bartrams garden.org.

It's not easy to find Bartram's Garden. The best way to get there may be to take the No. 36 trolley from City Hall, which stops just below the garden's entrance at Fifty-fourth Street. If you're driving, your best bet is to call for directions from your specific location or check out the comprehensive directions on its Web site.

timeforabreak

The 1784 Continental Congress adjourned a session specifically to visit Bartram's garden.

If you're still in the mood to be outdoors, or if you are a bird-watcher, head to the *John Heinz National Wildlife Refuge at Tinicum* (Eighty-sixth Street and Lindbergh Boulevard), not far from Bartram's Garden. Despite the fact that this is an industrial part of Philadelphia and near a busy airport, this has been a favorite spot for bird-watching. It was created thirty years ago by an act of Congress, designed to protect the last remaining freshwater tidal wetland in Pennsylvania. In 1991 the refuge was named after John Heinz, a late senator who had worked hard to preserve the Tinicum marsh. The refuge has become a major stopover on the Atlantic flyway and is now a resting and feeding area for an estimated 280 species of birds, 80 of which nest here. Visitors can also see fox, deer, muskrat, turtles, fish, frogs, and a wide variety of wildflowers. The marsh is one of the few places in the state where the endangered red-bellied turtle and southern leopard frog can be found. Several wide trails that branch off from the Cusano Environmental Education Center provide easy walking and biking. Canoeing and fishing are allowed in designated areas. The refuge grounds are open all year from 8:00 A.M. to sunset. The Environmental Center is open daily from 8:30 A.M. to 4:00 P.M., free of charge. If you're coming from Bartram's Garden, make a left on Lindbergh and it's a straight shot 3.5 miles ahead. The Route 37 bus passes the corner of Eighty-fourth Street and Lindbergh. Call (215) 365–3118 or go to http://heinz.fws.gov.

Just east of the airport, right on the Delaware River, is *Fort Mifflin,* which has served several important roles in the country's history. It's a little hard to put yourself into a historic mood with jumbo jets flying low overhead, but looking at the water, you can understand why a fort was established in this strategic location by the Delaware River at the mouth of the Schuylkill. Fort Mifflin stood as a first line of defense throughout the nineteenth century. It was a key battle at Fort Mifflin that held off British forces and allowed George Washington's troops to retreat to Valley Forge. After Washington's defeat at Brandywine in 1777, a force of 20,000 British troops, led by General William Howe, marched back into Philadelphia to regroup and get fresh supplies waiting on a fleet of ships on the Delaware. But while Howe and his troops had been fighting at Brandywine, rebel forces led by General Thomas Mifflin occupied and strengthened a partially built British fort guarding the waterways. Mifflin and about 400 soldiers held off a British onslaught for several days, inflicting heavy casualties on the British and delaying the supply ships. Though the fort finally fell back into British hands around November 16, winter had set in and Washington's troops had made it to Valley Forge.

Restored in 1795, Fort Mifflin was again manned during the War of 1812, though it saw no action. It was used as a prison camp during the Civil War, and although it was declared a National Monument after being disarmed in 1904, the fort was largely neglected until the city of Philadelphia took control in the 1960s. Now a National Historic Landmark, Fort Mifflin is one of the only remaining examples of a Revolutionary-era defense fortification system in the country.

The fort appears today as it did in 1834. You can take a self-guided or docent-led tour, and there are uniform and weapons demonstrations, as well as programs on the life of a soldier. The complex includes bombproof, vaulted casements; an arsenal with 4-foot-thick walls that was originally used as a prison; a number of batteries; a blacksmith shop; soldier and officers' quarters, as well as a northeast bastion; and a sweeping view of Philadelphia and the Delaware. In all, eleven buildings have been restored. Open from 10:00 A.M. to 4:00 P.M. daily from May through November. Tours start hourly at 10:00 A.M. from the flagpole. There are reenactments throughout the year. Call for a schedule. To get to Fort Mifflin, take Island Avenue to Enterprise Avenue, where you'll make a left. Then turn right on Fort Mifflin Road. The entrance to the fort is about a mile ahead on the left. Admission is $6.00 for adults, $5.00 for seniors, and $3.00 for children. Call (215) 685–4167 or visit www.fortmifflin.com.

Now *That's* a Pretzel

You think the soft pretzels you buy on the street corner are larger than your average pretzel? Try this one on for size; Joe Nacchio, a baker at South Philadelphia's Federal Baking Company, holds the record for making the world's largest pretzel. It weighed in at forty pounds and was 5 feet across. Bring on the mustard!

Places to Stay on South Street and in South Philadelphia

Your overnight options in South Philadelphia are pretty much confined to the major hotels near the airport. Your best bet is to stay in Center City, from which you can easily explore South Street and South Philly.

One quaint option lies just south of South Street:

Shippen Way Inn,
418 Bainbridge Street;
(215) 627–7266 or
(800) 245–4873

There are only nine rooms in this colonial B&B, which is owned and operated by a sister-and-brother team. It's a country inn right in the heart of the city. Housed in a restored 1750 building, the rooms are furnished with antique furniture and hand-made quilts, and each has a private bath. There's a patio and garden where you can have your complimentary breakfast if the weather is nice. The front room has a fireplace, and you're welcome to the wine and cheese kept in the refrigerator. It's as romantic as you'll get in this part of town. There's a parking lot right across the street, but the cost of parking is not included. Moderate.

Places to Eat on South Street and in South Philadelphia

Django,
526 South Fourth Street;
(215) 922–7151
This upscale BYOB isn't quite as hard to get into now that the original owners have moved on. The food is terrific and the space is elegant and more sophisticated than its South Street environs would have you believe. The menu is seasonal and changes frequently, but regulars always rave about the cheese plate. Open Tuesday through Sunday from 5:30 to 10:00 P.M. Moderate.

AUTHOR'S FAVORITE PLACES TO EAT ON SOUTH STREET AND IN SOUTH PHILADELPHIA

Dante & Luigi's
762 South Tenth Street at Catharine;
(215) 922–9501

Dmitri's
795 South Third Street at Catharine;
(215) 625–0556

Geno's
1219 East Ninth Street;
(215) 389–0659

John's Roast Pork
14 Snyder Avenue;
(215) 463–1951

Pat's
1237 East Passyunk Avenue;
(215) 468–1546

Shank and Evelyn's Luncheonette
932 South Tenth Street;
(215) 629–1093

Southwark
701 South Fourth Street;
(215) 238–1888

Tony Luke's
39 East Oregon Avenue;
(215) 551–5725

Tre Scalini
1533 South Eleventh Street;
(215) 551–3870

Lauletta's Grille,

1703 South Eleventh Street;
(215) 755–5422

Housed in a refurbished luncheonette, Lauletta's has earned a reputation as one of the best bargains in the city. At this BYOB you start off with roasted pepperocini, olives, and bread. The Mediterranean food is sophisticated, but the prices are down-home. Regulars rave about the homemade pastas and the seafood specials, and the owner's mother still makes her famous rice pudding. Open Tuesday through Thursday from 5:00 to 10:00 P.M.; Friday and Saturday from 5:00 to 10:30 P.M.; and Sunday from 4:00 to 9:00 P.M. Moderate.

Melrose Diner,

Fifteenth and Passyunk Avenue;
(215) 467–6644,
www.melrose-diner.com

If you're hungry in the middle of the night and not in the mood for a cheesesteak, you can always head to the Melrose Diner, a South Philly classic. The Melrose inhabits a fifty-four-seat Paramount diner, which has been dishing up traditional diner food around the clock since the 1950s. The waitresses call you "hon," and you can't beat the buttercream cake. Open all day, every day. Inexpensive.

Pif,

1009 South Eighth Street;
(215) 625–2923

Pif is a sign of the changing times that are starting to come to the Bella Vista neighborhood of South Philadelphia. It's a French country restaurant in the land of pasta and red sauce, but dining crowds agree it's a welcome addition. Just a block away from the Italian Market, this tiny BYOB is cozy, and though there's nothing special about its decor, the food is fabulous. Owner David Ansill heads to the Italian Market each morning and that day's menu depends on what strikes his fancy. There's an average of five appetizer and five entree choices, finishing up with a selection of cheeses and desserts prepared by Ansill's French-born wife. Open Tuesday through Saturday from 5:30 to 10:00 P.M. Moderate.

Ralph's,

760 South Ninth Street;
(215) 627–6011,
www.ralphsrestaurant.com

It's the character of this restaurant and the characters who run it that continue to bring people to Ralph's, which has been in the same family since it opened more than one hundred years ago. What's been consistent all those years is good, old-fashioned Italian food and reasonable prices. Ralph's is known for its red sauce, or "red gravy," as they call it in this part of town (yes, they even pick what they call "gravy tomatoes"). The restaurant has been in the same former boardinghouse since 1915; the original tile floor was uncovered and restored during a renovation several years ago. It's loud and cash only. Open Sunday through Thursday from noon to 10:00 P.M., Friday and Saturday from noon to 11:00 P.M. Moderate.

Victor Cafe,

1303 Dickinson Street;
(215) 468–3040,
www.victorcafe.com

If you're an opera lover, this is the place for you. Every twenty minutes or so, the waiters and waitresses put down their trays and break out in song. Most are voice students at the Curtis Institute of Music, so this is the real thing. In fact, founder Victor DiStefano began his life in Philadelphia by setting up a gramophone shop in 1918. People in the neighborhood would come and enjoy a spumoni while listening to Victor's beloved operas. When times got tough in the 1930s and Prohibition was repealed, the family got a liquor license and DiStefano's Gramophone Shop transformed into Victor Cafe, "The Music Lovers' Rendezvous." You come for the experience more than the food, which is standard Italian fare. A bit of movie trivia: Victor Cafe was transformed into a boxing-themed restaurant owned by Rocky Balboa in the *Rocky* series' final installlment. Open Monday through Thursday from 5:00 to 10:00 P.M., Friday from 5:00 P.M. to midnight, Saturday from 4:30 P.M. to midnight, and Sunday from 4:30 to 10:00 P.M. Expensive.

HELPFUL WEB SITES

www.south-street.com   www.phillyitalianmarket.com

Benjamin Franklin Parkway, Fairmount, and Fairmount Park

Many guidebooks talk about the riches of the Benjamin Franklin Parkway and Fairmount Park, but few people take—or even have—the time to truly explore the treasures to be found in this part of town. There's really so much to see here, and you should pace yourself. You know how tired your eyes—not to mention your feet—can get after several hours in a wonderful museum. And this is where the lion's share of Philadelphia's museums are located. While the performing arts are clustered along South Broad Street, the Benjamin Franklin Parkway is known as Museum Mile. For an overview of this elegant boulevard, you need only stand atop the steps of the Art Museum ("*Rocky* style," if you must) and take in the view. Designed to be Philadelphia's Champs-Élysées, the wide parkway extends from City Hall to the Philadelphia Museum of Art and is lined with trees, bright flags, and neoclassical buildings housing the city's top artistic treasures. This was the setting for the Philadelphia show in the worldwide Live 8 concerts, which drew an estimated crowd of 800,000 in July 2005.

Looking ahead, the Parkway is adding more jewels to its crown. After much drama and many courtroom battles, plans appear to be in place to move the world-class collection of the Barnes Foundation in nearby Merion to a new building on

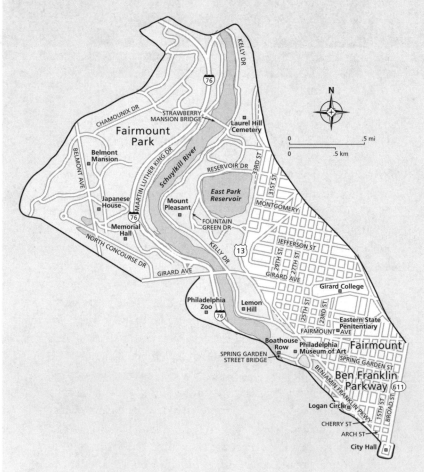

Museum Mile, at the current location of the Youth Study Center. And there are still hopes of establishing a Calder Museum, which would honor the sculptural work of three generations of Calders: the well-known twentieth-century artist Alexander Calder, whose father, Alexander Stirling Calder, was responsible for the Swann Fountain in Logan Circle, and his father, Alexander Milne Calder, who created City Hall's towering statue of William Penn. A site was chosen at Twenty-second Street and the Parkway, where several of Calder's sculptures are currently installed, but the plan has been put on hold while fund-raising and logistical issues are worked out.

Regardless, there certainly is plenty to see here already. To set the stage for your exploration of the Parkway, begin at Kennedy Plaza across from City Hall (Fifteenth Street and JFK Boulevard). Here you'll find Robert Indiana's famous **LOVE sculpture,** which has been called the most plagiarized piece of artwork in the country. The sculpture was originally on loan for the bicentennial cele-bration in 1776, but there was such a public outcry when it was later removed that the owner of the Philadelphia 76ers basketball team paid for its permanent installation. A recent redesign and renovation of the plaza was controversial, since LOVE Park, as it's also called, had become a major destination for skate-boarders. The city agreed to install skateboarding equipment at recreation cen-ters throughout the city, but many young people are still fuming about the loss of what was said to be one of the premier skateboarding sites in the country.

The Cathedral of Saints Peter and Paul (Eighteenth Street and Ben-jamin Franklin Parkway) is the seat of the Roman Catholic Archdiocese of Philadelphia. Built between 1846 and 1864, the cathedral was designed by Napoleon Le Brun, who also designed the Academy of Music, and John Not-man, who was responsible for its Palladian facade. The Italian Renaissance influences are also apparent inside, where the dome was painted by Constan-tino Brumidi, who painted the dome of the Capitol in Washington. The side

AUTHOR'S FAVORITES ON THE BEN FRANKLIN PARKWAY AND IN FAIRMOUNT

Cedar Grove	Pavilion in the Trees
Eastern State Penitentiary	Philadelphia Museum of Art
Fairmount Water Works	Swann Memorial Fountain
Mount Pleasant	View from Belmont Plateau

One Percent for Art

As you walk around downtown Philadelphia, it can seem like you are being bombarded with art—some of it wonderful, some of it quite terrible. You can thank the city's 1-percent-for-art rule. This regulation requires planners and architects to set aside 1 percent of the cost of a building for decoration on any building constructed within the city limits. That can be a sculpture, a mural, bas-relief, whatever. Whether the art is your taste or not, you can certainly say one thing: There's a lot of it.

chapels were turned into a series of shrines during a 1950s renovation. Call (215) 561–1313 for more information.

The cathedral fronts **Logan Circle** and its **Swann Memorial Fountain,** one of the city's most beloved and photogenic locations. Though certainly circular now, this is actually one of William Penn's original squares. The fountain was the work of Alexander Stirling Calder, and its three figures represent the city's three main waterways: the Delaware River, the Schuylkill River, and Wissahickon Creek. On hot summer days it's not unusual to see children romping in the fountain's cool waters. If this is a return trip to Philadelphia for you, you may notice something different about Logan Circle. The lovely stand of giant paulownia trees that surrounded the fountain and burst into purple bloom each spring had to be removed in 2005 because of old age. Though they have been replaced with new trees, it will be a few years before the landscaping grows to regal proportions.

The imposing twin structures on either side of Nineteenth Street north of the Parkway are the Family Court building and the **Free Library of Philadelphia.** Even if you're not looking to check out a book, it's worth it to step into the library. Display cases in the entrance hall showcase exhibits, frequently featuring the library's impressive rare book collection. Fund-raising is underway for a planned $120 million expansion of the library, designed by renowned architect Moshe Safdie. Open Monday through Wednesday from 9:00 A.M. to 9:00 P.M., Thursday through Saturday from 9:00 A.M. to 5:00 P.M., and Sunday from 1:00 to 5:00 P.M. Tours can be arranged by calling (215) 686–5322; for more information visit www.library.phila.gov.

The Shakespeare monument in front of the library was created by Alexander Stirling Calder in 1928, with Hamlet and Touchstone the fool representing Tragedy and Comedy. You may notice that Shakespeare's name is spelled two different ways on the sculpture; the last time the Bard wrote his name, he reportedly spelled it "Shakspere." Just around the corner on Twentieth Street, the Friends of the Free Library operate the **Book Corner** (311 North Twenti-

Rodin Museum

eth Street), a terrific used-book store where you can pick up books on just about every subject imaginable, as well as a few music selections. The Book Corner also sponsors an annual poetry festival, writers' readings, and children's performances. Open Monday through Saturday from 10:00 A.M. to 6:00 P.M. Call (215) 567–0527 for more information.

Anchoring the grand stretch of the Parkway from Twentieth Street to the Art Museum are two large marble monuments that honor the soldiers, sailors, and marines of the Civil War. To the right, you pass the Youth Study Center, the site chosen as the home of the Barnes Foundation.

Visitors on their way to the Museum of Art sometimes pass up the ***Rodin Museum*** (Twenty-second Street and Benjamin Franklin Parkway), an astonishing collection of the works of Auguste Rodin. The famous *Thinker* draws you into this small museum, which contains 124 of Rodin's sculptures, donated to the city by philanthropist Jules E. Mastbaum in the 1920s. This is the largest collection of Rodin's work outside of France. Many of the sculptures are placed in a lovely formal garden outside, including *The Gates of Hell,* on which Rodin

No Ordinary Bird

One of Philadelphia's oddest treasures is hidden away in the Rare Book Department on the third floor of the Free Library. Grip, a stuffed raven, was a beloved pet of Charles Dickens, played a role in his serialized novel *Barnaby Rudge,* and may well have been the inspiration for Edgar Allan Poe's famous poem *The Raven.* When Grip died in 1841 (possibly from eating lead paint), Dickens had him mounted, and a trail of collectors finally led to the Free Library. He was recently declared a Literary Landmark by the American Library Association.

worked for thirty-seven years before his death in 1917. Open Tuesday through Sunday from 10:00 A.M. to 5:00 P.M. Admission is $3.00. Call (215) 763–8100 or log on to www.rodinmuseum.org.

Just below the Museum of Art lies **Eakins Oval,** named for native son Thomas Eakins, one of the country's most-loved painters. He is best known, at least in Philadelphia, for his images of crews rowing on the Schuylkill. Here sits Philadelphia's version of the Washington Monument. Created by German sculptor Rudolph Siemering, Washington rides on horseback above four fountains representing four great waterways of America—the Mississippi, the Potomac, the Delaware, and the Hudson. The thirteen steps at the base represent the original thirteen colonies.

You'll need lots of time to take in the treasures at the **Philadelphia Museum of Art.** Be sure not to miss several galleries often overlooked by visitors who concentrate only on the paintings and sculpture. Sunkaraku—a ceremonial teahouse—is tucked away in Gallery 244 in the Asian Art Collection. The museum purchased Sunkaraku from Ōgi Rodō, the architect who constructed it using elements from an eighteenth-century teahouse. It is the only work of Rodō's outside of Japan. The museum also holds collections from closer to home, including an extensive display of Pennsylvania German artifacts and a room devoted to Shaker furniture. Open Tuesday through Sunday from 10:00 A.M. to 5:00 P.M. and Friday evening until 8:45 P.M. Wednesday night happenings throughout the year incorporate music and film and have become quite popular. Admission to the museum is $12.00 for adults, $9.00 for seniors, and $8.00 for children and students. Pay what you wish all day on Sunday. Call (215) 684–7500 or go to www.philamuseum.org.

Fairmount

One of Philadelphia's nicest residential areas adjoins the Art Museum grounds. The Fairmount section is a small, compact neighborhood bordered by the Park-

Daring Diana

The copper statue of Diana inside the great hall at the Philadelphia Museum of Art was originally built as a weathervane for the tower of the first Madison Square Garden in New York. Designed by Augustus Saint-Gaudens in 1886, the goddess of the hunt originally wore a billowy drape to catch the wind. At the time, Diana marked the highest point in the New York skyline. She was a little too unwieldy as a weathervane, however, and was taken down in 1892.

TOP HITS ON THE BEN FRANKLIN PARKWAY AND IN FAIRMOUNT

Academy of Natural Sciences	Please Touch Museum
Eakins Oval	Postcard view of Boathouse Row
Franklin Institute	Rodin Museum
Philadelphia Museum of Art	Shofuso
Philadelphia Zoo	

way and two historic structures—Girard College and the fascinating Eastern State Penitentiary. The last decade has seen this area transformed into one of the most desirable addresses in town, with renovated row houses and an abundance of restaurants and neighborhood taverns. Fairmount opens its doors during an annual house tour in May, but it is pleasant to wander around this neighborhood any time of year or to slip away from the museums and have lunch here.

As you walk up Twenty-fifth Street, you pass a dramatic building belonging to the Art Museum. Sporting an elaborate art deco facade, the building once housed the Reliance Standard Life Insurance Company. It has been renovated and expanded with new galleries for the museum's photography collection, modern and contemporary design, and costume and textile displays. The newly renamed Ruth and Raymond G. Perelman Building is scheduled to open in fall 2007. If you continue on North Twenty-fifth Street you come to two of the neighborhood's best restaurants. *Figs* (2501 Meredith Street) is a recent upscale BYOB that quickly became one of the most popular dining spots around. The colors and cuisine of the Mediterranean take center stage, with its Moroccan-born chef overseeing the kitchen. If the weather's nice, you can grab a table outside. Fish specials, in particular, get rave reviews. Finish off with fig ice cream. Open Tuesday through Friday from 11:00 A.M. to 2:30 P.M. and Saturday and Sunday from 10:30 A.M. to 2:30 P.M. for lunch; Tuesday through Saturday from 5:00 to 10:00 P.M. for dinner. Call (215) 978–8440. Moderate.

Just up the street is *Aspen* (747 North Twenty-fifth Street), another corner tavern and restaurant that's worked its way into the neighborhood's heart. There's a small dining room behind the bar that serves a full dinner menu, but the real winner here is the bar menu, which is available until 1:00 A.M. every night of the week. Talk about a neighborhood service. There are sophisticated appetizers and salads available as well as entrees like New York strip steak

Girard College

Despite its name, Girard College, 2101 South College Avenue in the Fairmount section, is actually a school for children in grades one through twelve. It was established in 1848 in the will of Stephen Girard, a wealthy banker, to educate "poor white male orphans." The boarding school now accepts boys and girls of any race from families headed by a single parent or guardian, with all students receiving full scholarships. The school's Founder's Hall looks more like a temple surrounded by huge Corinthian columns. It took fourteen years to build and at the time was one of the most expensive buildings in the world. The Girard campus also had a starring role in the movie *Annapolis,* in which it portrayed the U.S. Naval Academy. Call (215) 787–2600 or log on to www.girardcollege.com.

and pan-blackened tuna that would suffice at any restaurant. If you have room, be sure to try the fried cheesecake for dessert. Open from 5:00 to 10:00 P.M. Sunday through Thursday and from 5:00 to 11:00 P.M. Friday and Saturday; the bar menu is available from 5:00 P.M. to 1:00 A.M. nightly. Call (215) 232–7736 or visit www.aspenphilly.com.

If you're here when it's light outside, take a stroll down the 2500 block of Aspen Street, a unified block of homes built in 1875 that are distinguished by their terrace gardens and mansard roofs.

In many ways the Fairmount section is defined by the ***Eastern State Penitentiary*** (2000 Spring Garden Street), a behemoth landmark with a fascinating history. When it was built in 1829, it was considered the ultimate in prison design and was used as a model around the world. (It was also, at $780,000, the most expensive building in America to date.) At that time the prison's location was on a farm more than a mile outside the city limits. Visitors today are often surprised to find it right in the middle of a bustling urban neighborhood, a stone's throw from the business district.

Eastern State's radial design reflected a revolutionary new Quaker concept in prison reform in the early nineteenth century. The idea was to replace brutality and physical punishment with isolation and introspection. Long cell blocks extend like spokes from a central hub, all of which is surrounded by walls 30 feet high and 12 feet thick at the base. Each prisoner was kept alone in a private cell, unable to communicate with any other person, and no one was allowed to sing, whistle, or read newspapers. Individual cells had heat, running water, and a flush toilet, something even the White House couldn't say at that time. There was a private exercise yard outside each cell, surrounded by a 10-foot wall, which prisoners could use for one hour a day. They were given manual jobs such as weaving and shoemaking, and a single skylight provided the cell with the light of God. The Quakers believed that enough time and solitude would make the criminals see the error of their ways and lead to a true penitence (thus the new word "penitentiary").

Not everyone approved of the new philosophy of punishment. When Charles Dickens visited America in 1842, he wanted to see just two things— Niagara Falls and Eastern State. He was not impressed, writing, "I hold this slow and daily tampering with the mysteries of the brain to be immeasurably worse than any torture of the body." In the end, some prisoners went stark, raving mad, and the system was deemed a failure. Closed and abandoned in 1971, the penitentiary sat vacant and deteriorating for years, as preservationists fought off a number of development proposals. In 1984 the city handed control of the facility to the Pennsylvania Prison Society, a direct descendant of the Quaker reform organizations, and the site is now open for historic tours. It also roars back to life around Halloween, when it hosts one of the city's favorite and spookiest haunted houses. The prison has also played host to numerous art installations and performances. A recent $1 million renovation stabilized the roof, meaning visitors no longer have to wear hard hats, but there's no doubt this is a rustic experience that some have compared to visiting an Old World ruin. The penitentiary is open for tours Wednesday through Sunday from 10:00 A.M. to 5:00 P.M. from April to November. A visitor area includes a small museum with artifacts from the early days. You can take a self-guided tour of the prison; guided tours are offered on the hour. No children under seven are allowed onto the site. Admission is $9.00 for adults, $7.00 for seniors, and $4.00 for children. Call (215) 236–3300 or log on to www.easternstate.org.

Just across the street from Eastern State is a fun place to eat. Housed in a renovated fire station (complete with the brass fire pole), ***Jack's Firehouse*** (2130 Fairmount Avenue) offers down-home cooking with an upscale twist. Owner Jack McDavid, usually seen in overalls and a "Save the Farm" cap, began his career in Philadelphia at the renowned Le Bec Fin and made it big appearing on the *Grillin' & Chillin'* show on the Food Network. He also owns the popular Down Home Diner in the Reading Terminal Market. McDavid insists on using only locally grown and raised products and swears he even makes his own mayonnaise and ketchup. The theme here is "haute country." Try the buffalo or other game meats you won't see other places, and don't miss the black-eyed pea and hog jowl soup. Open Monday through Saturday for lunch from 11:30 A.M. to 4:30 P.M. and dinner from 5:00 to 10:30 P.M. Sunday brunch is served from 11:00 A.M. to 3:00 P.M., with dinner on Sunday from 5:00 to 10:00 P.M. Call (215) 232–9000 or visit www.jacksfirehouse.com. Moderate.

If you want something lighter or need a cup of coffee, try down the street at the cleverly named ***Mugshots*** (2100 Fairmount Avenue). You can grab a quick breakfast or a wrap for lunch, or try one of their fresh-squeezed juices or smoothies. You can even check your e-mail at a computer. Open Monday through Friday from 6:30 A.M. to 10:00 P.M., Saturday from 8:00 A.M. to 9:00 P.M., and Sunday from 8:00 A.M. to 5:00 P.M. Call (215) 514–7145 or visit www.mugshotscoffeehouse.com.

It's hard to miss the large community garden that occupies the block between Wallace, North, Eighteenth, and Nineteenth Streets. Surrounded by a custom-made wrought-iron fence, this is a shining example of the many neighborhood garden co-ops throughout the city.

As you wander around Fairmount, you notice a preponderance of the murals for which Philadelphia has become so well known. The city's *Mural Arts Program* (1729 Mount Vernon Street) is headquartered here in a house that was occupied by painter Thomas Eakins's family in the mid-1800s. Besides overseeing the city's more than 2,000 murals, the program offers arts education classes from its newly expanded headquarters and maintains gallery space devoted to mural arts. Open Monday through Friday from 9:00 A.M. to 5:00 P.M. A wonderful option for visitors wanting to see some of this amazing urban art are weekly Saturday tours that depart from the Independence Visitor Center. Tours leave at 11:00 A.M., exploring a different section of the city each week. The trolley tours run every Saturday from April through October; the cost is $20 for adults, $17 for students and seniors, and $10 for children. Call (215) 685–0750 or visit www.muralarts.org for more information.

As you head back to the Parkway, take the time to wander a few blocks of Green Street, a particularly lovely residential section of Fairmount.

If you have young children, you'll love the *Please Touch Museum* (21 North Twenty-first Street), a museum made just for kids. They call it a museum, but it's really more like a giant play area, where children can have so much fun they won't even realize they're learning something. Work is under way to convert historic Memorial Hall in Fairmount Park into a much larger home for the Please Touch. For now its home is a playfully renovated storefront building. It's aimed at children seven years or younger and includes areas where kids can shop for and prepare their own play food in a kid-kitchen, drive a city bus, use a miniature crane to guide cargo onto a ferry on a replica of the Delaware River, or romp with life-size creatures from the books of Maurice Sendak. Open seven days a week from 9:00 A.M. to 4:30 P.M. (5:00 P.M. in the summer). Admission is $9.95 per person. Call (215) 963–0667 or go to www.pleasetouchmuseum.org.

You come now to the *Franklin Institute* (222 North Twentieth Street), Philadelphia's renowned science museum. It's perfectly clear from the start for whom this museum was named—the 20-foot-high, marble Benjamin Franklin National Memorial sits smack in the middle of the entry rotunda. This hallowed space was the site of many celebrations in 2006 when Philadelphia celebrated Franklin's 300th birthday. The Franklin Institute is one of the city's most popular destinations for visitors and locals alike; generations of Philadelphians have memories of the giant pendulum and the famous walk-through heart. Not quite so well known are two exhibits you should seek out: Franklin—He's Electric explores Ben Franklin's lesser-known inventions, such as his glass harmonica and bifocals; and Space Command, the perfect place for any kid who has fantasies of becoming an astronaut. Be sure to ask about the wide variety of daily shows and demonstrations that take place throughout the museum, and take time to ride the sky bike. A park out back offers interactive activities in a playground like setting from 10:00 A.M. to 3:00 P.M. from May through September. Admission is $13.75 for adults and $11 for children and seniors, but it goes up for some special exhibits and if you want to see shows at the museum's IMAX theater. Call (215) 448–1200 or log on to www.franklininstitute.org for information about special exhibitions.

A block from the Franklin Institute is *St. Clement's Episcopal Church* (Twentieth and Cherry Streets), a beautiful church designed by John Notman in 1859. (The entrance to the church and its gardens is actually off Appletree Street.) The church is noted for the triptych on its high altar and the wrought-iron gates on the Lady Chapel, which were designed by Samuel Yellin. Visitors are welcome to look around when services are not in session. Call (215) 563–1876 or visit www.s-clements.org.

At Twentieth and Race Streets, the *Moore College of Art* exhibits work from students and nationally known artists in two galleries. Founded in 1848 as the Philadelphia School of Design for Women, Moore was the first industrial arts school for women, originally focusing on textile design. In 1931 the state gave the school the go-ahead to grant Bachelor of Science in Art Education degrees, making it the first independent art school in the country allowed to award degrees. Open Tuesday through Friday from 10:00 A.M. to 5:00 P.M. and Saturday and Sunday from noon to 4:00 P.M. No admission fee. Call (215) 965–4045 or visit www.thegalleriesatmoore.org.

Next door is the *Academy of Natural Sciences* (1900 Benjamin Franklin Parkway). The Academy is best known for its exhibits of stuffed birds and animals, but things are a little more cheerful in the live butterfly exhibit. If you have children, be sure to visit Outside-In, an often-overlooked, hands-on exhibit on the top floor where kids can crawl under a pond, look for fossil footprints, and sift through sand for shark teeth. Open Monday through Friday from 10:00 A.M. to 4:30 P.M. and weekends and holidays from 10:00 A.M. to 5:00 P.M. Admission is $10.00 for adults, $8.25 for seniors, and $8.00 for children. Call (215) 299–1000 or log on to www.acnatsci.org.

The statue in front of the **Four Seasons Hotel** (1 Logan Square) depicting Polish military hero Thaddeus Kosciuszko was given to the United States by the people of Poland during the bicentennial celebration as a sign of friendship between the two countries. The national memorial honoring Kosciuszko is located at Third and Pine Streets in Society Hill.

Nestled within the Four Seasons is what many people insist is still the best restaurant in town. **The Fountain** has been on the best-restaurant list for so long that surveys keep coming up with new categories for it. One was "the best restaurant in which to propose." You can't beat its outstanding views of the Swann Fountain, elegant decor, and extensive wine cellar. If you're looking for an elegant Sunday brunch, this is the place to go. Breakfast is served from 6:30 to 11:00 A.M. Monday through Friday, 7:00 to 11:00 A.M. Saturday and Sunday. Lunch is offered daily from 11:30 A.M. to 2:15 P.M., and dinner is served from 5:45 to 10:00 P.M. The remarkable Sunday brunch is available from 11:00 A.M. to 2:15 P.M. Also inside the Four Seasons is the Swann Lounge, which offers an oh-so-civilized afternoon tea with finger sandwiches and pastries. Call (215) 963–1500. Very expensive.

For something way more casual, head to **Mace's Crossing** (1714 Cherry Street), a headstrong tavern that refused to leave this prime location when developers were planning to build a large apartment building on the site. As you can see, they were forced to build around the bar. Though very small, Mace's Crossing has an upstairs dining room that offers above-average bar food at reasonable prices. If the weather's nice, you can eat on the patio, which provides great people watching. Open daily from 11:00 A.M. to 2:00 A.M. Call (215) 564–5203. Moderate.

Fairmount Park

In 1681 a man named Thomas Holme sketched out the first map of the area surrounding William Penn's new city. His effort—A Mapp of Ye Improved Part of Pensilvania in America, Divided into Countyes, Townships and Lotts—shows a prominent hill sketched to the north of the city, near the banks of the Schuylkill River, which he designates "Faire Mount." Over time, what came to be called Fairmount Park grew to be the largest city park in the country—8,700 acres—and Philadelphians remain fiercely proud of it. They jog, in-line skate, and bike here daily on generous paths on either side of the Schuylkill. Summer days find a variety of picnics taking place, and on summer nights the fishermen come out and softball, rugby, and even cricket leagues fill its fields. If you live here long enough, you learn your way around the park, but a first-time visitor is often thrown off course by its winding roads and circuitous paths. A good map is a must and can be picked up at the visitor center.

Another must for most of the park is a car. If you're exploring on foot, stick to the areas around the Art Museum. The river is bounded by roads on each side: Martin Luther King Drive to the west and Kelly Drive to the east, though most longtime Philadelphians still refer to them as "West River Drive" and "East River Drive." Most roads in the park lead to one of those drives. As a rule the signs for roads in the park are not great, but you can count on signs pointing you to specific locations.

Start your visit to the park by climbing to the gazebo behind the Art Museum and taking in the view. You can see the Schuylkill and Philly's famous boathouses and get a firsthand look at the ***Fairmount Water Works.*** This classical group of buildings was built in the early 1820s to alleviate the growing city's water supply problems. With a reservoir where the museum now stands (the original "faire mount"), the system pumped water from the newly dammed river in what was, at the time, the most sophisticated water system in the world. When the river became too polluted early in the twentieth century, the mill house was turned into an aquarium, but that was abandoned in the 1960s and the site was left to deteriorate. In the 1970s the Junior League of Philadelphia began a long crusade to bring the Water Works back to life. The job was nearly completed when a New Year's Day 2002 fire severely damaged the engine house. Though the setback pushed plans back a year, renovations are completed and the Water Works has taken on its rightful mantle as a Philadelphia destination. The engine house has been transformed into the ***Water Works Restaurant,*** an upscale dining spot with a view that can't be beat. The menu is contemporary American, with some Mediterranean accents thrown in here and there. Open for lunch and dinner daily from 11:00 A.M. until 11:00 P.M., with Sunday brunch beginning at 10:00 A.M. For more details call (215) 236–2011 or go to www.thewaterworks

Fairmount Water Works

S-C-H-U-Y-L-K-I-L-L

You thought your spelling bees were tough. It's one of the first words expected to roll off the tongues of Philadelphia schoolchildren, and most natives do eventually learn how to spell it. Schuylkill—the river and the expressway—are integral to life in Philadelphia. The word has its origins as *schuyl kil,* from the Dutch for "hidden creek." Early Dutch explorers approached the area from the Delaware, where apparently the waters of the Schuylkill were hidden by vegetation. The correct pronunciation is "skool-kil," though "skool-kul" will do, and you'll hear lots of variations around town: "Skook'll" is a popular one for old-timers. And just ask people who commute on the expressway: They'll swear it's "sure kill."

restaurant.com. Expensive. Downstairs, an interpretive museum run by the Philadelphia Water Department, the ***Fairmount Water Works Interpretive Center*** explains just how the Water Works functioned in the early days. Open Tuesday through Saturday from 10:00 A.M. to 5:00 P.M. and Sunday from 1:00 to 5:00 P.M. Admission is free. Outbuildings house an upscale souvenir store and a gallery featuring local artists' interpretations of the Water Works and other Fairmount Park sites. The Water Works complex can be reached from Water Works Drive off Kelly Drive. Call (215) 685–4908 or visit www.fairmountwaterworks.com.

After the dam was built for the Water Works, the calm waters upriver were the perfect spot to build boathouses for the rowing clubs that had long used the Schuylkill River. These Victorian boathouses today constitute ***Boathouse Row***—Philadelphia's postcard shot—particularly at night when they are outlined in lights. In reality the houses are little more than glorified garages for the clubs' long, sleek shells, but they are an integral part of the Philadelphia landscape, as are the scullers who glide over the river. The Schuylkill now plays host to several competitions each year, including the Dad Vail each May—the world's largest intercollegiate regatta. Call (215) 978–6919 or go to www.boathouserow.org. The best views of Boathouse Row and the Art Museum are from the west side of the river. Unfortunately, that sometimes means going 55 miles an hour on the Schuylkill Expressway, though there is a spot on Martin Luther King Drive where you can pull over for your photograph.

Spread throughout Fairmount Park are a group of historic houses, many of which were built as country retreats for wealthy merchants in colonial Philadelphia. These houses have been preserved and most are open to the public from April through December. Trolley tours of the houses are offered Wednesday through Sunday, leaving from the Art Museum at 10:45 A.M. and 1:45 P.M., at a cost of $20.00 for adults and $13.00 for children and seniors. Or you can take your own self-guided tour, paying $3.00 per person at the door. Around the holidays the houses get all decked out for Christmas, and the museum offers popular candlelight tours. Find out more at www.philamuseum.org/collections/parkhouse.

Closest to Boathouse Row is **Lemon Hill** (Lemon Hill Drive), the property of financier Robert Morris, who signed the Declaration of Independence and was a major funder of the American Revolution. Morris eventually went bankrupt, and the property was sold to merchant Henry Pratt, who built the current house in 1800 and planted the lemon trees that give the estate its name. This was the first of the Fairmount Park houses to be acquired by the city, and it currently serves as headquarters for the Colonial Dames of America. Noted for its oval rooms, the home features unique concave doors and period furnishings. Open Wednesday through Sunday from 10:00 A.M. to 4:00 P.M., April through mid-December. Admission is $3.00. Call (215) 232–4337.

Back on Kelly Drive you come to the **Ellen Phillips Samuel Memorial,** three terraces of sculpture designed to symbolize the history of America. The southern terrace represents the settling of the colonies, the theme of the central plaza is expansion and immigration, and at the third plaza, the figures of the *Laborer,* the *Poet,* the *Preacher,* and the *Scientist* represent the diverse strengths that built the nation.

Turning onto Fountain Green Drive where you see the statue of Ulysses S. Grant will take you to the **Smith Memorial Playground** (Reservoir Drive), which is worth a visit if you have children five or younger. Generations of Philadelphians have memories of going down the huge wooden slide, which can fit ten across. The 44-by-12 foot slide and its surrounding playground was shut down in 2003 when it was determined that it didn't meet current safety standards. Cries of protest went up, and fund-raising for improvements got a

Dueling Dragons

It isn't only the college crews who control the waters of the Schuylkill River. In recent years the ancient Chinese tradition of dragon boat racing has been making a comeback. Teams are composed of twenty people who paddle to the beat of a drum in a brightly painted boat decorated with the carved head and tail of a dragon. Philly's men's team is frequently at the top of national competitions. The women's team now has members ranging from their twenties to their seventies.

Those Graceful Kellys

Grace Kelly is one of the most famous people to come out of Philadelphia, but originally it was her father who was the famous one. John B. Kelly—a millionaire owner of a brick company—honed his rowing skills on the Schuylkill. In 1920 he won two Olympic sculling titles on the same day, bringing home gold medals in single and double sculling contests. He and his partner won the doubles again in 1924, a first-time achievement for American sculling teams. In Fairmount Park a statue of John Kelly now graces Kelly Drive, which was renamed from East River Drive in his honor. At about the same time that his daughter Grace was marrying Prince Rainier of Monaco, someone remarked that Kelly—then president of the Fairmount Park Commission—had a larger domain than Rainier, since Fairmount Park covers 6 square miles, whereas Monaco covers less than 1 mile.

huge boost from a woman who remembered the slide from her youth. Strawberry Mansion native Ida Newman donated $300,000 to renovate the giant slide, which is now named after her daughter, Ann. In all, Smith Playground raised $2.2 million in less than two years, and the refurbished slide and brandnew playground equipment opened for business in 2005. Administrators are now turning their attention to renovating the mansion playhouse, which offers three floors of activities for young children. The house was built in 1899 by a wealthy Philadelphian in memory of his son. It never served as a residence—Richard Smith built it expressly so that children of Philadelphia would have a safe place to play, free of charge. The playhouse is open year-round from 10:00 A.M. to 4:00 P.M. Tuesday through Sunday for children five and younger. The playground is open 10:00 A.M. to 4:00 P.M. Tuesday through Sunday from April through October. There is no charge. For more information, call (215) 765–4325 or visit www.smithplayhouse.org.

Nearby is **Mount Pleasant** (Mount Pleasant Drive), a stately Georgian home at the end of a tree-lined road. Built in the 1760s by Scottish sea captain John Macpherson, the home is almost completely symmetrical, including its two outbuildings. In 1779 the house was sold to Benedict Arnold, who was prevented from ever living there by the treason charges against him. Macpherson hired the best woodworkers he could find, and it shows, particularly in the downstairs hallway. Mount Pleasant has been part of Fairmount Park since 1868 and recently underwent a painstaking, year-long preservation project. For now the house is being shown unfurnished, which allows visitors a chance to appreciate its construction details and sweeping views of the Schuylkill River. Open Tuesday through Sunday from 10:00 A.M. to 5:00 P.M. Admission is $3.00. Call (215) 763–8100.

You pass by the **Rockland Mansion,** a Federal house that has recently undergone major renovations. Now the headquarters of the Psychoanalytic Center of Philadelphia, Rockland is open to the public by appointment only. Next comes **Ormiston,** a late-Georgian brick home built in 1798 for a wealthy lawyer. Maintained by the Royal Heritage Society of the Delaware Valley, the house has period furnishings and features changing exhibits during the summer and the holidays that focus on British heritage in the area. Hours vary. Call (215) 763–2222.

Turn left on Randolph Drive and circle around to **Laurel Hill,** which was home to many distinguished Philadelphians over the years. Built in 1760, this Georgian brick home is kept up by the Women for Greater Philadelphia, a group of volunteers who conduct special programs and tours of the main floor. Laurel Hill is open Wednesday through Sunday from 10:00 A.M. to 4:00 P.M. from July through mid-December and Saturday and Sunday from 10:00 A.M. to 4:00 P.M. from April through June. Admission is $3.00. Call (215) 235–1776 for more information.

Crossing Reservoir Drive to Dauphin Street brings you to **Woodford,** at the eastern edge of the park. Originally built in 1756, Woodford is a classic Georgian house noted for its three-part Palladian window on the second floor. This floor was added in 1772 by owner David Franks, who held firm to his British loyalties. After the Revolution all of Franks's property, including Woodford, was seized. The building is maintained by the trustees of the estate of Naomi Wood, a Philadelphian whose extensive collection of colonial furniture was installed here as a permanent exhibition. A fire in 2003 seriously damaged the house and

Better to See It Now Than Later

One of the most fascinating places in Fairmount Park—and in an eerie, Gothic way, the most lovely—is the **Laurel Hill Cemetery,** which looks out directly over the Schuylkill. Though its seventy-four acres were originally laid out by architect John Notman in the 1830s, there now appears to be little order, and one gets the feeling that families competed for the most elaborate monuments and obelisks. There are house-size mausoleums for some of Philadelphia's most famous families, and some site owners even provided seating areas for those who came to visit. Laurel Hill was the first cemetery to be named a National Historic Landmark, and there's even a booklet for sale at the gatehouse, *Guide to the Famous and Blameless in Laurel Hill Cemetery,* that includes a detailed map of the artwork—as well as the graves. The main entrance is on Ridge Avenue between Thirty-fifth and Clearfield Streets. Open Monday through Friday from 8:00 A.M. to 4:30 P.M. and Saturday from 9:30 A.M. to 1:30 P.M. Call (215) 228–8200.

Honoring a Legend

Facing Fairmount Park near the Woodford historic home is the *John Coltrane House* (1511 North Thirty-third Street), where the great jazz musician composed many of his early works. Coltrane's cousin Mary Alexander (honored in Coltrane's song "Cousin Mary") still lives in the house and does her best to keep up with maintenance. Now the official headquarters of the John W. Coltrane Cultural Society, the house is the setting for occasional concerts and workshops throughout the year. Call (215) 763–1118.

its contents but allowed curators to restore Woodford with an eye toward historical accuracy and design flairs. Open Tuesday through Sunday from 10:00 A.M. to 4:00 P.M. Admission is $3.00. Call (215) 229–6115 for information.

Just behind Woodford is *Strawberry Mansion,* the largest of the park's historic homes. The oldest part of the house, the Federal-style center, dates to 1788, when it was built by Judge William Lewis, a prominent lawyer. After Lewis's death, the house was sold to Judge Joseph Hemphill, who added the two large Greek-Revival wings. The home got its name after being bought by the city of Philadelphia in 1871. Thanks to its wonderful location overlooking the Schuylkill, a restaurant opened here as a destination for excursion boats. The house specialty was strawberries and cream, ergo Strawberry Mansion. The mansion stands in stark contrast to the urban neighborhood bordering the park here, also known as Strawberry Mansion. The house is currently closed for renovations. Call (215) 228–8364.

If you turn left as you leave Strawberry Mansion, you will circle around by the Robin Hood Dell East outdoor amphitheater and come to the Strawberry Mansion Bridge, which takes you to the western side of Fairmount Park. Take Ford Road to Chamounix Drive. You'll pass *Ridgeland,* another eighteenth-century house that has been converted into a Wellness Center that offers support to cancer victims.

At Belmont Mansion Road turn left and get your cameras ready for a terrific view of the Philadelphia skyline. The *Belmont Plateau* provides the most scenic shot you can get, as well as outstanding sledding in the winter and classic competition for distance runners. Built in 1743, the Palladian *Belmont Mansion* across the street was home to William Peters, a friend of William Penn's, and his son Richard, who served as Secretary of the Board of War during the Revolution. His list of visitors to Belmont reads like a Who's Who of the Founding Fathers. Once a stop on the Underground Railroad, the mansion is being turned into a house museum highlighting the story of the Peters family and

Shofuso

their connection to the anti-slavery movement. For more information call (215) 878–8844 or visit www.belmontmansion.org.

As you come down Belmont Mansion Drive and cross (carefully!) Montgomery Drive, you approach a wonderful, often-overlooked section of Fairmount Park. This is the area where the Centennial Exposition was held in 1876. There were one hundred buildings that went up for the event, but they weren't built to last, and only two remain. The area that was developed as the centennial's showcase garden is now the ***Horticultural Center*** (North Horticultural Drive). Though not a major botanical garden, it's a beautifully landscaped arboretum and hosts displays inside its vast greenhouses. Look closely for the ***Pavilion in the Trees,*** a 1993 piece of installation art by well-known woodworker Martin Puryear. The canopied pavilion overlooks Landsdowne Glen, a naturalized area in the arboretum. An old pond now sprouts irises, cattails, and tulip trees. The Horticulture Center grounds are open daily from 9:00 A.M. to 5:00 P.M. from October through June and until 6:00 P.M. July through September. A display house that was built for the Bicentennial in 1976 on the site of the original Horticultural Hall is open daily until 3:00 P.M. For more information call (215) 685–0096 or visit www.fairmountpark.org/hortcenter.asp.

Also in the Horticultural Center is ***Shofuso,*** a Japanese house surrounded by traditional gardens with a small waterfall and a koi pond. A model of an early seventeenth-century residence, the house is connected to a ceremonial teahouse by a wooden bridge. Originally from the Metropolitan Museum of Art, the house was extensively refurbished for the 1976 bicentennial by a specialized team of craftsmen from Japan. Open Tuesday through Friday from 10:00 A.M. to 4:00 P.M. and Saturday and Sunday from 11:00 A.M. to 5:00 P.M.,

May to October. Admission is $4.00 for adults and $3.00 for seniors and children. For a schedule of special tea ceremonies and origami demonstrations, call (215) 878–5097 or go to www.shofuso.com.

From the Horticultural Center it's a short drive via Belmont Avenue to **Memorial Hall** (Forty-second Street and North Concourse Drive). This was one of the centerpieces of the Centennial Exposition, and it is the only large structure from that celebration still standing. (The small Ohio House that you pass on Belmont Avenue is the other remaining building.) President Grant was on hand to dedicate Memorial Hall to the soldiers of the Revolution. The beautiful copper dome glows warmly in the evening and can be seen for miles around. After the centennial, Memorial Hall served as the art museum until the current structure was completed, and it is said to have been the inspiration for New York's Metropolitan Museum of Art. The building is being reborn as a new home to an expanded Please Touch Museum, which will include a restored carousel and a 40-foot-high interpretation of the Statue of Liberty torch by found-object artist Leo Sewell.

Heading east on North Concourse Drive, you pass the **Smith Civil War Memorial Arch,** which honors Union generals who hailed from Pennsylvania. Well, almost all of the sculptures are of generals. There among the military brass is a life-size statue of moveable type–founder Richard Smith, looking official in his work apron. Who's Richard Smith? He's the one who gave the money to build the memorial. Smith also donated the money for the Smith Playground on the east side of Fairmount Park.

Two of the park's nicest historic houses are tucked away in this corner of Fairmount Park. **Cedar Grove** (Cedar Grove Drive) is a charming country house that served as a summer home to five generations of a large Quaker family. Originally built in the city's Frankford section, the house was dismantled and moved to its present location, stone by stone, in 1927. The house's warm kitchen is built around a large fireplace and includes a built-in unit for heating water. Open year-round Tuesday through Sunday from 10:00 A.M. to 5:00 P.M. Admission is $3.00. Call (215) 763–8100.

The Whispering Benches

Although many people visit the Smith Civil War Memorial Arch in Fairmount Park to admire the huge archway and many wonderful sculptures, some Philadelphians know the memorial only as the place where the "whispering benches" are. If you're there, try it. Have one person sit at the end of one of the curved stone benches at the arch's base. If that person turns to the bench wall and whispers, someone sitting at the other end of the bench can hear what's being said as plain as day.

The Animals Were an Afterthought

There's a reason the Philadelphia Zoo—the country's oldest—is called a "zoological garden." That's because in the beginning the plan was to create a Victorian pleasure garden. The animals were only added later to make things a little more interesting. To this day, the zoo's collection of trees and plants is almost as impressive as its roster of animal inhabitants.

On a cul-de-sac not far away is *Sweetbriar,* built in 1797 by merchant Samuel Breck, who little knew that one day a busy expressway would roar by downhill. Breck went on to serve in Congress. His elegant, Federal-style home features long windows that stretch to the floor. Open Wednesday through Sunday from 10:00 A.M. to 4:00 P.M., July through mid-December. There is a $3.00 admission charge. Call (215) 222–1333.

Wrapping up your tour of Fairmount Park is the *Philadelphia Zoo* (3400 West Girard Avenue), the oldest zoo in the country. It's not hard to find now that they have an enormous ride that sends a huge balloon high above the park and the Schuylkill Expressway. The zoo's manageable size can be a plus if you have young children, because everything is close together. While there be sure to take note of Solitude, a 1784 home built for William Penn's grandson John, which quietly takes in all the surrounding action. There are all sorts of bells and whistles at the zoo—from swan boat rides to simulators that take you on a 3-D ride through the African plains—but they'll cost you, and after all you're here to see the animals. The latest attraction to open at the zoo is Big Cat Falls, a $20-million naturalistic exhibit that is home to African lions, leopards, jaguars, pumas, and tigers. Fall 2007 will see the opening of the McNeil Avian Center, which will showcase not only the birds themselves, but also the role Philadelphia plays on the migratory superhighway. Plans are also underway for a new children's zoo. Open daily from 9:30 A.M. to 5:00 P.M. (closes at 4:00 P.M. December through February). Admission is $16.95 per adult and $13.95 for children ($10.95 November through February); no charge for children under two. If you want to ride the Zooballoon as well, it will cost you $26.95 for adults and $23.95 for children ages two through eleven. Or, if you prefer just to ride the Zooballoon and leave the animals for another day, that option is $12.00 per person; children under two are free. The balloon climbs to about 400 feet and provides great views of Fairmount Park and the skyline. Each trip up (and down!) lasts about 15 minutes. Call (215) 243–1100 or log on to www.philadelphiazoo.org.

Places to Stay on the Ben Franklin Parkway and in Fairmount

Best Western Center City,
501 North Twenty-second Street;
(215) 568–8300
It's not much to look at, but the prices are right and the location is great. The rooms have been recently renovated, and children under eighteen are free. Still, double check before heading out because developers have their eyes on this prime location. Moderate.

Chamounix Mansion,
West Fairmount Park;
(215) 878–3676,
(800) 379–0017,
www.philahostel.org
If you don't mind staying in a youth hostel, Chamounix affords you the opportunity to sleep in one of Fairmount Park's historic houses. The house is a restored 1802 Quaker estate, so there's lots of charm, but it's hard to find and you have to share bathrooms. Inexpensive.

Four Seasons,
1 Logan Square;
(215) 963–1500,
www.fourseasons.com/philadelphia
The ultimate in luxury. Built right on Logan Circle in 1983, the Four Seasons has 364 rooms, including 103 suites, all furnished in Federal-style reproductions. Expensive.

Hotel Windsor,
1700 Benjamin Franklin Parkway;
(215) 981–5678,
www.windsorhotel.com
The Windsor offers a mid-price suite option in a great location for exploring Center City as well as the Parkway. You can get a studio or one-bedroom; ask for one with a private balcony. Moderate.

Places to Eat in Fairmount

The Bishop's Collar,
2349 Fairmount Avenue, Fairmount;
(215) 765–1616,
www.thebishopscollar.com
The name refers to a nickname for a perfectly poured pint of Guinness, and this long, narrow pub even offers some long, narrow pews as seating. But that's about as ecclesiastical as it gets. Some nights there's live music, and when there isn't, they pump up what is said to be the best jukebox in town. The menu is standard bar fare, with an outstanding turkey chili. Open Monday from 3:00 P.M. to 2:00 A.M. and Tuesday through Sunday from 11:00 A.M. to 2:00 A.M. Moderate.

AUTHOR'S FAVORITE PLACES TO EAT IN FAIRMOUNT

Aspen
747 North Twenty-fifth Street;
(215) 23–ASPEN,
www.aspenphilly.com

Figs
2501 Meredith Street;
(215) 978–8440

The Fountain
1 Logan Square;
(215) 963–1500

Jack's Firehouse
2130 Fairmount Avenue;
(215) 232–9000

Mace's Crossing
1714 Cherry Street;
(215) 564–5203

Water Works Restaurant
640 Water Works Drive;
(215) 236–9000,
www.thewaterworksrestaurant.com

HELPFUL WEB SITES

www.philamuseum.org/collections/
parkhouse

www.fairmountpark.org

Illuminare,
2321 Fairmount Avenue,
Fairmount;
(215) 765–0202,
www.illuminare2321.com
This is as fancy as it gets in
Fairmount. The row house
has been completely reno-
vated, with stained glass,
tile, and woodwork details,
as well as a patio complete
with fountains. It may seem
a bit much since the menu
is mostly brick-oven pizzas
and pastas. Try the spicy
linguine with lobster and
scallops. Open for lunch
Monday through Saturday
from 11:30 A.M. to 3:00 P.M.
Dinner is served Monday
through Thursday from 5:00
to 9:30 P.M., Friday and Saturday from 5:00 to 10:30
P.M., and Sunday from 5:00
to 9:00 P.M. Sunday brunch
is available from 11:00 A.M.
to 3:00 P.M. Moderate.

London Grill,
2301 Fairmount Avenue,
Fairmount;
(215) 978–4545,
www.londongrill.com
Another great dining option
after a day at the museums,
this is also a local favorite.
There's plenty of good drink
and live music on Thursday

and Saturday nights, but the
menu is a solid step above
bar food. Kid-friendly, too.
Open daily from 11:30 A.M.
to 2:00 A.M. except for Saturday, when it doesn't serve
lunch. Moderate.

Rembrandt's,
741 North Twenty-third
Street,
Fairmount;
(215) 763–2228,
www.rembrandts.com
Rembrandt's is a popular
neighborhood spot for several reasons: It's a great
neighborhood bar that
serves a late bar menu, and
the dining room is elegant
and offers a terrific Sunday
brunch, accompanied by
live music. If you sit in the
bar, you got to enjoy a great
view of the skyline. The lunch
and tavern menus are offered
Monday through Friday starting at 11:30 A.M. Dinner is
served Monday through
Thursday from 5:30 to 10:00
P.M., Friday and Saturday
until 11:00 P.M., and Sunday
from 5:00 to 9:00 P.M. A
Sunday brunch is served
from 10:30 A.M. to 2:30 P.M.
A late-night menu is available
every night from 11:30 P.M.
until 1:00 A.M. Moderate.

Rose Tattoo Cafe,
1847 Callowhill Street,
Fairmount;
(215) 569–8939,
www.rosetattoocafe.com
Some people come here just
for the flowers. The restaurant is packed with plants
and flowers and retains the
wrought-iron railings from
its earlier life as a New
Orleans–type eatery. It's very
romantic. Go for the roasted
duck with sun-dried cherry
sauce, and save room for
the crème brûlée, with different flavors offered nightly.
Open for lunch Monday
from 11:30 A.M. to 3:00 P.M.
and Tuesday through Friday
from 11:30 A.M. to 4:00 P.M.
Dinner is served Monday
through Thursday from 5:00
to 10:00 P.M. and Friday and
Saturday from 5:00 to 11:00
P.M. Moderate.

North Philadelphia and the Northeast

North Philadelphia and what locals call the Great Northeast are linked by geography, but little else. Although vastly different in ethnic, religious, and social makeup, both communities are uniquely Philadelphian. North Philadelphia is an expansive area centered along North Broad Street running from Spring Garden Street to Roosevelt Boulevard. Its population is primarily African American, with a strong Latino community in the Fairhill neighborhood. Roosevelt Boulevard is the major artery through the Northeast, an overwhelmingly white, working-class region of more than 400,000 residents.

Many people avoid North Philadelphia, scared away by its areas of poverty and neglect. To the casual visitor, those areas may dominate, and this is not the safest part of Philadelphia—visitors should show caution. Although you can look around North Philadelphia and see abandoned cars and boarded-up row houses, you can also focus on vacant lots that neighborhoods have transformed into abundant vegetable gardens and playgrounds for the children.

There is also history embedded in these vibrant urban communities. The Independence Visitor Center has even started conducting tours of neighborhoods in North Philadelphia, pointing out significant places and the importance

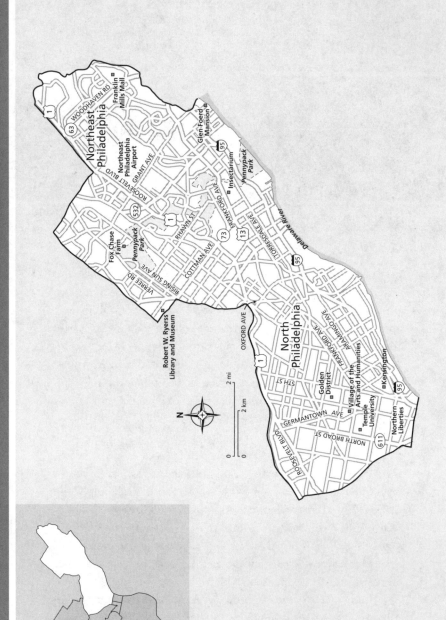

Philadelphia played in the struggle for civil rights. Visitors may feel more comfortable taking this approach. Ask at the visitor center on Independence Mall for more details.

This is not a pretty ride. It is not always a fun ride. People in colonial costumes don't appear to tell you interesting stories. But it is a real ride.

Fishtown and Kensington

As rents increased in trendy Old City, many residents sought refuge just north of there in the neighborhood known as Northern Liberties, a long-dead manufacturing community near the Delaware that's now considered one of the hottest areas in the city. Many architectural gems have their original detailing and are being restored. It's hard to walk a block in Northern Liberties these days without encountering the sounds and sights of construction. It's become a magnet for restaurants, galleries, condominiums, and shops. In fact some people say the rents in Northern Liberties are now too expensive, and they are migrating even farther north and east, into sections of neighborhoods known as **Port Richmond, Fishtown,** and **Kensington.** The *Philadelphia Inquirer* went so far as to dub this suddenly hip area "Port Fishington."

These neighborhoods make for an interesting mix of up-and-comers and old-time Philadelphians. Some families have lived in these row homes for decades and talk of buying them for just a few thousand dollars. They can't believe how high the housing prices are now, but to people used to the rents in other corners of the city, the area is a bargain. That is, except for the waterfront. A number of luxury condominium projects are being built on the Delaware River near Spring Garden Street, including Philadelphia's first foray into the empire of Donald Trump. Much of this development has been spurred by the planned construction of three slot casinos on that section of the riverfront.

AUTHOR'S FAVORITES IN NORTH PHILADELPHIA AND THE NORTHEAST

Fox Chase Farm	Tierra Colombiana
Insectarium	Village of the Arts and Humanities
Standard Tap	Wagner Free Institute of Science

A Simple Statue Marks the Spot

Despite all the monuments around the historic district, William Penn actually landed along the banks of the Delaware about a mile north in what is now the Fishtown neighborhood. A simple monument marks the site in a small park—Penn Treaty Park—where Columbia Avenue intersects Columbus Boulevard. The statue of William Penn on top of City Hall faces northeast, directly toward this spot.

Part of what has brought new life to Fishtown and Kensington is the **Yards Brewing Company** (2439 Amber Street), the only brewery within the city limits, which set up shop here in 2001. It's not easy to find, but Yards does offer free tours of the brewery on Saturdays between noon and 3:00 P.M. The entrance is off Martha Street near Hagert, just west of Frankford Avenue. There's not much here, but you do get free samples in the tasting room and visitors are welcome to BYOF (as in food). Plus, in one of the city's great bargains, you can buy a case of their fresh-brewed beer for well below market price. Call (215) 634–2600 or log on to www.yardsbrewing.com for more information.

At Frankford and Norris you'll find the funky **Rocket Cat Cafe** (2001 Frankford Avenue), which has been called the hub of Fishtown's resurgence. This coffee shop/art gallery has become a popular local hangout. The building was rehabbed and now houses studio space for artists upstairs. The husband-and-wife owners sometimes open their doors to live music acts as well. A neighborhood group known as the New Kensington Community Development Corporation envisions this part of Fishtown as the Frankford Avenue Arts Corridor, and the idea seems to be taking hold. Witness the **Bambi Project** (1817 Frankford Avenue), which was established in 2005 by two bartenders and former art students. They call it an art gallery and art consignment shop, where artists in the area can sell their wares. Open Thursday, Friday, and Saturday from noon to 6:00 P.M. Call (215) 423–2668 or go to www.bambiproject .com to learn more.

At Frankford Avenue and Girard, you'll find **Johnny Brenda's** (1201 Frankford Avenue), the latest pub effort of the pair behind Northern Liberties' popular Standard Tap. They took over an old neighborhood bar, keeping the name but sprucing up the joint. It still has some dive-bar elements like a jukebox and a pool table, but the beer is good—they only serve draft and it's all local, including Yards from up the street. The food is above par too, with such choices as garlicky pork tenderloin, grilled octopus, and lamb kabobs. Open daily from 11:00 A.M. to 2:00 A.M. Call (215) 739–9684 or go to www.johnny brendas.com.

Northern Liberties

At Girard you shift into **Northern Liberties,** which roughly stretches from Girard to Spring Garden Street and from Sixth Street on the west to the Delaware River on the east. The main street here, so to speak, is North Second, which is lined with bars and restaurants. The quintessential neighborhood hangout is **Standard Tap** (901 North Second Street), a pub with great food. Northern Liberties is also known for its music scene. Options range from weekend jazz at **Liberties** (705 North Second Street), a restored tavern with an over-the-top Victorian bar, to the more divelike **Ortlieb's Jazz Haus** (847 North Third Street), which has music every night from Tuesday through Saturday. If dancing is your thing, the hottest nightclub in Northern Liberties is **Shampoo** (417 North Eighth Street), a former warehouse that's been converted into a huge club. There are eight bars and three dance floors. In the summer there's an outdoor dance area as well. Open Wednesday through Sunday from 9:00 P.M. to 2:00 A.M.; the crowds on Fridays are predominately gay. Call (215) 922–7500 or go to www.shampooonline.com for more information. The newest entry into Northern Liberties entertainment is **NorthBowl** (909–915 North Second Street), offering seventeen lanes of bowling and opportunities to shoot some pool. Call (215) 238–BOWL or visit www.northbowlphilly.com.

The southern edge of Northern Liberties claims several historic sites. First is the **German Society of Pennsylvania** (611 Spring Garden Street), which boasts the largest collection of German materials in the United States outside a university. The Joseph Horner Memorial Library houses 70,000 German-language books, pamphlets, and manuscripts; it specializes in nineteenth-century works, particularly in the areas of history, travel literature, popular literature, religion, and children's books. There is also a collection of thousands of German-American documents, with special emphasis on Pennsylvania, making this a popular stop for genealogists. The society is located in a grand 1888 building, which is listed on the National Register of Historical Places. Hours are limited and varied, so for specifics call (215) 627–2332 or visit www.germansociety.org.

Just across Seventh Street is the **Edgar Allan Poe Historic Site** (532 North Seventh Street). Operated by the National Park Service, this site consists of three buildings and a park area and includes a number of exhibits on Poe's life. Poe lived in Philadelphia after marrying his thirteen-year-old cousin (the inspiration for his poem "Annabel Lee"), and they lived with her mother for several years. The family resided at several addresses, but the house on Seventh Street is the only one to survive. It was while living in Philadelphia that Poe wrote some of his most famous stories, among them "The Fall of the House of Usher", "The Tell-Tale Heart", and "The Murders in the Rue Morgue." If you've got the spine for it, descend into the basement, where there's a false fireplace. Many believe this sparked Poe's imagination and inspired "The Black Cat", in which a husband plots to murder his wife and hide her body behind just such a false fireplace. Open from 9:00 A.M. to 5:00 P.M. (last tour at 4:00 P.M.) Wednesday through Sunday. Call (215) 597–8780 or visit www.nps.gov/edal.

Of architectural interest is *Guild House* (711 Spring Garden Street), one of the earliest works of Philadelphia superarchitect Robert Venturi. Completed in 1964, Guild House is considered an important milestone in the development of his postmodernist style.

North Philadelphia

One of the things you notice as you drive through North Philadelphia is the large number of wonderful old churches and synagogues. Though many are in need of repair, most have stood the test of time and still serve vital congregations. On North Broad Street just above Spring Garden Street is *Congregation Rodeph Shalom* (615 North Broad Street), which bills itself as the oldest Ashkenazic congregation in the Western Hemisphere. Inspired by the great synagogue of Florence, Italy, Rodeph Shalom is one of the only synagogues in this country built in the Byzantine-Moorish style. The stained-glass windows gracing its sanctuary represent one of the few remaining collections from the renowned D'Ascenzo Studio, and the entrance foyer houses a collection of Jewish ritual and ceremonial art dating back to the 1700s. Rodeph Shalom is also home to the *Philadelphia Museum of Jewish Art* (entrance on Mt. Vernon Street), which aims to present contemporary art that "illuminates the Jewish experience." The museum maintains a permanent collection of works by a variety of artists and organizes special exhibits several times a year. Open Monday through Thursday from 10:00 A.M. to 4:00 P.M., Friday from 10:00 A.M. to 2:00 P.M., and Sunday from 10:00 A.M. to noon. Admission is free. For further information call (215) 627–6747 or visit www.rodephshalom.org.

On Franklin Street between Seventh and Eighth Streets is the *Ukrainian Catholic Cathedral* (830 North Franklin Street), which is only forty years old but was designed to resemble the Hagia Sofia Cathedral in Istanbul. The impressive dome dominates the neighborhood and is layered with tiny, Venetian-glass tiles made by fusing twenty-two-karat gold into glass. To learn more call (215) 922–2845 or visit www.ukrcathedral.com.

Another landmark in Philadelphia's religious history is the *Divine Lorraine Hotel* (North Broad Street and Fairmount Avenue). Now just a shadow of its former self, it was once the epitome of luxury. In 1948 it became one of the first integrated hotels in the country when it was purchased by charismatic civil rights pioneer Father M. J. Divine. Father Divine's Peace Mission Movement's central operations were also located here. A number of plans to restore the hotel have fallen through, so for now it sits unoccupied.

At Broad and Thompson you'll find the legendary *Blue Horizon Boxing* (314 North Broad Street), which has been called the best place to watch a fight in America. It's said that "the Blue" is to Philadelphia boxing what the cheesesteak is to Philadelphia cuisine. This famous fight club, where *Rocky V* was filmed, is finally undergoing a long-delayed renovation and its ring is back in business. Its owners hope to add a museum of Philadelphia boxing memorabilia and renovate the club's ballroom, which has long been used for wedding receptions and other large gatherings. Call (215) 763–0500 or visit www.legendarybluehorizon.com.

Just up Broad Street at Master Street is the *Freedom Theatre* (1346 North Broad Street), the country's largest African-American theater. Founded in 1966, the Freedom has grown from a small community theater to one with a repertory company that draws national attention. The company performs four productions a year in its space in the historic Edwin Forrest Mansion, and a total renovation of the theater was completed in 2000. A Performing Arts Training Program provides formal training to local students. Call (215) 765–2793 or go to www.freedomtheatre.org.

One block north across the street you will see *Progress Plaza* (1501 North Broad Street). It doesn't look like much—it's basically a strip mall—so you might not know why you're looking at it. But in its time, Progress Plaza was quite a remarkable development. The brainchild of the Reverend Leon Sullivan, a civil rights leader, the shopping center opened in 1968 in an effort to give African Americans more opportunities to own and operate their own businesses. The project was financed by North Philadelphia residents who bought shares of the development; $360 got you 4,000 shares. The shopping center recently got a multimillion-dollar infusion for renewal, and renovations are ongoing.

A Beloved Saint

Many Catholics have made the journey to the *Shrine of Saint John Neumann* (1019 North Fifth Street), where the body of this beloved saint lies in full view in a glass case beneath an altar in the basement of the Redemptorist St. Peter and the Apostle Church. Neumann was bishop of Philadelphia for eight years in the 1850s, during which time he ministered to Philadelphia's growing immigrant population, helped immensely by his knowledge of eleven languages. He was canonized by Pope Paul VI in 1977. Call (215) 627–3080 or log on to www.stjohnneumann.org.

Another First for Philadelphia

According to the United States Travel and Tourism Administration, Philadelphia is one of the leading cities for African-American tourism in the United States. It's not an accident: the city has made a concerted effort to promote its multicultural attractions and its role in the history of the civil rights movement. There's North Philadelphia's Freedom Theatre, the African-American History Museum, and Philadanco, a world-renowned dance company featuring African-American choreographers and dancers. There is discussion now about building a monument near Independence Mall honoring slaves in colonial America.

You now enter the area of North Philadelphia dominated by ***Temple University,*** the Philadelphia area's largest school, serving more than 30,000 students. One of the state's three public universities, Temple is very much an urban school and its presence is felt throughout the city. It encompasses seventeen schools and colleges, including schools of law, medicine, pharmacy, podiatry, and dentistry, and has its own medical center. As a cultural center Temple has much to offer the community. The Esther Boyer School of Music and the Department of Dance sponsor the Greater Philadelphia Concert Series, which annually stages more than 200 recitals, concerts, master classes, and lectures both at Temple and at venues around Philadelphia. Most are free. Faculty, guest artists, and students regularly perform in the school's Rock Hall (1715 North Broad Street). (Call 215–204–8307 or visit www.temple.edu/music for a schedule.) The Temple Theater Department (1301 Norris Street) presents six plays each season in two theaters and sponsors staged readings of each year's winners of the Philadelphia Young Playwrights Festival (215–204–1122, www.temple.edu/theater). Though currently located at a suburban Elkins Park campus, Temple's Tyler School of Art plans to relocate to the main campus in the coming years and continues to maintain galleries on the main campus and in Old City.

Much of the large-scale entertainment on Temple's campus takes place at the ***Liacouras Center*** (1776 North Broad Street), home to the university's famed basketball teams. A hulking 10,000-seat arena located just off Broad Street, the center also hosts a full range of concerts and exhibitions throughout the year. Call (215) 204–2424 or log on to www.liacourascenter.com.

If you're hungry—or thirsty—drop by the ***Draught Horse*** (1431 Cecil B. Moore Avenue), a pub just around the corner from the Liacouras Center. It's your basic college bar loaded with Temple memorabilia, but the food is decent and there are twenty beers on tap. Open Monday and Tuesday from 11:30 A.M. to midnight, Wednesday through Friday from 11:30 A.M. to 2:00 A.M., and Saturday from 4:00 P.M. to 2:00 A.M. For more information call (215) 235–1010 or visit www.draughthorse.com.

Architecturally, Temple has several sites of particular interest. At Broad and Ontario Streets is the **Baptist Temple** for which the school is named. Conceived by the university's founder and first president, Pastor Russell Conwell, the temple was finished in 1891; two years later it had become the largest Baptist church in America. Conwell founded Temple College in 1888, relying entirely on the personal contributions of Baptists in the area. The congregation sold the building to the university in 1974, and after years sitting empty, it's now undergoing a slow renovation. There's talk of converting the space into a performing arts venue for the university's art, theater, music, and dance program.

Just to the north is **Mitten Hall** (1913 North Broad Street), another architectural gem, this one a Collegiate Gothic structure built in 1931. In addition to the stone edifice, leaded glass, and ornately carved ceilings, Mitten Hall has a secret detail most people miss: Stone renditions of the mascot owl are chiseled into the outside corners, but you have to look up to see them—they're 30 feet from street level. It helps to be across Broad Street.

Just 2 blocks west of Broad Street and the center of Temple's campus is the fascinating **Wagner Free Institute of Science** (1700 West Montgomery Avenue), which has been called a museum of a museum. Founded in 1855 as

There's Nothing Painless about It

There's one thing at Temple University you may not want to do, but you really should—just like visiting the dentist. The dental school is so proud of its *Historical Dental Museum* (3223 North Broad Street) that it recently built a brand-new, expanded facility to house its collection of historic dental paraphernalia. This should send you right for your toothbrush and floss. On display are dental instruments dating back to the 1700s, the country's first known dental chair, early X-ray machines, and what the museum calls "innovative electric drills." There's also a re-creation of a Victorian dental office, complete with life-size dental technicians and sound effects. The highlight, without question, is Painless Parker's Bucket of Teeth. Edgar R. R. "Painless" Parker was a champion of tooth pullers, and he saved each and every bicuspid to prove it: The museum includes a bucket filled with thousands of pulled teeth. He once pulled 357 teeth in one day, which he strung as a necklace. Parker operated thirty West Coast dental offices, sometimes alongside a circus, in the early part of the twentieth century. He ended up making a fortune, despite the fact that the American Dental Association labeled him "a menace to the dignity of the profession." Temple wasn't as quick to disown Parker, a graduate of its School of Dentistry. Open Monday through Friday from 8:30 A.M. to 4:30 P.M. Call (215) 707–2816 or visit www.temple.edu/dentistry/museum.htm.

LaSalle Treasures

North Philadelphia's **LaSalle University** (1900 West Olney Avenue) offers a number of interesting attractions to visitors. The campus includes the adjoining former estates of Philadelphia's esteemed Wister family and Charles Willson Peale, the colonial painter whose portraits are on display in the historic district's Second Bank of the United States. There are occasional tours of these historic buildings. LaSalle's president lives in the main house of the Peale farm, and hidden inside a stone outbuilding on the property is an authentic Japanese tea house, one of only a few on a college campus. The tea house was designed by Japan's Urasenki tea foundation at the behest of a former LaSalle faculty member who was in training to be a tea master. Tea ceremonies are held regularly and are open to the public. La Salle's art museum is also open to the public Tuesday through Friday from 11:00 A.M. to 4:00 P.M. and Sunday from 2:00 to 4:00 P.M. Though small, the museum has an impressive collection of European and American paintings, drawings, and sculpture, as well as a grouping of rare illustrated Bibles. LaSalle can be reached by taking North Broad Street; 1 mile north of Roosevelt Boulevard turn left on Somerville Avenue, then right on Ogontz Avenue. Ogontz intersects with Olney Avenue near the entrance to the campus. For more information call (215) 951–1000. Maps to the campus are available at www.lasalle.edu.

a natural history museum offering free programs to the public, the institute has maintained its collections exactly the way they were originally laid out. The display cases themselves are antiques, and many of the labels date back to the 1880s. The building—designed by John McArthur, Jr., who also designed City Hall—is undergoing renovation, but its Victorian details are being kept intact, and it is listed on the National Register of Historic Places. The collection includes more than 100,000 specimens, including founder William Wagner's extensive mineral collection. Open Tuesday through Friday from 9:00 A.M. to 4:00 P.M. As the name implies, the museum is free, though donations are accepted. Call (215) 763–6529 or go to www.wagnerfreeinstitute.org.

About a half-mile north on Eighteenth Street is the Gothic ***Church of the Advocate*** (1801 West Diamond Street), an important institution in Philadelphia's civil rights movement. In the 1960s the church became known as the "Freedom Church" because it provided space to many groups others would not welcome, such as the Black Panthers and the National Black Power Convention. Its leaders also strongly supported women's rights, and it was here that the first ordination of women in the Episcopal Church took place. The church also serves as a majestic home for ***Art Sanctuary,*** a community group that works to bring regional and national artists, writers, and prominent speakers to the African-American community. Art Sanctuary has an outstanding record of attracting such well-known figures as Nikki Giovani, Sonia Sanchez, Ntozake Shange, and Terry McMillan. In just a few years, its annual Celebration of Black Writing has grown into a popular series that attracts thousands of participants each February. Call (215) 232–4485 or visit www.artsanctuary.org.

Back on Broad Street is the *Philadelphia Doll Museum* (2253 North Broad Street), the country's first black-doll museum. Here you will find more than 300 dolls, some dating from the early nineteenth century, including African, European, and American folk art dolls. Creator Barbara Whiteman uses her collection to illustrate how blacks were perceived throughout history. The dolls range in size from small figurines to full-size figures. Many are homemade creations; there's even one made of chicken bones. Open Thursday through Saturday from 10:00 A.M. to 4:00 P.M. and Sunday from noon to 4:00 P.M. Admission is $4.00 for adults and $3.00 for seniors and children under twelve. Call (215) 787–0220 or visit www.philadollmuseum.com.

There are two separate communities within the confines of North Philadelphia that are shining examples of how people can come together to change the character of their communities. People talk about urban despair. These are communities that care.

East of Broad Street, in an area bordered roughly by Germantown Avenue, Cumberland, Huntingdon, and Eleventh Streets, is the *Village of the Arts and Humanities.* Since its extremely humble beginnings in 1985, the village has transformed a neighborhood at the heart of Philadelphia's so-called badlands drug culture into a bright spot of hope. More than 150 lots that once held burned-out row houses or were left to the weeds have been turned into gardens and playgrounds, open spaces, and even a two-acre tree farm. It all began when Lily Yeh, a Chinese landscape painter looking to do something different, was offered free rein and a vacant lot in North Philly. She painted a mural on the wall of the building next door, then used a small grant from the Pennsylvania Council on the Arts to begin work on the lot. Enlisting the help of neighborhood children and adults, Yeh turned the abandoned lot into a park, of sorts. Because there was no money in the budget for trees, they created their own with concrete, at first

TOP HITS IN NORTH PHILADELPHIA AND THE NORTHEAST

Edgar Allen Poe Historic Site	Temple University
Franklin Mills Mall	Wagner Free Institute of Science

trying unsuccessfully to paint them, then turning to mosaics as a more permanent solution. They built a low, scalloped adobe wall, which has become a signature for the village, and concrete love seats covered with mirrored tile.

Working steadily and thoughtfully, Yeh continued her work, and people
began to notice. A neighborhood man who had sold drugs to support his own
habit—James "Big Man" Maxton—was persuaded to help because he liked to
draw. Just like the lots, Maxton was transformed by the experience, came clean,
and became the village's chief mosaic artist. Early on, Maxton executed Yeh's
vision of an Angel Alley. The neighborhood was poor—median family incomes
of $10,000—and dangerous, and Yeh thought it needed spiritual protection.
She painted larger-than-life angels on a wall, and Maxton brought them to life
in mosaic. These are no willowy angels in white, however; inspired by
Ethiopian icons, they are powerful warriors, with black and red faces and
strong swords, to stand guard over the neighborhood. The work of the village
expanded, as did its mission. Yeh quit her professorship at the University of the
Arts to give the village her full attention. Slowly but surely, vacant lots were
made green, mosaic sculptures sprouted up in the most unexpected places,
and abandoned housing was renovated and put to use. The village began programs in the area's schools and housing projects to involve the residents.
Through grants and donations, crews from the neighborhood have been paid
to help restore the buildings. The village also runs classes in art, dance, and
theater; a hallmark of its efforts is a rite-of-passage program for teens that cul-
minates with a coming-of-age festival each August. It has forged partnerships
with schools, businesses, and even Philadelphia's professional football team,
the Eagles, who built a playground for the neighborhood.

Yeh's mission spread overseas. She spent months in Kenya and the Ivory
Coast working with villagers to build parks and murals in slums. When Yeh
retired in 2004, she founded Barefoot Artists, an organization that promotes art
and community revitalization in countries around the world. James Maxton
passed away in 2005. From their humble beginnings, the village now employs
a full-time staff of sixteen and works with an annual budget of $1.3 million.

This is still a struggling, inner-city neighborhood, and there is still poverty
and neglect. But a visit to the Village of the Arts and Humanities is a moving
experience, as you witness this oasis of trees, flowers, murals, and mosaics
where once there was only urban blight. Most symbolic is the village's Medita-
tion Park, where an entire wall of an abandoned building was plastered with a
striking Tree of Life, and the neighboring lot was turned into a quiet courtyard.
The village's headquarters is at 2544 Germantown Avenue. You can park near
there and spend time wandering around in that area, where most of the development is located. The village will arrange for guided tours for groups, but it

needs at least two weeks' notice. The 23 bus and the Broad Street subway line serve the area, though you may not feel safe wandering too far afield. Still, as you drive away from the village, you will be pleasantly surprised to find a corner vegetable garden or a mosaic animal popping up blocks away. Call (215) 225–7830 or go to www.villagearts.org.

Fairhill

From the Village of the Arts and Humanities, travel to the city's vibrant Latino community in the Fairhill section of the city by getting on Germantown Avenue, then turning right onto Lehigh Avenue. At the intersection with North Fifth Street, you'll see a bright, three-story mural on your left that signals your arrival at *Taller Puertorriqueño* (2721 North Fifth Street), a cultural and community center. When established in 1974, its mission was to preserve and foster Puerto Rican artistic and cultural traditions. Now its Cultural Awareness Program, run from an educational building a block away, offers area children low-cost classes in literature, theater, visual arts or dance, as well as summer enrichment programs. A gallery at the center invites international artists to exhibit their work and conduct workshops with the children, and a theater space serves as a venue for performances and community meetings. There's also a bookstore devoted to Latin and Puerto Rican cultures, where you can find toys, clothes, music, and a wide variety of bilingual materials. Call (215) 426–3311 or log on to www.tallerpr.org.

Fifth Street is the center of this community, which the locals refer to as "El Centro de Oro"—the *Golden District.* The 5 blocks extending north from Fifth and Lehigh are referred to as the "Golden Block" and feature a variety of brightly painted Puerto Rican restaurants, novelty shops, and grocery stores. Banners

What's That Overhead?

Drive around the Philly neighborhoods where kids grow up—South Philly and North Philly mostly—and you find yourself wondering what in the world is hanging from those wires overhead. They're shoes. In Philadelphia it's what you do with a worn-out pair of sneakers—toss 'em over the telephone wires. Now a little research will turn up theories about what this means: that it marks a spot where you can buy drugs or identifies gang territories, that it's a memorial ritual when someone dies or marks an important moment in a girl's romantic life. But in Philadelphia the consensus seems to be that you do it just because it's always been done.

Planting Seeds of Change

Fairhill is a perfect neighborhood in which to appreciate the transforming powers of the Pennsylvania Horticultural Society's Philadelphia Green program. As you drive around you notice numerous vacant lots with just a few trees surrounded by a simple wooden fence. What you don't see are the mounds of trash and debris that used to be there. The Philadelphia Green program has used this simple formula to clean up thousands of vacant lots around the city, working in close partnership with community-based organizations. One shining success story is the Las Parcelas gardens (2138–64 North Palethorpe Street). When this vacant lot was transformed into a vibrant garden and gathering place in the late 1980s, the community took notice. Since then nearby Norris Square Park (Emerald and North Mascher Streets), once known as "Needle Park," has been given new life and now houses playground equipment, a pergola, and many benches that are filled on summer days.

and flags wave over this congested commercial center. Though the area has always had a lot of character, it hasn't always had financial resources, but that is starting to change. The district has seen a recent infusion of government money and is undergoing some positive development. A sparkling new public school recently opened, and factory space is being converted to offices.

Latin American music lovers flock to **Centro Musical** (464 West Lehigh Avenue), a clearinghouse for Latin music, instruments, and a variety of gifts with a Puerto Rican flair. This is where to go for your salsa, merengue, and bachata, as well as congas, timbales, and tamboras. Open Monday through Saturday from 9:00 A.M. to 8:00 P.M. Call (215) 425–7050.

The **Asociacion de Musicos Latino Americanos (AMLA)** (2726 North Sixth Street) is a major force behind the development in this area. It was founded in 1982 as a vehicle for spreading a love of Latin music and culture. The group runs a school offering instruction in Latin music and provides instructors for workshops in community schools. But AMLA's mission extends further into community development. The group is raising funds to build a multiuse cultural center that will house its music school and a 500-seat performance space at Fifth and Huntingdon Streets. Call (215) 223–3060 or go to www.amla.org.

End your visit to the Latino community with an authentic, south-of-the-border meal at **Tierra Colombiana** (4535 North Fifth Street), just south of Roosevelt Boulevard. This Cuban-Colombian restaurant gets big points for having huge portions of authentic food at reasonable prices. Start with a *batidos de frutas* (fruit smoothie), maybe guava for a change. The appetizers can be a meal in themselves. For variety try the *picada*—an assortment of Colombian sausages, corn patties, fried pork ribs, beef empanadas, and sweet and fried plantains. There's plenty for a group. Don't pass up the plantain fritters with garlic sauce. For dessert try the *las tres leches* (three-milk cake) or *flan de leche*. It's open for breakfast, too! Be patient with the service; this is an authentic Latino restaurant, and language can be a barrier. Open daily from 7:00 A.M. to 11:30 P.M. An upstairs nightclub is open Thursday through Saturday from 8:00 P.M. to 2:00 A.M. Call (215) 324–6086. Moderate.

The Northeast

You're now set to explore the Greater Northeast. This is a wide area, much of it block upon block of stone-faced row houses, a sight in and of itself. Northeast Philadelphia is a testament to the immigration of Europeans in the nineteenth century, when Irish, Italian, Polish, and German immigrants developed neighborhoods reminiscent of their homelands. The area is still home to many Ukrainians, Russians, and other Eastern Europeans, as well as a thriving Jewish community. In recent years, there has been an influx of Portuguese, Indians, and Pakistanis also. By one estimate there are thirty-seven languages spoken by students at the local high school. The Northeast is home to many firefighters, police officers, city and government workers (the IRS has a huge, unwelcoming facility right off Roosevelt Boulevard), postal workers, and teachers.

In terms of attractions, they are there and worth seeking out, but they're far apart and not necessarily conducive to an easy day of sightseeing. The key road in the Northeast is Roosevelt Boulevard (Route 1), which travels the length from the Schuylkill Expressway to the Pennsylvania Turnpike and beyond. In Northeast Philadelphia, all roads lead to Roosevelt.

About 2 miles from Tierra Colombiana is **Friends Hospital** (4641 Roosevelt Boulevard), the country's first private psychiatric hospital. Founded in 1813 as "The Asylum for Persons Deprived of the Use of Their Reason," the hospital each year treats more than 5,000 inpatients ranging from children to senior citizens. From its earliest days the hospital strived to create an environment that fostered calm and healing. The one-hundred-acre grounds are beautifully landscaped and include shaded walks and a stream. Friends is closed to the public except for Mother's Day, when it celebrates Garden Days and welcomes visitors into its quiet oasis from noon to 5:00 P.M. There's a $2.00 admission fee, but that includes a free azalea. Call (215) 831–7817.

Tucked away on the third floor of the hospital's Scattergood Building is the **Museum of Nursing History.** This small archival museum displays artifacts and documents from the early days of nursing, including a collection of nursing instruments from the early 1900s and an original letter from Florence

Nightingale. It also maintains a collection of nursing caps and uniforms, some dating as far back as World War I. The collection is on view Monday through Friday from 9:00 A.M. to 5:00 P.M. For further information or to arrange for a guided tour, call (267) 235–3901 or visit www.nursinghistory.org.

Hidden among the row houses of the city's Frankford section is the **Grand Army of the Republic Museum and Library** (4278 Griscom Street). This unique collection of Civil War artifacts and documents was started by a chapter of Civil War veterans. Now headquartered in an eighteenth-century brick house, this museum displays numerous Civil War relics, including tree stumps from the Chickamauga battlefield, each embedded with a cannonball, and a strip of the bloodstained pillowcase from President Lincoln's deathbed. Hours are limited, but the museum is usually open the first Sunday of the month from noon to 5:00 P.M. and on Tuesdays and Wednesdays from 10:00 A.M. to 2:00 P.M. It's wise to call ahead to confirm. You can find out more by calling (215) 289–6484 or going to www.garmuslib.org.

There are a lot of small bars and restaurants to explore in the Northeast, and everyone has their favorites. You can get a bite—or better yet, a beer—at **The Grey Lodge** (6235 Frankford Avenue). This is a classic neighborhood bar with a twist; its selection of microbrews (eight taps' worth) changes so often it actually posts updates on a Web site. The tomato pie is great if you're hungry. Every Wednesday night is quiz night, and the people there go all out if you happen to be around on a Friday the thirteenth. Open Monday through Thursday from 5:00 P.M. to midnight, Friday and Saturday from 11:00 A.M. to 1:00 A.M., and Sunday from 11:00 A.M. to midnight. Call (215) 624–2969 or visit www.grey lodge.com. Inexpensive.

If you're in the mood for seafood, head around the corner on Robbins Avenue to the original **Chickie's and Pete's Cafe** (4010 Robbins Avenue), a Northeast Philly standard. Although there are other Chickie's and Pete's locations

A Pioneer in Psychiatry

Dr. Benjamin Rush, a signer of the Declaration of Independence, is considered the father of American psychiatry and was largely responsible for the founding of Friends Hospital. The Surgeon General of the Continental Army, Rush had long been concerned about the treatment of what he called "mad people." This led the Philadelphia Yearly Meeting to set up Friends Hospital in Frankford to treat people "deprived of their reason." Rush's likeness is still used in the logo for the American Psychiatric Association.

throughout the city, this is the original. Locals swear this is the best place for crabs in the city. The mussels are a good bet, too, and don't miss the house specialty—crab fries. Open weekdays from 11:00 A.M. to midnight and weekends from 11:00 A.M. to 1:00 A.M. The bar is open until 2:00 A.M. daily. Call (215) 338–3060 or log on to www.chickiesandpetes.com. Moderate.

A third dining option in this neighborhood—and another Northeast Philly classic—is the **Mayfair Diner** (7373 Frankford Avenue), a few blocks farther north on the right. This is a perennial "Best of Philly" winner; it's squeaky clean, and you can get breakfast twenty-four hours a day. What more can you ask for? The diner food is a little on the expensive side, but when you've just got to have chipped beef or meat loaf and mashed potatoes, where else are you gonna go? Always open. Call (215) 624–4447. Inexpensive.

Continue north on Frankford Avenue to the **Insectarium** (8046 Frankford, between Rhawn Street and Welsh Road), a favorite field trip for elementary schools in the area and great for bug lovers no matter what their age. It's the only all-bug museum in the area, and really—how many all-bug museums are there anywhere? They're all here: hissing cockroaches, Japanese butterflies, tarantulas and scorpions, Goliath beetles, Indian walking sticks, African millipedes, and even something called a Human Face Stink Bug. The Insectarium is the brainchild of Steve Kanya, the proprietor of Steve's Bug Off Exterminating Company (the sign out front still says Steve's Bug Off, so that's what to look for). After a hard day spent exterminating, Steve would put a "catch of the day" display in his front window. Soon the bugs and rodents in the window were drawing more interest than Steve's exterminating services, and the Insectarium was born. Today the wonderful world of insects takes up two floors and includes 6,500 square feet of live and mounted insects from all over the world. There are interactive games, puzzles, microscopes, and a crawl-through spider web. But the real stars are the displays: a kitchen and bathroom crawling with cockroaches, a tank filled with glow-in-the-dark scorpions, a working beehive, and a live termite colony. You do have to pay real money for this pleasure: Admission is $6.00. Open Monday through Saturday from 10:00 A.M. to 4:00 P.M. Call (215) 335–9500 or log on to www.insectarium.com. The Insectarium can be reached by public transportation: Take the Market-Frankford line to the Bridge-Pratt stop at Frankford Terminal, then switch to the Frankford Avenue Route 66 bus, getting off at Welsh Road.

If you're a history buff, it's worth a visit to the **Robert W. Ryerss Library and Museum** in **Burholme Park**. Located right on the border of neighboring Montgomery County, the museum can be reached by continuing north on Cottman Avenue for about a mile and a half, then turning right on Central

Ryerss Mansion

Avenue. This was the country villa of a family of Philadelphia merchants who built an Italianate mansion and named it "Burholme" after an ancestral estate in England, which means "a house in a woodland setting." The grand home now houses several generations' worth of artifacts collected during the nineteenth century by the Ryerss family, who had a passion for traveling and collecting. There are paintings, sculptures, ceramics, weaponry, a Haskel pipe organ, Native American artifacts, and Japanese temple furniture. The museum is probably best known for its Asian art collection, which includes models of ships, costumes, and armor.

One word of warning: Some people think the Ryerss mansion is haunted, and, in fact, it does host an occasional murder-mystery night. If there are spirits hanging around, they are likely of the animal variety, since the Ryerss family was particularly fond of pets. Some are buried under a tree on the west side of the mansion, complete with headstones. One of those—Old Grey—was a favorite horse, whose portrait you can see hanging in the gallery inside. You can also get to Burholme Park by taking the R8 train to Fox Chase, where it's an easy walk from Ryerss station, which was at one time on mansion grounds.

The Take on Tastykake

Few things say "Philadelphia" like *Tastykakes*. These local favorites have been around since 1914, when they were marketed as "the cake that made Mother stop baking." Now they've even got a good mail-packaging service going for exiled Philadelphians in dire need of a Butterscotch Krimpet.

Open Friday, Saturday, and Sunday from 10:00 A.M. to 4:00 P.M. Call (215) 685–0544 or visit www.ryerssmuseum.org. Burholme Park also has a miniature golf course and a driving range, which you enter off Cottman Avenue.

Also hugging the Philadelphia/Montgomery County border is **Pennypack Park,** which you can reach from Verree Road. A narrow, winding, 1,600-acre park, Pennypack offers miles of hiking and bike trails, as well as bridge paths. Purchased by William Penn from the Lenni-Lenape Indians in 1684, the park also contains several historic structures: The Pennypack Baptist Church was built in 1688; the Pennypack Bridge at the southern end on Frankford Avenue (near the Insectarium) is one of the oldest stone bridges still in use in the country; and the Verree House on Verree Road was the site of a raid by British troops during the Revolutionary War. Also on Verree Road is the **Pennypack Environmental Center** (8600A Verree Road), which houses rotating exhibits as well as a collection of artifacts found in the region and serves as a head-quarters for the park's field trips and other activities. Open Monday through Friday from 9:00 A.M. to 4:00 P.M. Call (215) 685–0470 or go to www.phila parks.org/ppnat.htm.

Just across the street from the Environmental Center is **Fox Chase Farm** (8600 Verree Road), the only remaining working farm in the city of Philadel-phia. A visit here is a great family activity, with tours and craft workshops such as ice-cream churning, sheep shearing, and maple sugaring. This has been a working farm since the days of William Penn and is now part of the Fairmount Park System. There is a resident farmer, but the farm runs under a unique part-nership with Abraham Lincoln High School. Call (215) 728–7900 or go to www.foxchasefarm.org.

Heading back to Roosevelt Boulevard, this part of Northeast Philadelphia is primarily industrial, with major distribution centers for Nabisco and Pepsi Cola (which explains the sometimes wonderful smell in the air). Several major companies have facilities here. Philadelphia's second airport, the Northeast Philadelphia Airport, is located right off Roosevelt Boulevard and manages a busy schedule of charter and commuter planes.

A Creek Runs Through It

The Lenni-Lenape called Pennypack Park in the Northeast "Pennapeca," meaning "deep, slow-moving water." Chief Mettamincont sold the land bordering the creek to William Penn on June 7, 1684, and within three years there was a working gristmill on the creek. Many of the roads in the area, such as Verree Road and Paper Mill Road, began as paths to the mill.

If you're feeling hungry, especially if you're traveling with kids, stop in at *Nifty Fifties* (2491 Grant Avenue), just off the Boulevard before the airport. This is a popular chain diner that seems particularly appropriate in Northeast Philly, with its neon lights and checkered floor. Great burgers, freshly made fries, and milkshakes in any flavor you can think of are served. It opens early, too, if you want breakfast, and it has good omelettes. Hours are 6:00 A.M. to 11:00 P.M. Sunday through Thursday and until 1:00 A.M. Friday and Saturday. Call (215) 676–1950. Inexpensive.

If ice-skating is your thing, the area's newest skating center is located just past the airport. Affiliated with the city's professional hockey team, the *Flyers Skate Zone* (10990 Decatur Road) bills itself as a family entertainment center. The rink is open to the public from 12:30 to 2:30 P.M. every afternoon and at night on weekends. There's also a bustling video game arcade for when your ankles start to hurt. Call (215) 618–0050 or log on to www.flyersskatezone.com.

The Philadelphia city limits actually extend almost to the Pennsylvania Turnpike. The last stretch of Roosevelt Boulevard, past Woodhaven Road, is dominated by the former *Philadelphia State Hospital for the Insane,* or "Byberry," as it was known. Its doors have been barricaded for good, but at its peak it held 6,000 patients in some fifty buildings, despite the fact that it was designed for 3,000 patients. It is not one of Philadelphia's shining moments. There was overcrowding and rampant charges of patient mistreatment. Originally constructed in the early 1900s, Byberry eventually became the place where the unwanted were warehoused. The state took over in 1938 because conditions there were so bad, but ultimately the state decided the time for putting mentally ill patients in huge sanitariums had come to an end, and the door closed for good in 1990. Widespread asbestos problems made the site an environmental nightmare. While the city, state, and neighbors continue to squabble, current plans call for the site to be developed as a mix of office space, light industry, and residences.

tastytrivia

If one chicken laid all the eggs used in a single day of production at *Tastykake,* that chicken would be laying eggs for 572 years.

Tastykake uses 135,000 pounds of sugar each day. That's the equivalent of 27,000 store-bought five-pound bags.

Want to know how many Tastykake pies you would have to put end to end to make a mile? 14,080!

Peanut Butter Tastykakes are the company's most popular item. It bakes one hundred million of them every year.

Shopper's Paradise

It's worth the hunt to find *Material Culture* (4700 Wissahickon Avenue) if you like shopping. This wonderfully rich warehouse-type store features roomfulls of antique furniture, pottery, and handmade carpets from many cultures. The breadth of products and their affordability regularly draw designers from New York and Washington, even though many Philadelphians aren't even aware it's there. For directions or information call (215) 849–8030 or go to www.materialculture.com.

It's hard to know what it says about Pennsylvania, but according to the state, the *Franklin Mills Mall* is now the most-visited tourist attraction in the entire state. If you're a shopper, it's definitely a sight to behold: more than 200 stores, many of them outlets, and keep in mind that Pennsylvania doesn't have sales tax on clothing. The mall is easy to find from anywhere along Roosevelt Boulevard. Take the Woodhaven Road exit south and follow the signs. If you're coming from Center City, take I–95 north to exit 35 at Woodhaven Boulevard. There are also daily shuttle services from many Philadelphia hotels and the airport and train station. Among the dozens of outlets, the big draws are name brands like Kenneth Cole, Off 5th Saks Fifth Avenue, and Last Call from Neiman Marcus. For those who burn out on shopping, there's a fourteen-screen movie theater, and at the north end of the mall is *Dave and Busters,* the entertainment mecca with its signature drinks, food, and the "million-dollar midway," a video arcade with virtual reality games. Dave and Busters is open Monday through Wednesday from 11:00 A.M. to 1:00 A.M., Thursday through Saturday from 11:00 A.M. to 2:00 A.M., and Sunday from 11:00 A.M. to midnight. Call (215) 632–0333. Your dining options are pretty much limited to mall food. There are two food courts, as well as a Ruby Tuesday restaurant, China Buddha Inn, and Johnny Rockets, a 1950s-style diner. The mall is open from 10:00 A.M. to 9:30 P.M. Monday through Saturday and from 11:00 A.M. to 7:00 P.M. on Sunday. Call (215) 632–1500 or (800) 336–MALL or log on to www.franklinmills.com.

Making a real switch from the mall scene, head to *Glen Foerd Mansion* (5001 Grant Avenue) on the banks of the Delaware River just where the city meets neighboring Bucks County. Although there are plans to try to develop this stretch of the Delaware riverfront, for now, Glen Foerd is the highlight. You're immediately transported back to a more graceful time, as a tree-lined lane guides you through well-kept grounds to an Italianate mansion, the last surviving riverfront estate in Philadelphia. Built around 1853 as a summer estate for Charles Macalaster, a financier and adviser to eight United States presidents, the home was expanded around the turn of the century and landscaped in an English tradition, including a formal rose garden that still survives. The estate includes a carriage house, a garden house, and a boathouse integrated into the river wall, but the centerpiece is the mansion itself. A sweeping staircase, with a Haskel pipe organ on the first floor landing, rises three floors to an elaborate stained-glass dome. There's also a recently restored art gallery featuring paintings by Rembrandt, Constable, and Monet, among others. Also on display throughout the home are Oriental rugs, antique furniture, and a rare book collection. Open Tuesday through Friday from 10:00 A.M. to 2:00 P.M. Admission is $4.00. The estate is the site of concerts and other activities throughout the year. For a schedule call (215) 632–5330 or go to www.glenfoerd.org.

Having reached the edge of Philadelphia, it's a quick trip back to Center City on I–95, from which you can see the abandoned **Holmesburg Prison** off to your right. Since it opened in 1896, the ominous stone walls of Holmesburg have kept awful secrets. The prison is infamous for a host of medical experiments that were conducted illegally on inmates between the early 1950s and the mid-1970s. In exchange for a few dollars and without informed consent, inmates were exposed to a range of substances, which included chemical weapons and radioactive isotopes.

Hop off I–95 at the Allegheny Avenue exit if you want to try what a lot of people swear is the best pizza in Philadelphia. **Tacconelli's Pizzeria** (2604 East Somerset Street) in Port Richmond is so popular it asks customers to call

AUTHOR'S FAVORITE PLACES TO EAT IN NORTH PHILADELPHIA AND THE NORTHEAST

Draught Horse
1431 Cecil B. Moore Avenue;
(215) 235–1010,
www.draughthorse.com

The Grey Lodge
6235 Frankford Avenue;
(215) 624–2969,
www.greylodge.com

Johnny Brenda's
1201 Frankford Avenue;
(215) 739–9684,
www.johnnybrendas.com

Mayfair Diner
7373 Frankford Avenue;
(215) 624–4447

Nifty Fifties
2491 Grant Avenue;
(215) 676–1950

Tacconelli's Pizzeria
2604 East Somerset Street;
(215) 425–4983

Tierra Colombiana
4535 North Fifth Street;
(215) 324–6086

a day ahead to reserve pizza dough. No joke. Don't expect much more than good pizza though. This is strictly a family-style pizza joint. Go figure. Turn right on Allegheny after exiting I–95, make a left on Richmond Street, then, about a half-mile down, a right onto Somerset. Open Wednesday and Thursday from 4:30 to 9:00 P.M., Friday and Saturday from 4:30 to 10:00 P.M., and Sunday from 4:00 to 9:00 P.M. Call (215) 425–4983. Inexpensive.

HELPFUL WEB SITES

www.northernliberties.org   www.temple.edu

Places to Stay in North Philadelphia and the Northeast

Conwell Inn,
1331 West Berks Street;
(215) 235–6200,
www.conwellinn.com
There are several chain hotels along the upper stretches of Roosevelt Boulevard, but not much to recommend staying in North Philadelphia or the Northeast. If you want to stay near Temple University, the Conwell Inn is really your only choice. There are twenty-two guest rooms in a renovated historic building. Moderate.

Places to Eat in North Philadelphia and the Northeast

Chink's,
6030 Torresdale Avenue,
Northeast;
(215) 535–9405
Chink's is your best bet for a cheesesteak in the Northeast. It's a retro '50s soda parlor where you can sit in a booth, play something on a jukebox, and get a chocolate egg cream to go with your cheesesteak. Open Monday through Thursday from 11:00 A.M. to 9:00 P.M. and Friday and Saturday from 11:00 A.M. to 10:00 P.M. Inexpensive.

Country Club Restaurant and Pastry Shop,
1717 Cottman Avenue,
Northeast;
(215) 722–0500,
www.ccdiner.com
A longtime favorite diner in the Northeast, with a decidedly Jewish twist. The city's culinary community was astonished recently when the Country Club was awarded three out of four bells by the *Inquirer*'s notoriously picky restaurant critic, who called it the best traditional diner in the region. Start with the matzo ball soup and end with out-of-this-world cheesecake. Open Sunday through Thursday from 7:00 A.M. to 11:00 P.M. and Friday and Saturday from 7:00 A.M. to 1:00 A.M. Moderate.

Las Cazuelas,
426 West Girard Avenue,
Northern Liberties;
(215) 351–9144,
www.lascazuelas.net
You can't miss this Mexican
BYOB in Northern Liberties,
where bright colors draw you
into a warm environment that
has great affordable food
and even an occasional
strolling guitarist. Don't miss
the chicken mole—the house
specialty—and finish with a
cup of Mexican coffee. Open
Monday through Thursday from 11:00 A.M. to 9:00 P.M.,
Friday and Saturday from
11:00 A.M. to 10:00 P.M., and
Sunday from 11:00 A.M. to
8:00 P.M. Moderate.

Sovalo,
702–704 North
Second Street,
Northern Liberties;
(215) 413–7770
The husband-and-wife team
who run this restaurant spent
nearly a decade in the Napa
Valley, and it shows in the
cuisine, said to be inspired by Italy as well as Northern
California. The dishes change
weekly, sometimes even
daily, depending on what
ingredients are available and
fresh. Regulars say you can't
go wrong with the pasta
dishes. In the summer you
can sit at a sidewalk table
and take in the Northern Liberties scene. Open Monday
through Thursday from 5:00
to 10:00 P.M. and Friday and
Saturday from 5:00 to 11:00
P.M. Moderate.

The Northwest

It's tough to lump such a large area with so much to offer into one chapter. Each neighborhood in this northwest corner of the city has a distinctive personality and places to explore. It's equally impossible to see it all in one day. If that's all the time you have, make plans to come back. This off-the-beaten-path area of Philadelphia has it all: history, charm, culture, nature, shopping, food, and fun.

Manayunk

The word "Manayunk" rolls off the tongues of Philadelphia natives like it was nothing out of the ordinary. Granted it's one of the strangest names of a Philly neighborhood, derived from the Lenni-Lenape word *manaiung*, which translates as "where we go to drink." An apropos name indeed, since the modern manifestation of Manayunk is as a trendy neighborhood full of bars, restaurants, and upscale shops. Since it was named a National Historic District in 1983, Manayunk has embraced its reputation and its restoration. Many of the chic shops and restaurants are housed in buildings that once served as textile mills, which set up shop here because of the close proximity of the Schuylkill River and the Manayunk Canal. If you look

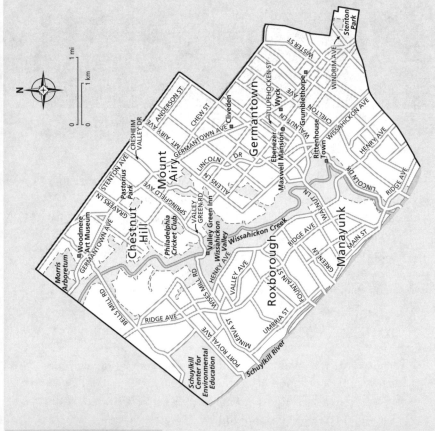

Let's Make This More Complicated

Manayunk was originally known as Flat Rock, named after the Flat Rock Bridge, which in turn was named after an area of flat rocks in the Schuylkill near the site. But apparently the locals didn't think the name was creative enough, so they changed it to Manayunk in 1824. They liked "Manayunk" better?

beyond **Main Street**—the epicenter of Manayunk's activity—you'll see the place real 'Yunkers call home. This is where the laborers lived during the Industrial Revolution; their bosses preferred the top of the hill, in places like Chestnut Hill and Germantown.

Today there are more than seventy shops and galleries and dozens of restaurants to choose from. Manayunk hosts several festivals throughout the year, with the largest being the Arts Festival held every May. The town is also known far and wide for the infamous "Manayunk Wall," a stretch of Levering and Lyceum Street that shoots up a 17 percent grade in just one-third of a mile. Racers in the Philadelphia International Championship Bike Race, held each year in June, have to make the climb ten times during the course of the 156-mile race. Manayunkers accommodate them by showering them with water and cheers during the climb.

It's not hard to get to Manayunk, but parking here is a notorious nightmare. There are several lots, but they fill up quickly. This is a situation where the numerous options of public transportation come in handy. The R6 Norristown Regional rail stops in Manayunk just 1 block from Main Street, and the Route 61 bus takes riders from Center City to Main Street. If you have access to a bicycle, that may be your best choice. The **Manayunk Towpath** lies along the 22-mile bikeway between Philadelphia and Valley Forge, paralleling the canal. It's a scenic ride

AUTHOR'S FAVORITES IN THE NORTHWEST

Cin Cin

Deshler-Morris House

Jake's

McNally's Tavern

Schuylkill Center for Environmental Education

St. Martin-in-the-Fields

Wissahickon Valley

Wyck

with historical signs pointing out old rail lines, canal locks, and other evidence of the town's history; plus it's a lot easier to park a bike than a car. There are also places in town where you can rent bikes. If you have to drive, take the Schuylkill Expressway to the Belmont Avenue/Green Lane exit, turning right to cross the bridge. For general information call the Manayunk Development Corporation at (215) 482–9565 or visit www.manayunk.com.

Once you get to Manayunk, you'd better like to eat or shop. It's a great place to do both, but there's not a whole lot else going on. Though it started as an artsy alternative to Center City, Manayunk's commercial strip has become more mainstream over the years, and unfortunately the chains have started to move in. You'll have to go to South Street if you want a truly hip experience in Philadelphia. It's not uncommon now to see a group of older suburban women gathering for lunch at one of the many fine restaurants that line Main Street.

Most of the action is in an 8-block stretch of Main Street, though retailers and restaurateurs in search of lower rents are starting to explore a few blocks in either direction. As you stroll Main Street, there's a certain sameness to most of the shops, not helped at all by the invasion of chains such as Pottery Barn, Chico's, and Ben and Jerry's. That sparkling, new ice-cream shop epitomizes the split personality of Manayunk, since it's just a block away from one of the town's longtime standards: a hole-in-the-wall water-ice place.

There are a few holdouts that keep the scene from getting too uppity: a busy animal clinic; a loaded-to-the-gills beauty supply store (Beans); and one of the town's original businesses, *A. I. Poland Jewelers* (4347 Main Street). Founded in 1899 in its current location, this family-owned business has survived the invasion of far more trendy stores selling jewelry. This is where you go to get your watch repaired or to buy your high school ring or the cross for a first holy communion, all plucked from original, dark wood display cases. The store saw some tough times in the 1950s and 1960s, but, as a family, they hung in there and have since seen a lot of upstarts pack up and leave town. "If you made a list of the retail stores that have come and gone in Manayunk in the past fifteen years, you'd have a pretty large volume of reading to do," says current owner Victor Ostroff. Open Tuesday through Thursday from 10:00 A.M. to 6:00 P.M., Friday from 10:00 A.M. to 7:00 P.M., and Saturday from 10:00 A.M. to 5:00 P.M. Call (215) 483–1316.

Most of the shops have funkier goods to purvey. A few of the most fun include *Latitudes Fine Craft Gallery* (4325 Main Street), which also stocks jewelry and gag gifts; *Belle Maison* (4340 Main Street), where you can deck out your home in luxury; and *Sweet Violet* (4631), a fun place to browse with girlfriends for all things feminine.

Manayunk, Take One

M. Night Shyamalan's movie *Unbreakable* (2000) was filmed largely at several Manayunk locations, including Pretzel Park and the United States Hotel on Main Street. The film stars Bruce Willis, who also starred in Shyamalan's breakthrough film *The Sixth Sense*. A native of nearby Conshohocken, Shyamalan continues to live in the Philadelphia suburbs and has given the city a big boost in its efforts to draw filmmakers to town. His movies *Signs* and *The Village* were also filmed in or around Philadelphia.

You don't need to get dressed up to dine in Manayunk, but the caliber of the cuisine and the clientele has risen over the years, and Main Street now boasts some of the finest restaurants in Philadelphia. The best is still **Jake's** (4365 Main Street), Bruce Cooper's New American restaurant that started Manayunk's dining renaissance in the 1980s. The regulars keep coming back for such favorites as sautéed veal medallions over lobster mashed potatoes and the award-winning crab cakes. The portions are adequate, the presentation outstanding. Be sure to save room for the cookie taco for dessert. Jake's isn't easy to miss—look for the pop-art table and wine bottle protruding over the sidewalk from the second floor. Open Monday through Thursday from 5:30 to 9:30 P.M., Friday from 5:30 to 10:30 P.M., Saturday from 5:00 to 10:30 P.M., and Sunday from 5:00 to 9:00 P.M. Lunch is served every day from 11:30 A.M. to 2:30 P.M., with Sunday brunch available starting at 10:30 A.M. Reservations are highly recommended. Call (215) 483–0444 or log on to www.jakesrestaurant.com. Expensive.

A more moderately priced Manayunk option—also a longtime favorite—is **Le Bus** (4266 Main Street). Known for its terrific breads, Le Bus has several take-out locations around town and a stall at the Reading Terminal Market, but the spot in Manayunk was the first to offer full-service dining. This is a homespun success story with a twist: Le Bus started almost two decades ago in an old yellow school bus parked near the campus of the University of Pennsylvania, dishing out sandwiches to the lunch crowd between classes. Its casual atmosphere makes Le Bus the perfect lunch spot for a break from shopping, and it's kid-friendly. Homestyle sandwiches—on their fresh bread, of course—are piled high. You can get down-home meat loaf or fried chicken, or more creative options such as a tasty Thai turkey salad. Le Bus is open Monday through Thursday from 9:00 A.M. to 10:00 P.M., Friday from 11:00 A.M. to 11:30 P.M., Saturday from 9:30 A.M. to 11:30 P.M., and Sunday from 9:30 A.M. to 10:00 P.M. Call (215) 487–2663 or visit www.lebusmanayunk.com. Moderate.

Roxborough

As you climb the hills away from Main Street, you come to the heart of where "real" Manayunkers live. Once you cross Manayunk Avenue, you're technically in neighboring Roxborough, which perhaps can best be described as Manayunk without Main Street. The two communities share the same ethos—as good, solid, working-class communities to raise families in. With so many row houses built on steep hills, the porch is central to life here.

If you want to eat away from the crowds in Manayunk, try Roxborough's **Adobe Cafe** (4550 Mitchell Street, a left off Green Lane). Moving up the hill from the restaurants of Manayunk, the prices drop significantly. This is a bargain, family-friendly, Tex-Mex restaurant if you don't like the scene on Main Street. Not only that, the food is good, the portions are big, and the margaritas can't be beat. Try the mushroom quesadillas with goat cheese or other great vegetarian choices, like spicy *seitan* or tofu-and-veggie kebabs. Every Monday is Fiesta Night, when you can get two dinner entrees and a bottle of wine or a pitcher of beer for only $25. Open Monday from 5:00 to 10:00 P.M. Other days it opens at 11:30 A.M. for lunch and closes at 10:00 P.M. Tuesday through Thursday, 11:00 P.M. on Friday and Saturday, and 9:30 P.M. on Sunday. Call (215) 483–3947. Moderate.

If you're in the mood for a change of pace, consider a visit to the **Schuylkill Center for Environmental Education** (8480 Hagy's Mill Road). (Turn left at Port Royal Avenue off Ridge, then right on Hagy's Mill Road. The No. 47 bus will get you to Cathedral Road, but the center's entrance is about a mile away.) It sure is out of the way, but it's a favorite place for local families to go explore the natural world in a manageable setting. There are 6 miles of winding trails, some with great views of the Philadelphia skyline; a butterfly house that's a hit in the spring and summer; a bird blind; and a pond. A hands-

Dueling Cheesesteaks

Roxborough has its own version of the famous South Philadelphia Pat's vs. Geno's cheesesteak war. Right across Henry Avenue from each other are two cheesesteak places that their proponents swear have the best cheesesteaks in town: **Chubby's** (5826 Henry Avenue) and **Dalessandro's Steaks** (600 Wendover Street). Chubby's claims to use better-quality meat, and it cooks to order. Fans swear Dalessandro's rolls are fresher. Take your pick.

What *Are* Those Lights?

You can't miss them at night as you fly or drive into Philadelphia from the west. More than a dozen broadcast towers perch on a high point in Upper Roxborough, carrying transmitters for television and radio stations and providing red beacons at night. The locals refer to it as the "antenna farm."

on Discovery Room has activities for the kids, and its Wildlife Rehabilitation Center provides treatment and a safe haven for thousands of injured birds and animals each year. Neighbors can rent a plot in a large community organic garden. It's open Monday through Saturday from 8:30 A.M. to 5:00 P.M. and Sunday from 1:00 to 5:00 P.M. Admission is $7.00 for adults and $5.00 for children. Call (215) 482–7300 or visit www.schuylkillcenter.org.

There's a convenient back way to Chestnut Hill from the Schuylkill Center. Hagy's Ford Road will take you to Spring Lane, which becomes Bells Mill Road after crossing Ridge Avenue. Bells Mill is a good way to approach the Wissahickon Valley and Chestnut Hill, where it ends. Another good way to enter the Wissahickon is from Henry Avenue, where Wises Mill Road heads down to the heart of Forbidden Drive.

Wissahickon Valley

You'll feel a complete change of pace in the **_Wissahickon Valley._** The city slips away as you enter this wooded gorge carved by the Wissahickon Creek. It's been a favorite recreation spot for Philadelphians for generations, at one point compelling Edgar Allan Poe to write: "Now the Wissahiccon is of so remarkable a loveliness that, were it flowing in England, it would be the theme of every bard."

The valley offers a true wilderness experience with high wooded bluffs and rock outcrops, but the best thing about it is you can enjoy it all from a relatively flat, winding carriage road known as Forbidden Drive (so named because cars are not allowed). This 5-mile path is perfect for walkers, joggers, horseback riders, and bicyclists, who certainly take advantage of it. Parking is not easy, but the city has finally gotten organized with some well-marked parking areas, one of which is off Bells Mill Road. (There's also convenient parking off of Valley Green Road.) You'll find the only covered bridge within the city limits of a U.S. city about three-quarters of a mile south of the Bells Mill entrance. There are also dozens of miles of dirt paths leading deeper into the valley. Trail maps are available at several locations, including at Valley Green Inn. Permits are required if you want to explore these areas by bicycle or horseback.

Just off Forbidden Drive at Valley Green Road is the **Valley Green Inn,** a charming inn that dates back to the 1850s. Although most people go more for the surroundings than the food, the current owners have made a push to improve the menu. They've also spent big bucks renovating and added a terrific outdoor patio. Sunday brunch is a favorite here, since you have time after to enjoy the Wissahickon. It's always crowded, but there's a reason. You can't beat it on a sunny Sunday. It's good to keep in mind that reservations are accepted. Dinner entrees have gotten more creative, including dishes like bourbon-soaked, cornmeal-coated catfish, named Drunken Colonel's Catfish. You'll need a hike after that meal. Take time after eating to feed the ducks that wait not-so-patiently by the creek across the path. Lunch is available Monday through Saturday from noon to 4:00 P.M. and brunch is on Sunday from 10:00 A.M. to 3:00 P.M. Dinner is served Sunday through Thursday from 5:00 to 9:00 P.M., until 10:00 P.M. on Friday and Saturday. Call (215) 247–1730 or visit www.valleygreeninn.com. Expensive.

You could spend an entire day exploring the Wissahickon and enjoying the beautiful surroundings. One place you should make time for is **Ritten-house Town** (206 Lincoln Drive—enter off Wissahickon Avenue), at the southern end of the Wissahickon. Many people, even Philadelphians, don't know it's there; it's easy to miss as you speed by on Lincoln Drive. A National Historic Landmark, historic Rittenhouse Town is the site of America's first paper mill, founded in 1690 by William Rittenhouse, a talented papermaker who had apprenticed in Germany. A small town sprang up around the mill and eventually grew to more than forty buildings, several of which are still standing. William Penn was said to be particularly proud of the mill because paper mills were new, even in England. The Rittenhouse family became an important force in the Revolution, supplying the paper for newspapers and pamphlets; paper was also used to make cartridges and gun wadding. It's also been reported that

TOP HITS IN THE NORTHWEST

Cliveden	Morris Arboretum
Cresheim Cottage Cafe	Valley Green Inn
Germantown Avenue in Chestnut Hill	Woodmere Art Museum
Main Street Manayunk	

Wissahickon Hide and Seek

Many people who grew up in Philadelphia have memories of the search to find the Indian in the Wissahickon. It's hard to find—you have to climb up a steep dirt trail. But there it is: a 12-foot-tall limestone Indian peering out over an outcropping of rock. It's known as Tedyuscung, after a Lenni-Lenape chief, even though that apparently isn't quite historically accurate. The statue originally stood in front of a tavern but was moved in 1910 to its current location, near the stone bridge at Rex Street.

during the Battle of Germantown in 1777, the Pennsylvania militia used Rittenhouse paper in its hats to make the uniforms look more formal.

A guided tour takes you back to the time of the mill. The visitor center is housed in the Abraham Rittenhouse Home, where you can see a working model of a colonial paper mill. Another home on the site—the 1707 Rittenhouse Home—was the birthplace of David Rittenhouse, the noted clockmaker and astronomer for whom Rittenhouse Square is named. You can also see the foundations of an early paper mill, which were just discovered in the 1990s, and find out that it was no easy thing making paper in the 1700s. The pulp had to be beat using a large hammer, and three hardworking men could put out only about 1,000 sheets a day. Today local artists on-site conduct a variety of papermaking workshops, which can range from Japanese papermaking to finishing techniques. Rittenhouse Town is open weekends from June through October from noon to 4:00 P.M. and by appointment the rest of the year. Admission is $5.00 for adults and $3.00 for children and seniors, though prices can vary for special programs, so it's wise to call ahead. There is no food service, but a picnic area is available. For a schedule and costs call (215) 438–5711 or log on to www.rittenhousetown.org.

There are several ways to get to the Wissahickon Valley using public transportation. The closest bus route is the No. 65, and the R8 rail line has stops at Tulpechocken. Call SEPTA at (215) 580–7800 for schedules and more information.

If you're driving to Chestnut Hill from here, follow Lincoln Drive until it dead-ends at Allens Lane. You can't help but notice the beautiful homes that line the road. And don't forget to look up as you go under the Walnut Lane Bridge high above. Connecting Roxborough and Germantown, the bridge was the world's largest poured-concrete structure when it was dedicated in 1906. If you are using public transportation, take the SEPTA R7 Chestnut Hill local train or the R8 Chestnut Hill West to the last stop. By bus, Route 23 along Germantown Avenue is your best bet.

Kelpius's Cave

It can seem like everything is hard to find in the Wissahickon. Add a hidden cave to that list. Located on a hill near Hermit Lane is the so-called Cave of Kelpius. Kelpius belonged to a religious sect known as the Tabernacle of the Mystic Brotherhood. After a split in the sect, Kelpius and his followers fled to the caves of the Wissahickon (dubbed "Burrow of Rocks," which became Roxborough in 1706), where they awaited the end of the world, which they believed would come in the year 1700. (It did not.) A marker at the cave declares that Kelpius was the first Rosicrucian master in America. The Rosicrucians (meaning rose and cross) are a worldwide group claiming to have secret wisdom dating to ancient Egypt.

Chestnut Hill

It doesn't get much more charming than Chestnut Hill. Still in the city limits—tucked into the northwest corner—this community feels more like some of Philadelphia's fabled suburbs on the Main Line. The center of the town is based along cobblestoned *Germantown Avenue,* a former Indian trail that today is lined with high-end boutiques, galleries, and restaurants. Some of the stores and taverns in town have been passed down through families for generations. Fanning off from Germantown Avenue are streets with lovely Colonial-Revival and Queen Anne houses.

Chestnut Hill was just a small village of farmers and millworkers until the commuter railroad came to town in the 1850s. Once that link to the city of Philadelphia had been established, it became much more appealing. Pennsylvania Railroad executive Henry Howard Houston saw the potential and pushed the area as a fashionable suburb set along the scenic Wissahickon Valley. Houston commissioned architects George and William Hewitt to design nearly a hundred homes, as well as an enormous inn and church. The area took off, and the streets are now lined with homes designed by virtually every significant Philadelphia architect of the time. The Chestnut Hill Historical Society produces a comprehensive architectural map that includes photographs of eighty of the town's more significant homes. All of Chestnut Hill has been named a National Historic District, and it remains a vibrant community.

While you can best explore Germantown Avenue by foot, it is helpful to have a car so you can see some of the more outlying areas. Though locals grumble about the parking, Chestnut Hill actually came up with a unique solution to its crowded streets. Several parking lots around town are staffed by retirees who greet you with a smile and a ticket that, once validated by a local business or restaurant, entitles you to reduced parking rates. Each validation sticker buys you a half-hour of free parking. The community once had the reputation of being a ghost town on Sunday, but most stores and restaurants are open now, and the town offers free parking as a Sunday incentive. The shopping district also sponsors several annual activities—the Fall for the Arts Festival in October and a Garden Festival in May.

To take Chestnut Hill from the top, arrive from Bells Mill Road, which dead-ends at Germantown Avenue. The shopping district is to your right, but wait—two of Philadelphia's best hidden treasures are off to your left. Follow the signs to the ***Morris Arboretum*** (9414 Meadowbrook Avenue—a circuitous but well-marked route to the entrance off Northwestern Avenue). Philadelphia has long been a draw for gardeners and horticulturists, who usually head south on Route 1 to Longwood Gardens and Winterthur. A visit to the University of Pennsylvania's Morris Arboretum is more intimate and relaxing, while still offering the stunning beauty of a well-maintained public garden. The arboretum's ninety-two acres are home to more than 6,000 shrubs and trees, which include some of Pennsylvania's oldest and largest specimens. Don't miss the Hamilton Fernery, a striking, curved, Victorian glasshouse in which hundreds of ferns grow in a miniature rock mountain near a grotto, waterfall, and rustic bridge. It's the only greenhouse of its kind in the country, and recently it has been restored to its original condition. You also won't find an equal to the arboretum's Garden Railway Display during the winter holidays. G-scale trains meander through an amazing landscape with a waterfall, bridges, tunnels, and historic buildings, all created with materials found in nature. There are picnic grounds if you want to grab a take-out lunch from one of the shops on Germantown Avenue. The arboretum is open daily from 10:00 A.M. to 4:00 P.M. and

Hamilton Fernery at Morris Arboretum

Will o' the WASP

It seems proper to note here in Chestnut Hill—Philadelphia's stronghold of the WASP lifestyle—that the acronym "WASP" was invented in Philadelphia. E. Digby Baltzell, a professor of sociology at the University of Pennsylvania (and an ardent WASP himself), coined the acronym when he tired of writing, over and over, "White Anglo Saxon Protestant" in his 1964 book *The Protestant Establishment*.

until 5:00 P.M. on weekends from April through October. Admission is $10.00 for adults, $8.00 for seniors, and $5.00 for students and children. Call (215) 247–5777 or visit www.morrisarboretum.org for more information.

Heading east on Germantown back toward Chestnut Hill, you'll see the **Woodmere Art Museum** (9201 Germantown Avenue) on your left. At one time the private estate of oil executive Charles Knox Smith, the Woodmere is one of the city's best small museums and the only one to focus on past and present art and artists from the Philadelphia area. Smith's will stipulated that his mansion become a museum, and his substantial collection of European and American paintings feel at home in the Victorian parlors. Impressive paintings and sculpture are complemented by a charming collection of decorative arts, including tapestries, porcelains, and Oriental rugs. The museum is open Tuesday through Saturday from 10:00 A.M. to 5:00 P.M. and Sunday from 1:00 to 5:00 P.M. There's a suggested donation of $5.00 or $3.00 for students and seniors. Call (215) 247–0476 or go to www.woodmereartmuseum.org.

Closer to town is the **Chestnut Hill Historical Society** (8708 Germantown Avenue), a good place to pick up information for your visit. Housed in a renovated Victorian, the society maintains changing exhibits of local interest and sponsors lectures and tours. Call (215) 247–0417 or visit www.chhist.org.

If you've spent the day hiking in the Wissahickon or Morris Arboretum, you may be ready for a stop at one of Chestnut Hill's most beloved hangouts, just down the street from the Historical Society—**McNally's Tavern** (8634 Germantown Avenue). Behind the green door is the quintessential neighborhood bar; McNally's has been in the family since 1921. Hugh McNally was a trolley driver, and his wife, Rose, noticed that when the line ended in Chestnut Hill, the drivers and trolley workers had a half-hour turnaround time and needed someplace to eat. Rose built a small corrugated shack, installed a potbellied stove so the men could get warm—there were no heaters in the trolleys back then—and put a pot of stew on the stove to cook. McNally's was one of the few restaurants in Chestnut Hill that served African Americans at the time, but it was a workingman's bar—no women allowed. Once Prohibition was lifted in 1933, McNally's added alcohol to the menu and the tavern became a popular gathering spot. There were some lean times in the 1950s, but the college crowd started to drop in, and now McNally's serves a lot of working professionals and families. The long, narrow room is lined by a solid wood bar that serves, among other things, McNally's Ale, brewed just for the tavern. McNally's offers a full menu, but you've got to have the "Schmitter," a perennial winner in *Philadelphia Magazine*'s best cheesesteak contest. It's a cheesesteak and then some, with onions, tomatoes, slightly burnt salami, and McNally's special sauce; it was named after a customer who drank only Schmidt's beer. All this for less than six bucks. Open Monday through Saturday from 11:15 A.M. to 11:00 P.M. and from noon to 8:00 P.M. on Sunday. Call (215) 247–9736 or visit www.mcnallystavern.com.

For something a little more exotic, just a few doors down is **Al Dana II** (8630 Germantown Avenue), a great BYOB where you can get authentic Middle Eastern food. The classics are terrific—tabbouleh, falafel, lamb, baba ghanough—or try the Holy Land chicken, which is served on flat bread and topped with perfectly sautéed onions, olive oil, and pine nuts. There are even chicken fingers for the kids. This may be a better family choice, because with all the garlic, it's certainly not a good date place! Call (215) 247–3336 or visit www.aldana2.com. Moderate.

For something decidedly more low-key to eat for lunch, look for the copper planter and sneak down the alleyway to the **French Bakery and Cafe** (8624 Germantown Avenue, rear; 215–247–5959), for great soups and sandwiches. Next door is **Monkey Business,** one of Chestnut Hill's consignment shops. This fifty-year-old shop is still staffed entirely by volunteers and offers some of the city's best bargain hunting. Call (215) 248–1835.

The upper part of Germantown Avenue is lined with the shops that bring the crowds to town. On the west side of the street, past the newsstand at the

Arrivederci

The stone you see in the beautiful homes in Chestnut Hill was local—Wissahickon schist—but many of the stoneworkers who built the homes were not. In fact, the population of Poffrabo, a small town in northern Italy, dropped by more than half between 1890 and 1905 when its stoneworkers and their families went en masse to build the estates of Chestnut Hill. They founded a club where they could gather and play boccie on their days off. The Venetian Club still exists today.

Wissahickon What?

Driving around the streets of the northwest you understand why the stone used to build these houses and walls—Wissahickon schist—was also known as Chestnut Hill Stone. Not only was the schist an excellent building material, it was also plentiful and easy to get, lying just 2 to 6 feet under the soil throughout most of the area.

train station, you have primarily chain stores, tucked tastefully away in unassuming buildings. Across the street it's a little more interesting, with smaller stores (go into the cheese shop for free samples) and *Robertson's* (8501 Germantown Avenue off East Highland Avenue). Known as *the* Philadelphia florist, Robertson's stands out with its wonderful summer window boxes and the Victorian glass-and-iron conservatory, which features fountains, statuary, and colorful tiles. An adjoining shop, Seedlings, sells high-end baby gifts, which is cute but makes for an odd mix.

At the corner of West Highland Avenue you'll find *Killian Hardware* (8450 Germantown Avenue), one of Chestnut Hill's old-timers that has remained mercifully unchanged. The hardwood floor is well worn and if you need it, you'll find it at Killian's. Even if you don't need it, Killian's has also cornered the vintage guitar collection in the area. Check out the window display. Call (215) 247–0945.

On this block you'll also find *Artisans On The Avenue* (8428 Germantown Avenue, 215–381–0582), a new and pleasantly unique shop that sells hand-made clothing and home accessories; the *Chestnut Hill Welcome Center* (8426 Germantown Avenue, 215-247-6696), which distributes directions and information about area attractions; and *Caruso's Market* (8422 Germantown Avenue, 215–247–4134), a small storefront that turns into a surprisingly large supermarket.

If you're feeling particularly civilized, you can stop and have tea at the *Women's Exchange* (8419 Germantown Avenue). When the weather gets nice, usually from April through October, tea is served in the garden including tea sandwiches, scones with lemon curd or jam, and hot or iced tea. Served Tuesday through Saturday from 11:00 A.M. to 3:00 P.M., but call (215) 247–5911 if the weather is iffy.

Just a few more stops if you're not tired of shopping. *Intermission* (8405 Germantown Avenue) is a truly unique store and a wonderful place to browse. Billing itself as the shop for the performing arts, this store stocks songbooks, scripts, Broadway posters, a wonderful collection of music boxes from around the world, and puppets, as well as jewelry, T-shirts, and even suspenders with musical themes and decorations. An area in the back has unusual toy selections and a great line of *Wizard of Oz* paraphernalia. The store also has a second location as the official gift shop of the Kimmel Center on the Avenue of the Arts. Open Monday through Saturday from 10:00 A.M. to 6:00 P.M. and Sunday from noon to 5:00 P.M. Call (215) 242–8515 or log on to www.intermission shop.com.

Then there's **O'Doodles** (8335 Germantown Avenue), which claims to be a toy store, but the grown-ups usually find something fun to go home with, too. This store used to be O'Donnell's, a well-established stodgy stationery store, but when a Staples moved in down the street, it reinvented itself and has been fabulously successful. While the toy train circles overhead, you can find high-end toys and specialty games. It stocks the latest children's books and has an "Around a Dollar" section, so you might actually get out with something left in your wallet. The staff also hosts play days, story times, and arts and crafts activities throughout the year. The store can get packed on weekends, so leave the strollers outside. Open Sunday through Friday from 9:30 A.M. to 6:00 P.M. and Saturday from 9:30 A.M. to 9:00 P.M. Call (215) 247–7405.

A school, church, and a few houses mark the transition to the "Bottom of the Hill," which provides a good opportunity to take a break from shopping and explore what else Chestnut Hill has to offer. For a quiet respite or a picnic, head to **Pastorius Park** at Lincoln Drive and Abington Avenue. Surrounded by lovely homes, the park doesn't have playgrounds or recreational facilities, so it's peaceful and quiet. There is an amphitheater, where local bands and orchestras perform weekly on summer evenings.

A leisurely drive around some of the side streets allows you to take in the wide range of wonderful residential architecture here. You see everything from huge stone mansions to lovely twins with their porches and small, well-tended gardens. In particular, you might enjoy the houses on Prospect Avenue and Crittenden Street; the early Victorians on Summit Street; the cluster of houses on Green Tree Street, all designed by Judson Zane; or the more modest cottages and older houses along Rex Avenue.

Two of Chestnut Hill's most architecturally significant houses are located on small streets around Pastorius Park, and they're totally unlike most of the stone homes that line the streets. The house at 8330 Millman Street, between West Hartwell and West Gravers Lanes, is known as the **Vanna Venturi House** and was designed by famous Philadelphia architect Robert Venturi for his mother. Radical when it was built in 1962, the house is starkly symmetrical and is now considered a landmark of twentieth-century architecture. Unfortunately, when the leaves are on the trees, the house is very difficult to see from the road, and it remains a private home.

Just across the street is Sunrise Lane, at the end of which you'll find the tiny *Margaret Esherick House* (204 Sunrise Lane). Also starkly modern, this house was one of relatively few designed by prominent modern architect Louis Kahn, who was on the faculty at the University of Pennsylvania. With its thick, stuccoed walls, the house is not very inviting, and you have to take for granted claims that the interior spaces receive abundant daylight, because the home is not open to the public.

On West Willow Grove Avenue at the corner of St. Martin's Lane is *St. Martin-in-the-Fields Episcopal Church* (8000 St. Martin's Lane). This beautiful church was built by the Houston family that developed the Chestnut Hill area in the late 1800s. Designed by George and William Hewitt, the church underwent an extensive renovation in 2000, when the interior was restored to its original appearance. Highlights include a Tiffany stained-glass window on the west side and the four-story bell tower, one of only two church towers in the Philadelphia area equipped for English change ringing (the other is St. Mark's on Locust Street in Center City). St. Martin's eight change-ringing bells were cast by the Whitechapel Foundry in London and installed here in 1980. Unlike traditional carillons, change-ringing bells do not play specific tunes. Rather they generate a cascade of sound, produced by a team of people who climb the tower and stand in a circle, each responsible for operating the bell suspended above, which swings a full 360 degrees when pulled. Visitors are welcome to listen in as the Philadelphia Guild of Change Ringers practice at St. Martin's on the first, third, and fifth Wednesday of every month from 7:00 to 9:00 P.M. Visitors are also welcome to visit the sanctuary during church office hours, usually daily from 8:00 A.M. to 4:00 P.M. Call (215) 247-7466 or visit www.stmartinec.org for more information.

Jolly Good Cricket

Though it has long since been pushed aside by other sports, cricket still has its enthusiasts in Philadelphia. Some of the area's most prestigious country clubs were founded as cricket clubs and still host matches. It's not unusual to see a pickup cricket game on the fields that front Memorial Hall in Fairmount Park. And each May the city plays host to the Philadelphia International Cricket Festival. The game is believed to have been introduced to the area in the 1830s by William Carvill, the landscape architect of nearby Haverford College, which still houses one of the most comprehensive collections of cricket memorabilia in North America.

Right next door you'll find the **Philadelphia Cricket Club** (415 West Willow Grove Avenue), a bastion of Philadelphia's high society days. The club was founded in 1854 by a group of English friends who had played cricket together while attending the University of Pennsylvania, but it did not find its permanent home in Chestnut Hill until 1883. At that time the club added lawn tennis and became the site of the National Women's Tennis Championship for more than thirty years. The club also hosted the Philadelphia Horse Show for many years, until neighbors started to complain about the large number of wood buildings and, no doubt, the smell. Still a posh, private club, the Cricket Club now offers an off-site, nine-hole golf course, indoor and outdoor tennis courts, and squash courts, in addition to its meticulously maintained cricket fields. Call (215) 247–6001 or visit www.philacricket.com.

Down the street is the **Wissahickon Skating Club** (550 West Willow Grove Avenue), a longtime destination for skaters in the Philadelphia area. You can take lessons or go when there are times for free skating. Call (215) 247–1759 or log on to www.wissskating.com.

Now head to the north side of Germantown Avenue to the **Gravers Lane Station** (300 East Gravers Lane), which was designed by Frank Furness in 1883. You have to walk around to the track side to see Furness's fanciful gabled tower. It's the only remaining Furness building in Chestnut Hill.

Nearby is another of Chestnut Hill's noted houses—**Anglecot** (401–409 East Evergreen Avenue). Meticulously restored and converted to condominiums in the 1980s, this Queen Anne house was designed by Wilson Eyre in 1883. Gables and unusual windows abound. Be sure to note the sundial above the entrance.

Heading back to Germantown Avenue, you approach the lower part of Chestnut Hill. It's safe to say that the shopping is better at the top of the hill, but the eating is better down here, where most of the restaurants of note are located. If you're in Chestnut Hill on a Thursday, Friday, or Saturday, be sure to check out the **Chestnut Hill Farmers Market** behind the hotel. It's one of the area's original farmers' markets, bursting with fresh fruits and vegetables, cheeses, desserts, flowers—the works. It's open Thursday and Friday from 9:00 A.M. to 6:00 P.M. and Saturday from 8:00 A.M. to 5:00 P.M. Locals rave about the Indian food available at the market's **Bhagya's Kitchen.** Call (215) 242–5905 for more information.

Take time to wander through **Garden Gate Antiques** (8139 Germantown Avenue, 215–248–5190), which is stuffed full of treasures. Its canine corner is the perfect place to head if you need a gift for the dog-lover who's already got it all. If you'd like a break, try the **Garden Gate Cafe** right behind the store.

It's a charming nook where you can sit outside on white Adirondack chairs if the weather is nice, or squeeze inside if it's not. Here you can get a light snack or a hearty bowl of soup. Open daily for lunch; cash or checks only.

For something a little sweeter, head across the street to ***Bredenbeck's Bakery and Ice Cream Parlor*** (8126 Germantown Avenue), a favorite Chestnut Hill mainstay. Though only in Chestnut Hill since 1983, the bakery traces its roots to an immigrant baker from Bavaria who set up shop in Northern Liberties in 1889. The old-fashioned ice-cream parlor is a family favorite, but watch those toppings—this can get to be an expensive outing. The cookies and cakes are pretty standard bakery fare, but the locals love it and the staff is friendly. This place is so popular it has even set up a Web site where people who've moved away can still order their bakery favorites. The bakery is open from 7:00 A.M. to 7:00 P.M. Monday through Saturday and from 8:00 A.M. to 5:00 P.M. Sunday. The ice-cream parlor is open daily from noon until 9:00 P.M. Call (215) 247–7374 or visit www.bredenbecks.com.

At 8130 Germantown Avenue you'll find the ***Stagecrafters Theater,*** a small gem of the local theater scene. This group was founded in 1929 by the Germantown Women's Club, who rented the space as a workshop for theatrical scenery. The building, which houses a 186-seat theater, is now listed on the National Register of Historic Buildings. Considering this is a volunteer-based organization, the group produces six first-rate plays a year. Call (215) 247–8881 or log on to www.thestagecrafters.org.

Probably the best restaurant in Chestnut Hill is ***Cin Cin*** (7838 Germantown Avenue). It's not much to look at from the outside, but the decor inside is warm and pleasant, and you're in for a delightful dining experience that's Chinese with unusual French twists. Co-owner Michael Weis owns several of the area's other top Chinese restaurants, but this counts as his best. Standards like the Peking duck are outstanding, and specials change seasonally and are always top-notch. Appetizer favorites include the Wild Mushroom and Goat's

The Jimmies Came Later

Philadelphia's own Bassett's was the first producer of ice cream in America. Founded in 1861, the company is still run by direct descendants of those first ice-cream makers. Their ancestor—Louis Dubois Bassett—began by selling his cold concoction from a stand at Fifth and Market, and he was right there when the Reading Terminal Market began selling food in 1893. Soon people began traveling through neighborhoods selling ice cream, the precursors to the trucks we still listen for today. At the time, they were known as "hokey pokey men."

Cheese Strudel and the Shrimp and Chicken Seaweed Roll. Some dishes, such as the rack of lamb, hardly seem Asian at all, but the restaurant adds its own touch with rosemary, lemon grass, thyme, and a special soy marinade. A grilled filet mignon is served with roasted shallots, mushrooms, and leeks in a Szechuan peppercorn sauce. For something a little spicier, try the sake wild-peppered chicken. For dessert you can't top the fried banana with crushed peanuts. Like all the good restaurants in Chestnut Hill, it can be crowded and noisy on a weekend night, but this one is worth the wait. Open Monday through Thursday from 11:30 A.M. to 10:00 P.M., Friday and Saturday from 11:30 A.M. to 11:00 P.M., and Sunday from 2:00 to 10:00 P.M. Call (215) 242–8800 or go to www.chestnuthillfood.com/cincin. Expensive (though some dishes are surprisingly moderate).

The consistent charm of Chestnut Hill falls apart a bit at the lower end, and you almost laugh (or cry) to see how they've tried to gussy up chain stores such as CVS, Staples, and—even worse—McDonald's. The community fought long and hard to keep such stores away, and you can tell why. Keep your eyes on the other side of the street and take the opportunity to step into **Night Kitchen** (7725 Germantown Avenue), a homespun bakery with the best oatmeal cookies around. You can also grab a slice of homemade pizza or a cup of veggie chili for a take-out lunch (215–248–9235 or www.nightkitchenbakery .com.) Right next door is another of Chestnut Hill's consignment shops— **Worth Repeating.**

Mount Airy

Leaving Chestnut Hill you move into Mount Airy, a primarily residential community that prides itself on being ethnically and racially diverse. Neighborhood organizations are particularly strong here and its small business district has undergone something of a transformation over the past several years. A nonprofit with a growing budget is in charge of sprucing things up, and new businesses are now a common sight along Germantown Avenue. To get a feel for the history of Mount Airy, take a brief tour of the **Gowen Historic District** just north of Germantown Avenue. Turn left on Gowen Avenue (at the Cresheim Cottage Cafe), and wander around the community that sprang up after the Mount Airy Station opened in 1882. In particular, the block of Boyer Street between Gowen and Mount Airy Avenues has a number of homes designed by Frank Furness.

A neighborhood treasure is located in the Mt. Airy Train Station. **Walk-A-Crooked-Mile Books** (7423 Devon Street) is stuffed to the gills with used books. You're sure to find something you want, and you can also get a cup of coffee or take in an occasional concert here. Open Monday through Friday from 6:00 A.M. (so you can get that coffee before you get on the train) to 6:00 P.M. and Saturday from 10:00 A.M. to 6:00 P.M. Call (215) 242–0854.

One of Mount Airy's hot spots is **North by Northwest** (7165 Germantown Avenue)—or NXNW as the folks there refer to themselves—an old, tin-ceiling store that's been converted into a down-home restaurant and venue for live music and dancing. An original art deco bar separates the stage area from a small piano terrace that's open when the weather is nice. The food is good and hearty, which is helpful, since you'll need energy for dancing later. There are homey favorites like meat loaf and pulled pork sandwiches on the entree menu, or you can go a little lighter and order from the tapas menu. The service can be slow, but the staff is young and friendly. Let the music menu be your guide. Tuesdays highlight jazz; Wednesdays are salsa nights, with dance lessons from 9:00 to 10:00 P.M. and dancing until 1:00 A.M. The bands get a little louder on the weekends, and Sundays are reserved for classics. Cover charges vary, as does the music: You can hear everything from jazz to blues to bluegrass and good-ole rock 'n' roll. Open Tuesday through Sunday from 5:30 P.M. to 2:00 A.M., with a late-night menu after 10:00 P.M. Call (215) 248–1000 or visit www.nxnwphl.com. Moderate.

If you want something more low-key, step into **McMenamin's Tavern** (7170 Germantown Avenue) across the street, a favorite local hangout complete with a checkerboard linoleum floor. The menu is standard bar fare, but it's good, and the beer selection is outstanding. Open Monday through Saturday from 11:30 A.M. to 2:00 A.M. and Sunday from 12:30 P.M. to 1:00 A.M. Call (215) 247–9920 or visit www.mtairy.org/mcmenamins. Inexpensive.

A relatively new hangout in the neighborhood is **InFusion** (7133 Germantown Avenue), a refreshing departure from the Starbucks saturation. This is truly a neighborhood coffee shop, as eclectic and politically correct as Mt. Airy itself. The walls are full of work by area artists and there's even an in-store "library" for browsing. You can grab a latte and a light breakfast or lunch and while away the hours with the locals. Open Monday through Friday from 7:00 A.M. to 8:00 P.M., Saturday from 7:00 A.M. to 6:00 P.M., and Sunday from 8:00 A.M. to 6:00 P.M. Call (215) 248–1718 or go to www.infusioncoffeeandtea.com.

For a more upscale meal, try **Umbria** (7131 Germantown Avenue), a tiny storefront that offers Mount Airy's most elegant meal. This small BYOB is decorated with the work of local artists and provides a quiet, romantic spot for dinner. The menu is not extensive, but there are a number of nightly specials. Try the sausage with figs. Open for dinner only, starting at 6:00 P.M., Wednesday through Saturday. Call (215) 242–6470. Expensive.

Also on Germantown Avenue in Mount Airy is the **Sedgwick Cultural Center** (7137 Germantown Avenue), a centerpiece of arts and entertainment in

Founding Families

The first settlers of Germantown were thirteen families from the lower Rhine, not far from Holland. They arrived on October 6, 1683, and were met by Francis Daniel Pastorius, who had come over several weeks earlier to scope out the land. They gathered in Pastorius's cave on the banks of the Delaware River, chose their plots of land, and then set about building dwellings before the winter arrived.

the area. The Sedgwick has an active theater schedule throughout the year; there's a folk music series and concert series for families with young children, and the Gallery of the Artists League of Mount Airy organizes exhibitions of the work of local artists. For schedules and hours call (215) 248–9229 or go to www.sedgwickcenter.org.

Germantown

You're now ready to explore Germantown. Though plagued by many of the problems of urban life, Germantown is, at heart, one of America's most historical communities. Germantown boasts the first documented protest against slavery, and the nation's first business association was formed here and still exists today, serving an active commercial district. Although there are signs of renewal here, particularly along Germantown avenue, some areas are still quite rundown, and visitors might be more comfortable exploring the avenue's historic houses in one of the guided tours offered by the Germantown Historical Society (215–844–0514 or www.germantownhistory.org).

The community is best known historically as the site of the Battle of Germantown, which saw General Washington's troops bear down on the British, culminating with a pitched battle at Cliveden mansion, where General Howe's troops had hunkered down. Though a defeat for the American rebels, the Battle of Germantown served to boost morale and helped to bring much-needed support from the French. This historic battle is colorfully reenacted each fall, and the historic houses along Germantown Avenue have become increasingly popular sites for visitors. These homes are open on very limited schedules, and they're not all open on the same days, though almost all are open on Saturday. You'll have to pick and choose and peek from the street at those that aren't open when you visit.

Start at **_Upsala_** (6430 Germantown Avenue), one of Germantown's finest examples of the Federal style. Built in the late 1760s by well-to-do tanner John

Cliveden

Johnson (and named after the family's Swedish hometown), the home was handed down through generations of descendants, who lived there until 1938. The house has been restored and is noted for its finely carved woodwork. Located on the "American" side of the road during the Battle of Germantown, Upsala was the perfect location for Washington's army to set up its cannons for the attack on the British troops barricaded across the street in Cliveden. The house is no longer open to the public.

Cliveden (6401 Germantown Avenue) is both an architectural gem as well as a pivotal site in the Battle of Germantown. The Georgian-style mansion was built in 1763 as a summer retreat by Benjamin Chew, chief justice of the Supreme Court of Pennsylvania. It remained in the Chew family until 1972, when descendants donated it to the National Trust for Historic Preservation. It was October 1777 when the Continental Army marched down Germantown Avenue, forcing British troops to seek the shelter of Cliveden's thick walls. Under heavy fire, Washington ordered a full-scale assault on the house, but withdrew in defeat after several hours, leaving bodies piled up on the doorstep. You can still see the scars of the battle today—cannon holes in the front facade, damaged statues on the front lawn, and a bullet hole inside a first-floor office. Today the home features original furnishings and decorative arts, exceptional examples of colonial Philadelphia craftsmanship. The six-acre site is nicely landscaped and includes a rare Franklinia, a tree discovered by Philadelphia botanist John Bartram in 1765 and named in honor of his friend Benjamin Franklin. (All Franklinias grown today descend from those propagated by Bartram in his southwest Philadelphia garden.) A restored carriage house serves as a reception area, where visitors can see changing exhibits and get information on special programs held throughout the year, including an annual reenactment of the Battle of Germantown. Open Thursday through Sunday from noon to 4:00 P.M., April through December. Admission is $8.00 for adults and $6.00 for students. Call (215) 848–1777 or go to www.cliveden.org.

If you're in Germantown on Thursday, Friday, or Saturday, consider stopping at the **Rib Crib** (6333 Germantown Avenue) for take-out barbecued bliss. Though nothing fancy, this place regularly tops the "best barbecue in Philadelphia" lists. The walls are covered with signed photos of the rich and famous, but it's the locals who keep Rib Crib going strong. There's an open charcoal-pit fire that's the center of the action. The ribs are great, but don't discount the chicken either. Open Thursday through Saturday from 11:00 A.M. to 2:00 A.M. Call (215) 438–6793.

Back to historic Germantown. In the next block you'll find what's known as the **Upper Burying Ground.** This is the oldest burial ground in Germantown—dating to 1692—where soldiers from the Battle of Germantown, the War of 1812, and the Civil War are buried. The dates carved into the stone wall represent years when the wall was built and repaired. The earliest grave belongs to Cornelius Teisen, who arrived in Germantown in 1684 and died in 1716 at the age of sixty-three. There's also a grave for Adam Shisler, who died in 1777 and whose tombstone informs us lived to "age 969 years." Today's stonecutters are a little more careful about proofreading their work. Adjacent to the burying ground is the **Concord School House** (6309 Germantown Avenue), a one-room schoolhouse built in 1775. It still includes the original bell, belfry, and schoolmaster's desk. Tuition in 1797 was $1.50 for a three-month quarter; by 1815, it had risen to $2.00. Back then, education was considered a privilege and unruly students were not allowed to attend. Just to show they were serious, the schoolroom still includes a stool with a dunce cap on it. The second floor was added in 1818 as a place to hold town meetings. These sites are open only by appointment. The charge is $3.00 for adults and $2.00 for students. Call (215) 843–0943.

Opposite the school on the corner of Washington Lane is the **Johnson House** (6306 Germantown Avenue). Built in 1768, the Johnson House served as a station stop on the Underground Railroad during the 1850s. Here the

Let the Light Shine

Tired of the dark, Philadelphia's citizens chipped in for a special tax to install a street lighting system in 1751—the first such lights in North America. Illuminated by whale oil, the first lights didn't work very well; they were very fragile and sent soot spewing all over. So Benjamin Franklin went to work and came up with a better system, using four flat panes and a funnel to draw out the smoke.

Quaker Johnson family sheltered runaway slaves on the third floor. Although many Philadelphia Quakers were involved in setting up safe havens, the Johnson House is the only accessible and intact Underground Railroad site in Philadelphia. It is believed that Harriet Tubman sometimes brought fugitive slaves here on her way to Lucretia Mott's home in nearby Cheltenham. Open Thursday and Friday from 10:00 A.M. to 4:00 P.M. and Saturday from 1:00 to 4:00 P.M. Admission is $5.00 for adults, $3.00 for seniors, and $2.00 for students. Guided tours are available by appointment. Call (215) 438–1765 or go to www.johnsonhouse.org. This is an appropriate place to ponder how past and present come together in Germantown. Directly across the street from Johnson House is a bright and shiny gas station, with a nearby bus stop. It takes some imagination indeed to think of what this street was like when the Johnsons lived here.

Turning right on Tulpehocken Street you'll enter the ***Tulpehocken Historic District,*** an elegant Victorian neighborhood of beautiful churches and a mix of historic mansions and smaller twins. Most have retained their original architectural details and are lovingly maintained. This area is bordered by Germantown Avenue, Tulpehocken Street, Wayne Avenue, and Walnut Lane. A highlight here is the ***Ebenezer Maxwell Mansion*** (200 West Tulpehocken Street), which may take you by surprise. When this house was built in 1859, Philadelphia's successful businessmen had no interest in Quaker understatement. Bring on the bells and whistles. An eclectic mix of Victorian, French, and even Gothic architectural touches, the home was slated for the wrecking ball

Urban Oasis

Often overshadowed by the Morris Arboretum up the street in Chestnut Hill, the *Awbury Arboretum* offers the largest and most peaceful open space in Germantown and has the distinct advantage of being free. This truly is a pocket of beauty in an often bleak urban landscape. The Awbury was once the summer estate of the Cope family, purchased by Quaker shipping merchant Henry Cope in 1852. The grounds were laid out in the 1870s under the oversight of horticulturist William Saunders, who also designed the Capitol grounds in Washington, D.C. There are 140 species of trees, many clustered together below rolling hills and open meadows. The original Hope House still dominates the property, with a Victorian kitchen garden out back. The Awbury is located off Chew Avenue (which roughly parallels Germantown Avenue) between Washington Lane and Haines Street and is open year-round from dawn to dusk. Call (215) 849–2855 or visit www.awbury.org for more information.

in the 1960s, but local preservationists and volunteers succeeded in turning it into a museum. Today it's the only authentically restored Victorian house-museum in the area and is complemented by two period gardens and the mansion's original wrought-iron fence. A visit takes you back to the time when the mansion and its surrounding homes constituted the suburban housing boom of the late 1800s. Central heat, running water, and indoor plumbing were the luxuries of the day. Displays in the house point out its Victorian design details as well as relate the story of how the house was saved and renovated. Open Friday through Sunday from 1:00 to 4:00 P.M., April through December. Admission is $5.00 for adults and $4.00 for students and seniors. Call (215) 438–1861 or go to www.maxwellmansion.org.

Back on Germantown Avenue, just below Pastorius Street, is the **Germantown Mennonite Church** (6119 Germantown Avenue). Built in 1770, the building is located next to the **Germantown Mennonite Historical Trust** (6133 Germantown Avenue), which provides information on the meetinghouse. Exhibits tell the story of the Mennonites' arrival in the area and include a variety of bibles and psalm books printed in Germantown in the 1700s. One of the most prized artifacts is the desk where the first known protest against slavery in America was written in 1688. The church is open by appointment only; there's a charge of $3.00 for adults and $1.00 for students and seniors. Call (215) 843–0943 or visit www.meetinghouse.info.

You head now to **Wyck** (6026 Germantown Avenue), perhaps Germantown's greatest treasure. One of Philadelphia's oldest properties, this estate was purchased in 1689 by a Swiss Mennonite, and the original house was incorporated into later structures. The British army used Wyck as a hospital during the occupation of Germantown, and the house later served as home to nine generations of the well-known Wistar and Haines families, prominent in the Quaker community. In 1824 a member of the Haines family hired William Strickland to alter the structure, and the home stayed in the family until the 1970s. It now serves as a living museum. Everything in the house was accumulated by Wyck's families over 300 years, and the cupboards are full of original porcelain and tea sets. A needlework family tree, carefully stitched by a descendant of the Haines family, hangs in the airy conservatory. Barnlike doors on both sides open to connect this wide hall to a garden of twenty-five varieties of historic roses, which continue to grow just as Jane Haines laid them out in the 1820s. Other garden beds on the property have been lovingly restored and are planted with perennials, heirloom vegetables, and herbs. The grounds also include early outbuildings that were part of Wyck's farm. Descendants of Wyck's original families are still actively involved in the preservation of this home. Open Tuesday and Thursday from noon to 4:30 P.M. and

Saturday from 1:00 to 4:00 P.M., April through December. Admission is $5.00 for adults and $4.00 for students and seniors. Call (215) 848–1690 or visit www .wyck.org.

Just opposite Wyck is what was once the **Green Tree Tavern** (6023 Germantown Avenue). Now a parish office for the First United Methodist Church of Germantown, the tavern was known by many names throughout its history. But it was the Green Tree in 1793 when Thomas Jefferson, then the country's first secretary of state, tried to find lodging at a home across the street. He wrote back to Washington, "According to present appearances, this place cannot lodge a single person more. As a great favor I got a bed in the corner of the public room of a tavern." High on a side wall near the roof you can see a stone lettered DSP 1748, put there by its builder, Daniel Pastorius, grandson of the founder of Germantown.

Several blocks later you come to Chelten Avenue, a busy commercial street that separates Upper Germantown from Lower Germantown. Farther on you'll find **Market Square,** a small park dominated by a Civil War memorial. The soldier rests on a piece of granite brought here from Devil's Den at Gettysburg. At one point this square was a hubbub of activity. Weavers sold their wares, and this was also where the prison and stocks were located. The church on the square was built in 1888 for the German Reformed Church. It was the third church building on that site, the first being where George Washington worshipped while he was in Germantown.

Overlooking the square is a church and the **Germantown Historical Society** (5501 Germantown Avenue), a wonderful resource for information about the area's history. A museum and library feature exhibits from the society's comprehensive collections. Particularly noteworthy is an abundance of historic clothing, everything from wedding gowns to mourning clothes. A courtyard in the back contains an original eighteenth-century fire pumper. The museum is open on Tuesday and Thursday from 9:00 A.M. to 5:00 P.M. and Sunday from 1:00 to 5:00

Say Cheese

Gilbert Stuart, the painter responsible for the famous Lansdowne portrait of George Washington, set up a studio on the second story of a Germantown barn in the late 1790s. He worked on the painting while Washington was in Germantown, and legend has it that Washington would get tired of posing and walk out to get an apple from a tree by the barn. The portrait now hangs in the National Portrait Gallery in Washington.

Grumblethorpe Blood Stains

If you need proof that Philadelphia's history was often violent, look no further than the floor of the seemingly genteel stone house called Grumblethorpe, home to Philadelphia's prominent Wister family. During the British occupation in 1777, the Wister family was sent packing and the home was occupied by General James Agnew. On the morning of October 4, Agnew was fatally shot while leading his troops down Germantown Avenue to counter a surprise assault by Washington's troops. Bleeding profusely, he was carried back to Grumblethorpe and placed on the floor of the front parlor. Despite obvious attempts to scrub or bleach the floor, Agnew's bloodstains are still clearly visible today.

P.M. Admission is $5.00 for adults and $4.00 for seniors and students. Call (215) 844–0514 or go to www.germantownhistory.org.

Facing the square across the street is the ***Deshler-Morris House*** (5442 Germantown Avenue). Built in 1773 by merchant David Deshler, this house became known as the "Germantown White House" in 1793 when President Washington moved in, fleeing the yellow fever gripping Washington. He held his cabinet meetings here with the likes of Alexander Hamilton and Thomas Jefferson. Washington and his wife, Martha, apparently liked Germantown life so much they returned to the house with the family in the summer of 1794 to escape the city heat. The bill for his two-month stay came to $201.60. Open Friday, Saturday, and Sunday from 1:00 to 4:00 P.M. Admission is free. Call (215) 596–1748 or visit www.nps.gov/demo.

Taking a break from revolutionary history for a moment, take note of the ***Cunningham Piano Company*** (5427 Germantown Avenue). Founded in 1891 by an Irish immigrant, this company switched from selling pianos to restoring them when times got tough in the Depression. You can tour the factory where the restoration work takes place. A historic marker outside the building notes that this was once Pine Place, the birthplace of Louisa May Alcott, author of the beloved *Little Women*. Call (215) 438–3200 or log on to www.cunningham piano.com.

Several blocks farther you come to ***Grumblethorpe*** (5267 Germantown Avenue). Built in 1744 as a country home for wine importer John Wister, Grumblethorpe became the homestead of Philadelphia's prominent Wister family for more than 160 years. A classic example of the period's domestic architecture, the house is constructed of Wissahickon stone and oak from Wister's lands. Throughout the eighteenth century, Grumblethorpe was known as "John Wister's Big House." The name Grumblethorpe didn't come along until the early nineteenth century, when it was lifted from an English novel one of the Wisters was reading. Maintained by the Philadelphia Society for the Preservation of Landmarks, the home has been restored and furnished with period pieces. The grounds include a colonial herb and vegetable garden. Open Tuesday, Thursday, and Sunday from noon to 4:00 P.M. from March through November. Admission is $5.00 for adults and $4.00 for students and seniors. Call (215) 843–4820.

The last of Germantown's historic treasures is a little more difficult to find than those that line Germantown Avenue and is not in a neighborhood you'd want to walk to. ***Stenton*** (4601 North Eighteenth Street) lies several blocks back from the Avenue and can best be reached by turning left on Windrim Avenue (just after you go under the train tracks) and then right onto North Eighteenth. What is now surrounded by abandoned factories and row houses was once the estate of James Logan, who stayed behind as William Penn's representative when Penn returned to England. Logan designed and built Stenton between 1723 and 1730, naming it after the Scottish birthplace of his father. Constructed in a square shape of solid brick, the house reflects Logan's high position in the community as well as his Quaker restraint. Logan furnished the house with pieces made in Philadelphia as well as English furniture of the William and Mary and Queen Anne periods. His son William succeeded him as attorney for Penn and added the kitchen wing together with "new" Philadelphia Chippendale and Sheraton pieces, many of which remain in the home. Shortly after William's death, the house was occupied for a brief period by General George Washington and then by Sir William Howe as his headquarters during the Battle of Germantown. Now maintained by the National Society of Colonial Dames of America, Stenton is a National Historic Landmark. The kitchen has been restored, and the adjoining eighteenth-century farm includes a barn display of early tools and farm equipment. The property also includes a small period garden and a greenhouse. Be sure to note the log house, which was built around 1790 as a barn and stood for many years at Sixteenth and Race Streets on the grounds of Friends Select School. The structure was moved to its present location in 1969 to preserve it. Open Tuesday through Saturday from 1:00 to 4:00 P.M., April through mid-December. Admission is $5.00 for adults and $4.00 for students and seniors. Call (215) 329–7312 or visit www.stenton.org.

Places to Stay in the Northwest

Chestnut Hill Hotel,
8229 Germantown Avenue;
(215) 242–5905,
www.chestnuthillhotel.com
This is your only hotel option in Chestnut Hill, but it's quaint and convenient. In the eighteenth century, the structure was a bar, but you'll sleep a little better there now. All twenty-eight rooms are furnished in colonial style, and most rooms have queen-size beds, some with four-posters. Moderate.

There are two B&Bs in Chestnut Hill:

Anam Cara Bed & Breakfast,
52 Wooddale Avenue;
(215) 242–4327,
www.anamcarabandb.com

Silverstone Bed & Breakfast,
8840 Stenton Avenue;
(215) 242–1471,
www.silverstonestay.com

Places to Eat in the Northwest

An Indian Affair,
4425 Main Street,
Manayunk;
215–482–8300
An elegant Indian offering, this BYOB has become popular for its affordable weekend buffet lunch. You may be tempted to make a meal out of the plentiful appetizers, but try the laziz pasliyan—lamb chops in a spicy curry sauce. The menu also offers numerous vegetarian dishes. If it's a cold day, grab a table in the back near the fire. Open for lunch Monday through Saturday from noon. to 3:00 P.M., with a Sunday brunch at noon. Dinner is served Sunday through Wednesday from 5:00 to 9:30 P.M. and until 11:00 P.M. Thursday through Saturday. Moderate.

Bob's Diner,
6053 Ridge Avenue,
Roxborough;
(215) 483–9002
Pay no attention to its location next to a graveyard; things here are lively and the breakfast is just what you need to get you started in the morning. It's a classic '50s diner with homestyle food, but the service is fast and the prices are very reasonable. It makes the best omelettes you'll find in Philadelphia. Open Monday through Thursday and Saturday from 7:00 A.M. to 9:00 P.M., Friday from 7:00 A.M. to 10:00 P.M., and Sunday from 7:00 A.M. to 8:00 P.M. Inexpensive.

Cafette,
8136 Ardleigh Street,
Chestnut Hill;
(215) 242–4220,
www.cafette.com
This restaurant is off even Chestnut Hill's beaten path, but it is a neighborhood favorite, and with good reason. Tucked away on a side street, Cafette is a homespun BYOB, and if you go when the weather is nice, you get to eat outside on a patio or in a small sculpture garden. Cafette serves great lunches of homemade soup and terrific, creative salads. Plus they try to keep everything on the menu under $15. Cafette is on Ardleigh Street, which parallels Germantown Avenue. Open Monday for lunch from 10:30 A.M. to 3:00 P.M., and Tuesday through Saturday from 10:30 A.M. to 9:00 P.M., Sunday brunch is served from 9:00 A.M. to 3:00 P.M. Moderate.

Cresheim Cottage Cafe,
7402 Germantown Avenue,
Mount Airy;
(215) 248–4365,
www.cresheimcottage.com
If you want historic atmosphere, this is your choice in Mt. Airy. Built in 1748, the cottage was the first house constructed along Germantown Avenue. It's been restored (you'd hope so!) into five intimate dining rooms and a patio that's great when the weather is nice. The food is seasonal American—adequate, but people come here more for the mood than the cuisine. Still, the roasted garlic soup is tasty, as are the crab and shrimp cakes. Hold on to your forks, though. There have been so many reports of a ghost in pink Victorian clothing that the owners have called her Emily and named one of the dining rooms after her. Open for lunch Tuesday through Saturday from 11:30 A.M. to 2:30 P.M. Dinner is served from 5:00

to 9:00 P.M. Tuesday through Thursday and on Sunday; hours are 5:00 until 10:00 P.M. Friday and Saturday. Sunday brunch is available from 10:00 A.M. to 2:00 P.M.

Hikaru,
4348 Main Street,
Manayunk;
(215) 487–3500
A great Japanese option—really the only one—in this part of Philadelphia. The first floor is teppan yaki if you like tableside theatrics. The food upstairs, especially the sushi, is authentic and great, if a lit-

tle pricey. Open for lunch Wednesday through Friday from 11:30 A.M. to 2:30 P.M., Saturday from noon to 3:00 P.M., and Sunday from noon to 9:30 P.M. Dinner is served Monday through Friday from 5:00 to 10:00 P.M. and Saturday from 4:30 to 11:00 P.M. Expensive.

Solaris Grille,
8201 Germantown Avenue,
Chestnut Hill;
(215) 242–3400,
www.solarisgrille.com
The food is great, but it can

be unbearably noisy on weekends. If the weather is nice, shoot for the patio. Start with the chopped salad, which includes asparagus, snap peas, cucumber, avocado, bacon, and blue cheese with a balsamic vinegar dressing. The best entrees are the straightforward dishes hot off the grill. Open Monday through Saturday from 11:30 A.M. to midnight and Sunday from 10:30 A.M. to 11:00 P.M. Moderate.

AUTHOR'S FAVORITE PLACES TO EAT IN THE NORTHWEST

Adobe Cafe
4550 Mitchell Street, a left off Green Lane;
(215) 483–3947

Al Dana II
8630 Germantown Avenue;
(215) 247–3336,
www.aldana2.com

Cin Cin
7838 Germantown Avenue;
(215) 242–8800,
www.chestnuthillfood.com/cincin

Garden Gate Cafe
8139 Germantown Avenue;
(215) 248–5190

McMenamin's Tavern
7170 Germantown Avenue;
(215) 247–9920

McNally's Tavern
8634 Germantown Avenue;
(215) 247–9736,
www.chestnuthillfood.com/mcnallys

North by Northwest
7165 Germantown Avenue;
(215) 248–1000,
www.nxnwphl.com

Rib Crib
6333 Germantown Avenue;
(215) 438–6793

Umbria
7131 Germantown Avenue;
(215) 242–6470

Valley Green Inn
Valley Green Road;
(215) 247–1730,
www.valleygreeninn.com

HELPFUL WEB SITES

www.manayunk.com

www.chestnuthillpa.com

www.wissahickonjournal.org

www.philadelphiahistoricnw.org

West Philadelphia

Once you cross over the Schuylkill River heading away from Center City, you've entered West Philadelphia, a diverse area where you can find some of the best brains around. Here are the city's major colleges and universities, dominated by the University of Pennsylvania, the city's largest private employer, which explains why the area is also known as *University City.* The area surrounding Penn transitions into street after street of row homes, and some neighborhoods are among the poorest in the city. However, in recent years the university has made substantial progress in spreading its influence—and its dollars—into the development of surrounding communities.

Numerous SEPTA buses and trolley lines, as well as the El, run through West Philadelphia, though visitors have an easier transportation solution. The Loop through University City—or LUCY, as it's known—has minibuses that circle from 30th Street Station to various sites around University City between 6:00 A.M. and 7:00 P.M. daily.

It is at *30th Street Station* (Thirtieth and Market Streets) that you'll want to begin your tour of West Philly, whether or not you are traveling by train. The station is a beautiful example of train stations like they used to build them. Designed by Graham, Anderson, Probst, and White, 30th Street opened in

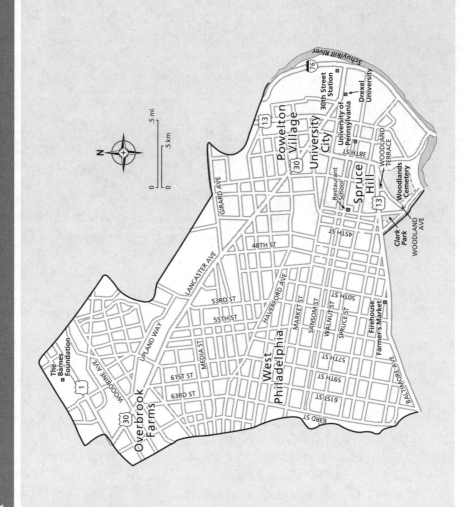

30th Street Station

1934, and it remains the second-busiest railway station in the country. The soaring main concourse, with its intricate, 90-foot-high ceiling illuminated by art deco chandeliers, is a welcome sight as travelers arrive from the tracks below. Movie fans recognize the station as the backdrop for the dramatic beginning of the movie *Witness.* There's also a food court if you need a quick bite to eat. Call (215) 349–3147 or visit www.30thstreetstation.com. The gleaming skyscraper next to the station is the Cira Center, one of Philadelphia's newest buildings, designed by Cesar Pelli.

Heading west, you come first to **Drexel University,** which is well known for its cooperative programs that find most students alternating semesters in classes with full-time work. Architectural highlights include the striking **Paul Peck Alumni Association Building** at Thirty-second and Market. Designed by Frank Furness in 1876 for Centennial Bank, the building has been impeccably renovated and includes a gallery space to exhibit pieces from the university's substantial art collection. Open Monday through Friday from 9:00 A.M. to 5:00 P.M. More remarkable artwork can be seen in Drexel's equally impressive Renaissance-style Main Building at Thirty-second and Chestnut. Built in 1890, this building is noted for its terra-cotta and wrought-iron detailing and features

AUTHOR'S FAVORITES IN
WEST PHILADELPHIA

Anne and Jerome Fisher
Fine Arts Building

Kelly Writers House

Rx

Thirtieth Street Station

White Dog/Black Cat

The Woodlands and cemetery

a skylit central court. On the third floor you'll find the historically restored *Westphal Picture Gallery,* which houses one of the university's treasures, an imposing, complex clock designed by David Rittenhouse (for whom Rittenhouse Square is named). This clock will tell you the time of day in hours, minutes, and seconds and it plays ten tunes. But Rittenhouse was not only an accomplished clockmaker, he was also a renowned astronomer. So it should come as no surprise that the clock also indicates the day of the week and date of each month, the phases of the moon, the orbit of the moon around the earth, the orbit of the earth around the sun, the signs of the zodiac, the equation of time, and the positions of those planets that had been discovered when Rittenhouse built it in 1773 (Uranus, Neptune, and Pluto came later). And you thought your Timex was enough. Open Monday through Friday from 3:30 to 5:30 P.M. Call (215) 895–0480 or log on to www.drexel.edu.

At Thirtieth and Walnut is the long-awaited *World Cafe Live* (3025 Walnut Street), a live-music mecca that draws primarily singer-songwriters to its two performance venues. You can listen and eat in its bistro-style concert rooms, though the music is usually better than the food. The club is named after the nationally distributed *World Cafe* radio show, which originates from WXPN, whose expanded studios are downstairs in the building. For concert listings call (215) 222–1400 or go to www.worldcafelive.com.

It is worth a slight detour to explore the neighborhood just north of Drexel known as *Powelton Village.* Long a neighborhood on the fringe, Powelton is probably best seen by car, so you can get an overview and take in its many architectural styles and attractive churches and homes. Many houses

Wistar: A Brainy Institute

Plenty of smart people have expanded their brains at the University of Pennsylvania's Wistar Institute. But it turns out a few of them left their brains there altogether. It seems a Wistar scientist named Dr. Edward Spitzka was convinced that if you compared the brains of scholars to those of uneducated or mentally ill people, you could discover much about human intelligence. So in the late nineteenth century, Spitzka succeeded in getting six esteemed citizens, Walt Whitman among them, to will their brains to Wistar for further study after their deaths. Modern science has refuted Spitzka's claims that he found significant differences between the brains. Some of the brains still reside in a closet at the Wistar Institute. Not so for poor Walt Whitman's brain. That had to be discarded after a clumsy lab assistant dropped the bottle containing it on the laboratory floor.

have been lovingly restored, while others have been left to the devices of Drexel fraternities.

If you're hungry, the 3600 block of Lancaster Avenue offers some good choices. Best among them is **Zocalo** (3600 Lancaster Avenue) if Mexican hits the spot. This isn't your average taco and enchilada place. The menu is creative and the ingredients are fresh. Try the shredded pork tacos with pineapple sauce and

collegetown

There are more colleges and universities in the Philadelphia area than there are in Boston. In fact, the city refers to itself as "one big campus" and even runs a Web site under that name: www.onebigcampus.com.

wash it all down with—what else?—a margarita. Open Monday through Thursday from noon to 10:00 P.M., Friday from noon to 11:00 P.M., Saturday from 5:30 to 11:00 P.M., and Sunday from 4:30 to 9:00 P.M. Call (215) 895–0139 or go to www.ucnet.com/zocalo. Moderate.

Just off thirty-eighth Street and Lancaster is the **East Africa Resource and Study Center** (3809 Pearl Street). This small exhibit space focuses on artifacts from the nomadic tribes of Ethiopia, Somalia, Eritrea, Sudan, Uganda, Kenya, and Tanzania. The center houses a complete nomadic shelter, photographs, sculpture, and textiles from East Africa and offers occasional discussions, performances, and films on East African culture. Open Saturday from 10:00 A.M. to 5:00 P.M. or by appointment. There is a $5.00 admission fee. For more information call (215) 382–3191 or go to www.eastafricacenter.net.

Market Street from Thirty-fourth to Thirty-eighth Streets is the center of what's known as the University City Science Center, a consortium of thirty academic and scientific institutions. Of note here is the **Esther M. Klein Gallery** (3600 Market Street), which features an Art in Science series focusing on artworks that explore technology and science. Open Monday through Saturday from 9:00 A.M. to 5:00 P.M. Call (215) 966–6188 or go to www.kleinart gallery.org.

West Philadelphia is also home to the **Institute of Contemporary Art** (118 South Thirty-sixth Street), which is often overlooked in favor of Philadelphia's better-known museums. Affiliated with the University of Pennsylvania, the institute highlights the work of emerging contemporary artists and has an impressive track record. It was the first museum to show works by Andy Warhol and performance artist Laurie Anderson. Open Wednesday through Friday from noon to 8:00 P.M. and Saturday and Sunday from 11:00 A.M. to 5:00 P.M. Admission is $6.00 for adults and $3.00 for children and seniors. Call (215) 898–7108 or go to www.icaphila.org.

You're now at the epicenter of the upscale commercial scene that has sprung up and, to a large extent, been sponsored by the University of Pennsylvania. Next to the Institute of Contemporary Art, at Thirty-sixth and Sansom, Penn recently ripped out a parking lot and put in a small urban park, with outdoor tables and chairs surrounded by hip stores and coffee shops. The Penn Bookstore, now a Barnes and Noble superstore, also relocated here. It's a great place to have a sandwich, maybe listen to some live music, and watch the college scene. If you're going to explore the Penn campus, it's best to take off from here on foot.

Who else but college students would eat cereal for every meal? It's possible at Penn, where the *Cereality Cereal Bar and Cafe* (3631 Walnut Street) tempts hungry co-eds. You get your choice of two cereals, toppings ranging from bananas to malted milk balls, and milk, all served in a Chinese take-out–type container and dished out by employees wearing pajamas. It's the place to go to relive the cereals of your youth. Count Chocula, anyone? Open Monday through Friday from 6:30 A.M. to 9:00 P.M., Saturday from 7:00 A.M. to 9:00 P.M., and Sunday from 8:00 A.M. to 5:00 P.M. Call (215) 222–1162 or go to www .cereality.com.

onyourmarks . . .

The *Penn Relays*—a highlight of the spring athletic season in Philly—first took place here in 1895. The relays were responsible for the first use of a baton and metric measurements in track events. Thousands of athletes now come to town each May for what is the oldest and largest competition of its kind.

Several of University City's best restaurants are hidden away on Sansom Street. Even if you don't eat there, you have to at least look into *Pod* (3636 Sansom Street), a fun, futuristic fantasy of a restaurant. The brainchild of restaurateur Stephen Starr, Pod is one of those restaurants that reviewers jump through all sorts of hyperbolic hoops trying to describe. Suffice it to say the seats light up, sushi comes by on a conveyor belt, and, if your party is five or more, you can sit in one of the private dining pods, which are equipped with do-it-yourself colorful lighting. The design budget for the space was reportedly $3.3 million. The food is Asian fusion and tasty, though overpriced for what you get, but you're paying more for the experience than anything else. Whether you have to go or not, be sure to check out the restrooms. Just look for the green lights. Open Monday through Thursday from 11:30 A.M. to 11:00 P.M., Friday from 11:30 A.M. to midnight, Saturday from 4:00 P.M. to midnight, and Sunday from 4:00 to 10:00 P.M. Call (215) 387–1803 or log on to www.podrestaurant.com. Expensive.

Sansom Street is also home to the *White Dog Cafe* (3420 Sansom Street), one of Philadelphia's most beloved restaurants. Housed in a rambling Victorian brownstone, the White Dog was founded in 1983 by Judy Wicks as a take-out coffee and muffin shop on the first floor of her house. The space grew in a piecemeal fashion from there, and though it's now quite large, the dining areas still have a homey atmosphere. Wicks has become not just a respected restaurateur, but a major civic and social activist. The White Dog manages to be politically correct without being annoying, largely because Wicks puts her money where her mouth is. She sponsors "sister restaurants," both in low-income neighborhoods in Philadelphia and in Third World countries. Every Monday night, the White Dog features speakers on issues of public concern. All this and great food, too. As befits a social activist, Wicks's menu is built around organic produce and what she calls "humanely raised meats." The menu spells out every ingredient, and there are often a lot of them, but the results rarely disappoint. One recent seasonal dinner special was described as "Pan Fried Pocono Springs Rainbow Trout in an Iroquois Corn and Brazil Nut Crust with Dark Rum Sauce; baked yams in coconut cream, snow peas sautéed with pink shrimp, sweet peppers, and grapefruit." You get the idea. Because the White Dog has managed to stay consistent and creative, it has quite a list of loyal customers, so you're well advised to call for reservations. Open Monday through Saturday from 11:30 A.M. to 2:30 P.M., then again from 5:30 to 10:00 P.M. (11:00 P.M. on Friday and Saturday). On Sunday, brunch is served from 10:30 A.M. to 2:30 P.M. and dinner from 5:00 to 10:00 P.M. Call (215) 386–9224 or go to www.whitedogcafe.com. Expensive.

Don't leave without taking time to wander through the ***Black Cat*** (3424 Sansom Street), the White Dog's sister store next door. Wicks has kept the individual rooms in this one-time residence, so the store is a series of alcoves filled with a wide range of eclectic gifts from home and abroad. Many of the items are

College Hall

made by Third World workers whose villages are supported by their efforts. Open Monday from 10:00 A.M. to 9:00 P.M., Tuesday through Thursday from 10:00 A.M. to 11:00 P.M., Friday and Saturday from 10:00 A.M. to midnight, and Sunday from 11:00 A.M. to 9:00 P.M. Call (215) 386–6664 or visit www.blackcatshop.com.

Thirty-fourth Street and Walnut provides the most logical entrance to the Penn campus. On this stretch of what's known as "The Green," you'll find two of the university's architectural treasures, as well as the often-photographed statue of Benjamin Franklin, who was behind the founding of Penn in 1792. The statue sits in front of **College Hall,** the ornate Gothic building that houses the university's administrative offices. The most spectacular building on campus is officially known as the **Anne and Jerome Fisher Fine Arts Building,** but it is usually simply called the "Furness building." The work of architect Frank Furness can be seen throughout the city, but many consider this his masterpiece. Red brick, terra-cotta, and fieldstone add rich texture to the building's exterior as well as to the skylit, four-story reading room that lies inside. The building's lower level houses the university's architectural archives, some of which are on display in the **Kroiz Gallery.** At the core of the archives is the work of Louis Kahn, the architecture school's most famous alumnus and former faculty member; but there are also drawings and models by more than 400 architects and designers. The gallery hosts four to six exhibitions a year. Open Monday through Friday from 9:00 A.M. to 5:00 P.M.; there is no admission fee. Call (215) 898–8323 or go to www.design.upenn.edu/archives.

didmorticia matriculate?

While wandering around the campus of the University of Pennsylvania, don't be surprised if you do a double take when you come to College Hall. The building—with its imposing towers and pinnacles—is said to have been the inspiration for the mansion of television's creepy *Addams Family.* Creator Charles Addams spent what were clearly formative years as an undergrad at Penn.

Several other buildings are worth visiting also. A wonderful Italian Renaissance building designed by Wilson Eyre houses **The University of Pennsylvania Museum of Archaeology and Anthropology** (3260 South Street). The museum has a fascinating collection of more than a million artifacts, many collected during hundreds of university-sponsored excavations around the world. You can see a twelve-ton sphinx; many fine examples of cuneiform, the world's first writing; and the always popular mummy collection. Open Tuesday through Saturday from 10:00 A.M. to 4:30 P.M. and Sunday from 1:00 to 5:00 P.M. Admission is $8.00 for adults and $5.00 for students and seniors. Call (215) 898–4000 or go to www.upenn.edu/museum.

And It Took a While to Reboot

If you're wandering around West Philly with your date book in your cell phone, give a nod of the old microchip to the University of Pennsylvania's Moore School of Electrical Engineering. It was in a vast room at Thirty-third and Walnut that two young engineers collaborated in the early 1940s to create the Electronic Numerical Integrator and Computer—now affectionately called **ENIAC**—which many consider the world's first all-electric computer. The top-secret military project was designed to speed up the tedious mathematical calculations necessary to produce artillery-firing tables for the army's war effort. ENIAC's specifications are astounding, especially considering that today a single, tiny microchip could do the job: 17,500 vacuum tubes linked by 500,000 soldered connections. It weighed thirty tons and filled a 50-foot-long basement room, but as with today's computers, things didn't always go as planned. Occasionally an insect would fly into the lab and short-circuit the program. That's how computer problems came to be known as "bugs." A small section of the historic computer lives on in the school's basement and was even fired up one last time on the occasion of its fiftieth anniversary. Though the dusty room is closed to the public, special arrangements to see ENIAC can be made by contacting Penn's Electrical Engineering School.

The **Richards Medical Research Building**—probably Penn's most architecturally famous building—is across campus at Thirty-seventh Street and Hamilton Walk. Although many today may find Richards unattractive, the building was responsible for establishing architect Louis Kahn's reputation as a groundbreaker when it was completed in 1961. With its heavy use of masonry and its unique engineering system, the building was considered a leap away from the glass and steel skyscrapers that up until then defined modern architecture. Ironically, this is one of the few buildings in the city designed by Kahn, a native Philadelphian.

Just behind the Richards Building is one of the university's hidden nooks known as the **Biopond.** Created in 1897 by a Penn botany professor, this five-acre oasis started as a botanical garden but has grown into more of a botanical forest. Winding pathways weave through towering trees and lush undergrowth, surrounding the pond that is the happy home of the neighborhood's fish, turtles, frogs, ducks, and even crayfish. Operated by Penn's Department of Plant Science, the Biopond includes a small picnic grove and several greenhouses. The university recently encountered fierce resistance from the public and its own community when it floated ideas about using the Biopond space for building expansion.

Many of Penn's cultural offerings come from the **Annenberg Center** (3680 Walnut Street). A complex of three theaters, the Annenberg plays host

Book Bazaars

As you might expect in an academic community, there are plenty of books to be had around Penn. The neighborhood supports two used bookstores, both run by Penn grads: *The Last Word* (3925 Walnut Street) is a relative newcomer; *House of Our Own Bookstore* (3920 Spruce Street) is a longtime favorite. Every nook and cranny of this midblock row house is stuffed with stacks of books. The title you're looking for is in there somewhere.

to theater, music, and dance performances and is the site of a very popular children's festival each May. Call for schedules (215–898–3900, www.annenberg center.org). The *Kelly Writers House* (3805 Locust Walk) is another major venue for cultural events at Penn, and it maintains an active schedule of talks by visiting writers, journalists, playwrights, and editors. Call (215) 573–WRIT or visit www.writing.upenn.edu/~wh.

As you would expect of a college neighborhood, there are numerous affordable places to get a bite to eat. But a favorite, uniquely Philadelphia solution for lunch is to grab it off the street—literally. Each midday finds a variety of food trucks lining up along Thirty-eighth Street, and while the aluminum-sided trucks may look plain, the food is anything but. You can get everything from crepes and Chinese to Mexican and Middle Eastern. Among the favorites of Penn regulars are *La Comadre,* a Mexican cart that sets up shop at Thirty-third and Spruce Streets; *Frita's,* which has great Greek food from its base on Thirty-third Street near Walnut; and *Yue Kee* on Thirty-eighth Street between Locust and Walnut, which some say offers the best Chinese food in West Philly. The truck with the longest line is usually a safe bet.

Fortieth Street between Walnut and Spruce Streets is what Penn refers to as Hamilton Square, and it's come a long way as part of the university's efforts to clean up the commercial district on its western border. Besides a general sprucing up, the strip got a big boost from the 2002 opening of a long-awaited multiplex theater at Fortieth and Walnut. *The Bridge: Cinema de Lux* features six screens that show a mixture of mainstream and independent first-run films, and the complex also includes a full-service bar and restaurant. If you want the ultimate college-bar experience, there's *Smokey Joe's* (210 South Fortieth Street), which refers to itself as the "Pennstitution." But as one Penn alum said, "I can't imagine why anyone would want to go there if you *weren't* a Penn student or alum."

A new hotspot for the Penn campus is *Strikes Bowling Lounge* (4040 Locust Street), a bowling alley and so much more. There are pool tables, big-screen televisions, hip lighting and a full-service restaurant and bar. Perhaps best of all, it offers the solution when you just have to try for a strike at three o'clock in the morning. Open Monday to Wednesday 11:00 A.M. to 2:00 A.M., Thursday and Friday from 11:00 A.M. to 4:00 A.M., Saturday from 9:00 A.M. to 4:00 A.M., and Sunday from 9:00 A.M. to 2:00 A.M. Call (215) 387–BOWL or visit www.strikesbowlinglounge.com.

If you're hungry, a better bet is several blocks away at the **Restaurant School** (4207 Walnut Street). Don't be scared away by the fact that the chefs here are still training. By the time they go on line in the kitchens of the school's four restaurants, they're ready for the real thing. The fanciest of the four, the Great Chefs of Philadelphia Restaurant, is located in a renovated mansion. The school constructed a faux European courtyard in back, at the center of a dining complex that also includes an Italian trattoria and a home-style American restaurant. Hours vary so it's best to call ahead. If you're there during the day, stop by the Pastry Shop and Cafe for an informal lunch of soups, salads, and light entrees, and take home something from the well-stocked pastry counter. The Pastry Shop is open Monday through Saturday from 7:30 A.M. to 6:00 P.M. There's free on-site parking. Reservations recommended for dinner. Call (215) 222–4200 or go to www.therestaurantschool.com. Moderate.

Right across Walnut Street from the Restaurant School is **St. Mark's Square,** a small street between Forty-second and Forty-third Streets to Locust. Historically certified, this block of row houses remains unchanged from when it was built. Anthropologist Margaret Mead lived here as a child. St. Mark's Square leads you to the former Philadelphia Divinity School between Forty-second and Forty-third Streets. These historic buildings have been joined by a $19 million, state-of-the-art building to form the campus of the new Penn-Alexander public school. The PreK–8 school was funded largely by the University of Pennsylvania and is being managed by Penn's Graduate School of Education. The idea is to prove that an urban public school can provide a top-notch education if it's well funded and well managed.

Where It All Began

The popular television show *American Bandstand* originated from Forty-sixth and Market at the WFIL studios, one of the first buildings in the country designed especially for television studios. Dick Clark, at the time a young disc jockey, became the show's host in 1956, and the show went national on ABC in 1957. At the time, record producer Phil Spector called Philadelphia "the most insane, the most dynamite, the most beautiful city in the history of rock and roll and the world."

This is the Spruce Hill section of West Philadelphia, and most of the homes you see in the blocks surrounding the Penn-Alexander school, both Italianate and Victorian, date from the mid-1880s. Many have been lovingly restored and colorfully painted. If you have a car, you'll enjoy meandering up and down streets taking in its charm. A center of Spruce Hill activity is the **University City Arts League** (4226 Spruce Street), a community art center that offers classes and workshops throughout the year and hosts gallery exhibitions showcasing the work of local artists and craftspeople. Open Monday through Thursday from 1:00 to 6:00 P.M., Friday from 1:00 to 5:00 P.M., and Saturday from 9:30 A.M. to noon. Call (215) 382–7811 or go to www.ucartsleague.org.

A favorite restaurant in this neighborhood is **Rx** (4443 Spruce Street), a cozy dining spot housed in a former corner pharmacy (thus the name) and decorated with apothecary relics from times gone by. The owner is ever present in this BYOB and aims to please with a reasonably priced menu featuring primarily free-range and organic ingredients. The menu changes daily depending on what's fresh, but some favorites like the grilled hanger steak and pine nut–crusted skate are constants. Dinner is served from 5:30 to 9:00 P.M. Tuesday through Thursday and until 10:00 P.M. on weekends. Brunch is available Saturday from 10:00 A.M. to 2:00 P.M. and Sunday from 10:00 A.M. to 3:00 P.M. Call (215) 222–9590. Moderate.

Rx has some new competition in the neighborhood that's generating a lot of buzz. **Marigold Kitchen** (501 South Forty-fifth Street) occupies a corner Victorian, and though it looks unassuming, its seasonal dishes are getting high marks for inventiveness. The food is getting such raves it might make sense to go with the tasting menu. The service gets high marks as well, in no small part because this is a BYOB that doesn't charge a corking fee. Open Tuesday through Saturday from 5:30 to 10:00 P.M. and for Sunday brunch from 10:00 A.M. to 2:00 P.M. Reservations are a must; call (215) 222–3699. Moderate.

After a good meal, head over to **Clark Park,** just around the corner from Marigold Kitchen (Forty-third Street and Baltimore Avenue). This park gets heavy use and hosts many festivals, most notably its annual May Fair, so maintenance is a constant struggle. It can look a little run-down, but there's a surprise inside. Clark Park is home to the world's only statue of **Charles Dickens.** Memorialized in bronze, Dickens appears with Little Nell, a beloved character he created in *The Old Curiosity Shop.* The statue was commissioned for the Chicago World's Fair, with the sculptor not knowing that Dickens's will had specified that he should be remembered by his writing alone; he directed that no monument or memorial bearing his likeness be created. When the fair was over and the statue was sent to England as a gift from the American people, Dickens's family

TOP HITS IN WEST PHILADELPHIA

Annenberg Center	Pod
The Bridge: Cinema de Lux	The University of Pennsylvania Museum of Archaeology and Anthropology
Institute of Contemporary Art	

refused to accept it, and it found its way to this corner of Philadelphia. In Clark Park you can also find the Gettysburg Stone, a monolith from the historic battlefield honoring Union soldiers who were treated at Satterlee Hospital, which once occupied part of the park's grounds. Visit www.clarkpark.info to find out more.

If you've eaten at Rx, you may be inclined to have another pharmaceutical experience, and there's one available nearby at the ***Marvin Samson Center for the History of Pharmacy*** (600 South Forty-third Street). This small, specialized museum is located in Griffith Hall of the University of the Sciences, a health sciences school that offered the country's first college of pharmacy. The university boasts more than 10,000 pharmaceutical and medical science artifacts, from which it organizes rotating exhibits. Open Monday through Friday from 9:00 A.M. to 5:00 P.M. (closed on Friday during the summer months). Admission is free. Call (215) 596–8721 or log on to www.usip.edu.

Take time to wander through ***Woodland Terrace,*** which is several blocks away off Woodland Avenue between Fortieth and Forty-first Streets. It's a charming block of twenty-one Victorian homes built by a speculative developer in the 1860s. A sign at No. 516 points out that this was the longtime home of prominent Philadelphia architect Paul Philippe Cret. Across Woodland Avenue you'll find the entrance to the ***Woodlands*** itself, a historic mansion surrounded by a rural cemetery. Though seemingly always under renovation, the mansion is worth a visit, as it is said to be an important house in architectural history. Built during the 1780s, the Federal-style mansion is noteworthy for its unique floor plan, with oval rooms at each end. It was designed by William Hamilton, grandson of the Hamilton who designed Independence Hall. The cemetery is almost as interesting as the home itself, with imposing obelisks and gravestones. Among those buried at the Woodlands are artist Thomas Eakins, Campbell Soup founder Joseph Campbell, Drexel University founder Anthony Drexel, and his father, Francis Drexel, whose classical mausoleum is the most elaborate in the cemetery. Admission to the Woodlands is free; guided tours are available for a small fee. The mansion is open Monday through Thursday from 10:00 A.M. to 3:00 P.M.; grounds are open daily from 9:00 A.M. to 5:00 P.M. Call (215) 386–2181 or log on to www.uchs.net/woodlands/woodlandshome.html.

Slowly but surely the neighborhoods radiating west from the University of Pennsylvania continue to show signs of renewal. On Baltimore Avenue you see evidence of that renaissance, with many Victorians colorfully painted in cheerful colors. There are also a number of ethnic restaurants. Of particular note is a string of African eateries and markets along Baltimore between Forty-fifth and Forty-eighth Streets. At the center of this revival is the *Calvary Center for Culture and Community* (801 South Forty-eighth Street), a nonprofit organization created by the Calvary United Methodist Church to help restore and make better use of its landmark Victorian building. After decades of neglect renovations are underway at the hundred-year-old church, which features the two largest Tiffany window ensembles in Philadelphia and two stained-glass domes. The Calvary Center sponsors numerous community events, including a spring arts festival and the Crossroads Music Series. It is also the new home of the *Curio Theater Company,* which is helping to raise funds to renovate the sanctuary. For more information on the Calvary Center, call (215) 724–1702 or visit www.calvary-center.org. For details on Curio's theatrical season, call (215) 525–1350 or visit www.curiotheatre.org.

Also in this neighborhood is the *Philadelphia Folklore Project* (735 South Fiftieth Street), an organization supporting folk arts and culture in the region. From this small row house, the nonprofit offers public programs, maintains a growing Philadelphia folklife archive, and offers services to artists and grassroots folk cultural agencies to support culture in the city's communities. You can find out more by calling (215) 726–1106 or by visiting www.folklore project.org.

Heading north now on Fifty-second Street, look for the *Philadelphia Beauty Showcase National Historical Museum* (510–514 South Fifty-second Street). A relative newcomer, this small, two-story museum pays tribute to Philadelphia's role in the development of the beauty industry. Visitors can view a large number of artifacts related to hair styling, makeup, and grooming, with one room dedicated to Madame C. J. Walker, who became the country's first African-American woman millionaire early in the twentieth century by developing and marketing her own line of beauty products. The museum is open by appointment Monday through Saturday from 10:00 A.M. to 4:30 P.M. Admission is $6.75. Call (215) 474–7533 to arrange for a visit.

At Fifty-second and Locust Streets, you'll find the *Bushfire Theatre Company* (224 South Fifty-second Street), a company that produces plays and improvisational performances to support African-American actors and play-wrights, both amateurs and professionals. Over the past several decades, the company has worked to transform the old 1901 Locust Theater and several adjoining buildings into an impressive theatrical facility in the middle of a down-at-the-heels urban shopping district. The complex now includes the Writers' Workshop Café, where new playwrights can have their work pro-duced; the Artist's Hut, which is devoted to children's theater; and Sassy's Salt Peanuts Café, which hosts small plays and blues and jazz performances. Bush-fire's artistic director Al Simpkins says the goal was to turn this section of Fifty-second Street into a "mini Avenue of the Arts," and he's gone so far as to construct a Walk of Fame out front, complete with sidewalk plaques honoring important figures in African-American theater. For more information call (215) 747–9230 or go to www.bushfiretheatre.org.

At Fiftieth and Walnut Streets is the ***Paul Robeson House*** (4949 Walnut Street), the last home of the African-American actor, singer, and human rights activist. The home is currently being restored and refitted into an interpretive center and historic house museum. On the first floor are ten life-size panels depicting Robeson at various stages of his life; the second floor features Robe-son's bedroom and areas for lectures and other activities hosted at the site by the West Philadelphia Cultural Alliance. Now a National Historic Landmark, the simple row house was Robeson's home from 1966 until his death in 1976. Open by appointment only. Call (215) 747–4675 or visit www.wpcalliance.org for further information.

Much farther off the beaten path, near the western edge of the city, lies one of Philadelphia's greatest treasures. Many people in the area have never been to the ***Barnes Foundation*** (300 North Latch's Lane, Merion); it may well be that the elite of European art circles know more about the Barnes than the Philadel-phians who have this jewel right in their own backyard. The reason for the secrecy has much to do with the strange story of how the Barnes came to be.

Technically, the Barnes is located in Merion, just 1 block in from the city limit. It was here on a quiet, tree-lined street that the eccentric Dr. Albert Barnes squirreled away one of the world's finest art collections. Barnes never intended for his amazing collection of nineteenth- and twentieth-century paintings to be open to the public, and he made a considerable effort to keep the works out of the sight of Philadelphia's art community. This collection, which includes more than a thousand major works by painters such as Renoir, Cézanne, Matisse, and van Gogh, was handpicked by Barnes, who made his fortune by inventing and marketing Argyrol, a silver-based eyewash used to treat eye infections. Born in 1872 to a poor Philadelphia family, Barnes attended camp revival meetings as a youth with his devout Methodist mother, and that is where he developed his appreciation for African-American culture. He was accepted to the elite Central High School, and by age twenty Barnes had a medical degree from the University of Pennsylvania Medical School. However, rather than practice medicine, he traveled to Germany to study chemistry, philosophy, and psychology.

While in Europe Barnes's interest in art flourished, and he began to purchase paintings; at the same time he was forming his own innovative theories about art and education. A friend from Central High, American painter William Glackens, traveled to Paris and purchased twenty paintings for Barnes, including van Gogh's *Postman,* Picasso's *Woman with a Cigarette,* and works by Renoir and Cézanne. Eventually Barnes was making his own buying trips abroad and expounding on his insights. In 1915 he published his first article, "How to Judge a Painting," in *Arts and Decoration.*

Central to Barnes's philosophy was compassion for the working man and equal rights for African Americans. He began to hang his newly acquired paintings in his factory to be studied and discussed by his workers, and he initiated educational discussion groups among his employees. It was his strong belief that all people should have access to art and education that led him to create The Barnes Foundation in 1922. His friend, the philosopher John Dewey, became the foundation's first director of education. Dewey's *Art as Experience* (1934) was dedicated to Barnes.

As the setting for the foundation, Barnes and his wife, Laura, purchased a thirteen-acre arboretum in Merion and hired the French architect Paul Philippe Cret to design the gallery, which was completed in 1925. The impressive building, designed in French Renaissance style, features seven exterior bas-relief sculptures. Barnes commissioned the Enfield Pottery Works to create intricate ceramic tile work in the vestibule, and Henri Matisse created a mural of dancing figures especially for the main gallery.

By 1929 Barnes had sold his company; the work of the foundation had become his life. He devoted himself full-time to collecting art of all types, which he arranged in the galleries in such a way as to reflect his theories. The amazing collection is still displayed as Barnes intended: Paintings by van Gogh, Picasso, Seurat, and Modigliani hang—unceremoniously unidentified—interspersed with iron hardware and household tools or folk art that Barnes believed shared similar aesthetics.

Barnes spent the rest of his life expanding his collection and concentrating on the foundation's educational mission. In 1940 Barnes and his wife established an arboretum school on the site, expanding their concepts of texture, form, and color into the natural world. For now, both the foundation and the arboretum continue to operate as centers of learning, reflecting Barnes's belief that his foundation was an educational institution, not a museum.

Barnes maintained a fierce rivalry with the art establishment at the Philadelphia Museum of Art, the University of Pennsylvania, and the Academy of Fine Arts. He banned certain critics from the galleries and refused to allow his collection to travel or to be photographed. As a final slap in the face to Philadelphia's art elite, Barnes's will left control of the foundation to Lincoln University, a small, predominately African-American college in nearby Chester County. He decreed that the university's board of trustees would nominate four of the foundation's five trustees. After his death in a car accident in 1951, the courts intervened and forced the foundation to open to the public. In 1993 the trustees approved a world tour of more than eighty pieces of Barnes's collection to help fund a $12 million renovation of the galleries. Following the tour, squabbles with neighbors and local zoning battles escalated, culminating in an Orphans Court ruling that the Barnes management be granted its petition to move the collection to a new site on the Benjamin Franklin Parkway's "museum mile." Plans now call for a building to be constructed on the site of the Youth Study Center on the Parkway between Twentieth and Twenty-first Streets, with Barnes's unique gallery layouts being duplicated in the new structure. The current timeline projects that a move is unlikely before 2009. Meanwhile groups vehemently opposed to the will vow to continue the fight until the moving vans come to cart away the masterpieces.

Public access to the foundation is still strictly regulated, but don't let that scare you away. It is a remarkable collection: old masters, modern European and American paintings, impressionists, postimpressionists, Oriental works, and an exceptional collection of African art. The emphasis is on impressionism—there are 180 paintings by Auguste Renoir alone. It can be overwhelming to take in all the paintings, which is why the Amish chests and antique hardware that punctuate Barnes's displays add so much to the experience.

Currently the galleries are open Friday, Saturday, and Sunday from 9:30 A.M. to 5:00 P.M. In July and August the schedule shifts to Wednesday, Thursday, and Friday from 9:30 A.M. to 5:00 P.M. (reflecting the foundation's insistence that the Barnes is a school, not a museum). Those hours may not sound restrictive, but there's a hitch: The court limits the number of visitors to 400 each day, so you need a prepaid reservation to get in. Call as far in advance as you can to reserve your spot. Because they limit the number of visitors, the galleries are rarely crowded, and you can have a leisurely visit. You need to go slowly to take it all in.

Don't overlook the arboretum during your visit to the Barnes. There are a remarkable range of plant species and varieties—more than 250 varieties of lilacs—and a lovely woodland area. The foundation recently added a new greenhouse and restored many of the gardens to their original 1930s plans, including a rose garden designed by Dr. Barnes.

If you're driving, from City Avenue turn onto Old Lancaster Road, then left onto Latch's Lane. SEPTA's bus 44 stops nearby, or take the R5 Paoli local to Merion Station, about half a mile from the foundation. Admission is $10.00. Call (610) 667–0290 or log on to www.barnesfoundation.org.

While you're in the area, take the time to explore the neighborhood of **Overbrook Farms.** Bounded roughly by City Avenue, Fifty-eighth Street, Woodbine Avenue, and Sixty-sixth Street, the entire community is listed on the National Register of Historic Places. This tract of land was purchased in 1887 for $425,000 and developed as a planned residential community, named Overbrook because the railroad tracks that bisect the neighborhood crossed over a brook. Developers promised fresh air, easy train access downtown, and elegant homes in what they called a "suburb deluxe." Many of the homes in the area have been well maintained and restored. Wide streets are lined with homes built in the arts and crafts, Gothic-Revival, and other late Victorian styles, with stained-glass accents and rich woodworking. Many architects who designed houses here, such as Horace Trumbauer, Chester Kirk, and William and Walter Price, went on to prominent careers. The community hosts an annual Open House Tour in April, which culminates in an elegant sit-down tea.

Most of the commercial district in Overbrook Farms is concentrated along Sixty-third Street near the SEPTA train station. One of the area's more interesting restaurants is housed in a building right next to the station. **DeBreaux's** (2135 North Sixty-third Street) may look like a tiny hole-in-the-wall, but its food has big, Southern flavors. The restaurant is indeed tiny—seating a maximum of fifteen—and even so, the service can be slow, particularly at lunch. But that's because owner Frances DeBreaux makes the food right. Try the chopped barbecue sandwich with a side of Tan's crazy rice or collard greens. Open Tuesday through Saturday from noon to 6:00 P.M. and Sunday from 2:00 to 8:00 P.M. Call (215) 877–4559. Moderate.

Places to Stay in West Philadelphia

The Gables Bed & Breakfast,
4520 Chester Avenue;
(215) 662–1918,
www.gablesbb.com
Located just off Clark Park, this B&B occupies an 1889 Victorian mansion, that is graced by a wraparound porch. There are five rooms with private baths; four rooms share baths. Ask for one of the corner rooms with a turret. Moderate.

Inn at Penn,
3600 Sansom Street;
(215) 222–0200,
(800) 809–7001,

www.theinnatpenn.com
Managed by Hilton Hotels, the new Inn at Penn offers deluxe accommodations smack in the middle of the upscale commercial district adjoining the University of Pennsylvania. Its 238 rooms come with such amenities as plush robes and data ports with Penn-Net access. Moderate.

Sheraton University City,
3599 Chestnut Street;
(215) 387–8000,
(888) 387–8000,
www.sheraton.com/
universitycity
The Sheraton isn't quite as well situated as the Inn at Penn, but it's been recently renovated, so it also offers the hi-tech amenities. Moderate.

Places to Eat in West Philadelphia

Abyssinia,
229 South Forty-fifth Street;
(215) 387–2424
Though it doesn't look like much from the outside, those in the know say Abyssinia serves the best Ethiopian food you'll find in Philadelphia. It's a communal eating adventure, so it may help to go with a group; plus, the entrees are huge, so it helps to share. Ethiopian food is spicy, but they'll accommodate your taste. Try the vegetarian combo. Open daily from 10:00 A.M. to midnight. Moderate.

AUTHOR'S FAVORITE PLACES TO EAT IN WEST PHILADELPHA

DeBreaux's
2135 North Sixty-third Street;
(215) 877–4559

Marigold Kitchen
501 South Forty-fifth Street;
(215) 222–3699

Restaurant School
4207 Walnut Street;
(215) 222–4200,
www.therestaurantschool.com

Rx
4443 Spruce Street;
(215) 222–9590

White Dog Cafe
3420 Sansom Street;
(215) 386–9224,
www.whitedogcafe.com

Zocalo
3600 Lancaster Avenue;
(215) 895–0139

HELPFUL WEB SITES

www.upenn.edu

www.drexel.edu

www.ucityphila.org

www.ucnet.com

La Terrasse,
3432 Sansom Street;
(215) 386–5000,
www.laterrasse.com
This longtime favorite is frequently filled with Penn students whose parents have come to town. The atmosphere manages to be casual and elegant at the same time, and the food is reliable, if not quite as good as at the White Dog down the street. You can grab a quick bite from the cafe menu at the long bar or linger over a full meal on the outdoor patio. Open for lunch Monday through Friday from 11:30 A.M. to 2:30 P.M.; open for dinner Monday through Thursday from 5:30 to 9:30 P.M., Friday and Saturday from 5:30 to 10:00 P.M., and Sunday from 5:30 to 9:00 P.M. Expensive.

Mokas,
3505 Lancaster Avenue;
(215) 222–4410
Home-style Greek cooking—

the basics, well done—and live blues or jazz on the weekends. When the weather is nice, you can eat outside under a grape arbor. Open Monday through Thursday from 5:00 to 10:00 P.M. and Friday and Saturday from 5:00 to 11:00 P.M. Moderate.

Nan,
4000 Chestnut Street;
(215) 382–0818
There are a lot of restaurants to choose from around Fortieth and Chestnut, but Nan is the best. It may not look like much from the street, but this small BYOB serves wonderful Thai-French fusion dishes that are quite reasonably priced. Regulars swear by the escargot and salmon. And save room for Nan's signature dessert—an apple puff pastry in caramel sauce. Open for lunch Tuesday through Friday from 11:30

A.M. to 2:30 P.M.; dinner is served Tuesday through Thursday from 5:00 to 10:00 P.M. and Friday and Saturday from 5:00 to 11:00 P.M. Moderate.

Penne,
3600 Sansom Street;
(215) 823–6222,
www.pennerestaurant.com
This is the new feature restaurant at the Inn at Penn (get it?), which refers to itself as both a "pasta laboratory" and "wine bar." Indeed the chefs whip up homemade pasta in an open kitchen, and the dishes don't disappoint. They are pricey and filling, though, so you may want to go with a half-portion. Open Monday through Friday from 11:30 A.M. to 10:00 P.M. Dinner only on the weekends, starting at 5:00 P.M. Expensive.

Appendix: Annual Events

Being a city of neighborhoods, Philadelphia has a year full of fun neighborhood events and celebrations. The list that follows outlines some of the top citywide annual events and larger community festivals. A complete list of activities can be found on the Web site of the Greater Philadelphia Tourism Marketing Corporation at www.gophila.com; look in the Events Calendar section.

January

Mummers Parade. There's nothing quite like it anywhere in the world. The Mummers Parade has been Philadelphia's unique New Year's celebration since the 1700s. Thousands and thousands of men (yes, mostly men) wearing outrageous costumes made of sequins and feathers strut their stuff in a parade that lasts well into the night. There's fierce competition among the clubs that participate: comics, fancies, string bands, and fancy brigades. After years of tinkering with the route of the parade, hoping to pick up the pace, the parade is once again back to its home on South Broad. A warmer option is Mummers Fest, an indoor festival at the Convention Center the week leading up to the parade. (215) 336–3050, www.mummers.com.

Chinese New Year. The streets of Chinatown come alive to welcome in the Chinese New Year, which occurs on the first day of the first Chinese lunar month (that can push this event into February). For two weeks there are festivities including dragon parades and fireworks, culminating on the fifteenth day with a Lantern Festival. www.phillychinatown.com.

February

Wing Bowl. In what is surely Philadelphia's most disgusting annual event, held the Friday before Super Bowl Sunday, the Wing Bowl sees thousands of unruly spectators crowd into the Wachovia Center to watch competitors stuff themselves with chicken wings.

Fat Tuesday on South Street. Things have gotten a little wild in past years, but police have restored relative order to the Mardi Gras celebrations on South Street. Still, expect some hard partying and large crowds. www.south-street.com.

Celebration of Black Writing. In just a few years, this annual event has grown in size and popularity and now attracts thousands to the Art Sanctuary in North Philadelphia for readings, workshops, and panel discussions with local and nationally known black writers. (215) 232–4485, www.artsanctuary.org.

March

Philadelphia Flower Show. The largest of its kind in the nation, the weeklong Philadelphia Flower Show is a true harbinger of spring each year. Even in its home at the Pennsylvania Convention Center—where it covers thirty-three acres—the show can get crowded, but it's worth the wait to get close to the featured displays, which are wonderfully created by nurseries, florists, and exhibitors from around the world. There are daily lectures and demonstrations, as well as a large marketplace. (215) 988–8800, www.theflowershow.com.

The Book and the Cook Festival. This festival continues to grow in popularity. Dozens of the world's leading cookbook authors descend on Philadelphia and team with the area's top chefs to create fabulous food. For each of the ten days of the festival, you can find up to ten restaurants offering unique meals, usually prix fixe, and have the opportunity to meet and chat with the guest author. (215) 545–5353, www.thebookandthecook.com.

St. Patrick's Day Parade. An estimated 25,000 participants wear the green to take part in this annual Irish celebration, which features marching bands, floats, and groups from many schools and Irish associations. The parade winds up South Broad Street and around City Hall, ending at Twenty-second Street and the Benjamin Franklin Parkway. www.philadelphiapatsparade.com.

April

Philadelphia Antiques Show. Held each spring at the Thirty-third Street Armory in University City, this show draws some of the country's most distinguished dealers. Proceeds benefit the University of Pennsylvania Medical Center. (225) 387–3500, www.philaantiques.com.

Philadelphia Film Festival. This full-scale international film festival offers first-time screenings of feature and short films, as well as workshops and festivals. (267) 765–9700, www.phillyfests.com.

Equality Forum. Billed as the nation's largest gay, lesbian, bisexual, and transgender symposium and festival, this weeklong event features lectures and panel discussions on a broad range of issues, as well as a wide variety of entertainment and social events. (215) 732–FEST, www.equalityforum.com.

Penn Relays. For more than one hundred years, the Penn Relays have marked the height of spring competition for athletes. It's the place to see Olympic track stars in the making. (215) 898–6121.

May

Philadelphia Open House Tours. Get a rare glimpse into some of the area's most spectacular homes and gardens. (215) 861–4971, www.friendsofindependence.org.

Jam on the River. This three-day music and food festival serves as the city's kickoff to summer. There's even a Junior Jam for children. (215) 636–1666, www.jamontheriver.com.

Broad Street Run. The 10-mile course takes runners through a variety of neighborhoods along Broad Street. www.broadstreetrun.com.

Dad Vail Regatta. The largest collegiate regatta in the country, the Dad Vail occurs in the second week of May, drawing college crews from around the country to the Schuylkill River. www.dadvail.org.

World's Largest Garden Party. Private gardens and historic houses open their doors for a series of special events throughout the month of May.

Philadelphia International Children's Festival. Musicians, storytellers, jugglers, and stage performers—all for the kiddie set—take center stage at several University of Pennsylvania venues. (215) 898–3900, www.pennpresents.org.

June

Odunde Festival and Marketplace. Philadelphia's oldest African-American community festival celebrates the African New Year with traditional foods, crafts, and music. Held in the area around Twenty-third and South Streets on the second Sunday of the month. (215) 732–8510.

Manayunk Arts Festival. This is the area's largest outdoor arts and crafts show, and it draws hundreds of thousands of people to the narrow streets of Manayunk. Arrive early to avoid parking nightmares. (215) 482–9565, www.manayunk.com.

The Philadelphia International Championship Bike Race. Considered by many to be the country's top cycling event, this is one of the richest single-day cycling races in the world. More than 130 riders compete on the Ben Franklin Parkway and Fairmount Park's Kelly Drive. The race is best known for its grueling climb up the "Manayunk Wall," a brutal 17 percent climb midway through each lap.

Islamic Heritage Festival. A morning parade leads to Penn's Landing, where you'll find music, boat rides, food, and games for the children.

Elfreth's Alley Fete Days. The first weekend in June, the homes along Elfreth's Alley open their doors to all. There are also colonial crafts and entertainment. (215) 574–0560, www.elfrethsalley.org.

July

Sunoco Welcome America Festival. It only makes sense that Philadelphia would throw the country's biggest birthday bash, with fireworks, concerts, and free events. The festivities actually begin about ten days before the fourth. (215) 683–2211, www.americasbirthday.com.

All About the Music Festival. Held in Wiggins Park on the Camden waterfront, just across the river from South Street, this three-day festival brings in some top singer-songwriters as well as rock and blues artists. (215) 898–6677, www.xpn.org.

August

Philadelphia Folk Festival. One of the country's oldest folk festivals, the Philly Folk Fest offers traditional and contemporary folk music, dancing, craft exhibits, food, activities for the kids, and on-site camping. (215) 242–0150, www.folkfest.org.

African-American Cultural Extravaganza. Festival Pier at Penn's Landing is the site of this celebration of African-American heritage. Live entertainment and an African marketplace set the festive tone.

September

Festival Puertorriqueño Fildelfia (Puerto Rican Week Festival). This festival has it all: a grand parade, food galore, music and dance performances, a mini-Olympics, even a pageant to see who will be crowned Miss Puerto Rico-Philadelphia. (215) 965–7676, www.elconcilio.net.

Labor Day Concert and Fireworks. The summer season wraps up with a concert and fireworks over the Delaware at Penn's Landing. (215) 928–8801, www.pennslandingcorp.com.

Philadelphia Live Arts and Philly Fringe Festival. This is a relatively new, favorite fall event for many Philadelphians. Highlighting alternative art and entertainment, the two-week festival offers hundreds of offbeat theatrical performances, concerts, dance, puppetry, and performance art—some of it downright strange. (215) 413–9006, www.pafringe.org.

Philadelphia College Festival. They call Philadelphia one big college campus, and that certainly is true for a week in September, when free concerts, entertainment, a scavenger hunt, and other activities officially welcome the area's college and university students. www.campusphilly.org.

October

USArtists. This three-day event at the Thirty-third Street Armory brings art dealers from around the country to Philadelphia. More than just an art exhibition, this event coincides with the **Philadelphia Artists Open Studio Tour,** where more than one hundred local artists open their studios to visitors. (800) 455–8312, www.usartists.org and www.post.cfeva.org.

Avenue of the Arts Festival. This free, weekend-long performing arts festival previews the cultural season and showcases performing arts groups and artists from throughout the region. (215) 731–9668, www.avenueofthearts.org.

Pulaski Day Parade. The Benjamin Franklin Parkway is the scene of this celebration on the first Sunday of October, which marks the beginning of Polish American Heritage Month. (215) 922–1700, www.polishamericancenter.org.

Columbus Day Parade. On the second Sunday in October, it's the Italian community that pulls out the stops for this colorful parade, held along South Broad Street. (215) 592–1713, www.sonsofitalypa.com.

November

Philadelphia Craft Show. Sponsored by the Museum of Art, this is billed as one of the finest crafts exhibitions in the country. The juried show features the work of almost 200 of the country's top artists in ceramics, jewelry, glass, furniture, wearable art, and more. (215) 684–7930, www.pmacraftshow.org.

Thanksgiving Day Parade. It may no longer be the largest, but it was the country's first, and Philadelphians still love it. Giant balloons, floats, bands—the works—welcome in the holiday season along Market Street and the Benjamin Franklin Parkway.

Philadelphia Marathon. Said to be the perfect race for first-timers, the route of the Philadelphia Marathon goes by some of the city's most scenic treasures. If a marathon's too much, there's also an 8K run. (215) 685–0054, www .philadelphiamarathon.com.

December

Fairmount Park Yuletide House Tours. A longtime favorite Philly tradition, the historic mansions of Fairmount Park are decked for the season. Go in the evenings for a candlelight tour. (215) 684–7509, www.philamuseum.org/collections/parkhouse/.

Elfreth's Alley Deck the Alley Holiday Celebration. A colonial Christmas is also the theme of the day as the homes on Philadelphia's famous Elfreth's Alley put on their seasonal best. Selected homes are open for tours. www.elfrethsalley.org.

The Pennsylvania Ballet Nutcracker. Say no more. (215) 551–7000, www.paballet.org.

There are many other holiday celebrations throughout the city, and *City Hall* gets its own big Christmas tree and lights up for the season. A traditional Philly holiday favorite goes hand-in-hand with Christmas shopping in Center City. Anyone who grew up in Philadelphia will have fond memories of the *Light Show* at Wanamaker's. The names have changed, but luckily the tradition remains. The Light Show—with Wanamaker's now Macy's—runs every even hour on the hour from 10:00 A.M. to 8:00 P.M. throughout December. Accompanied by the store's famous organ, a wall of 100,000 lights puts on a spectacular show. A little tacky, but traditionally delicious.

New Year's Eve at Penn's Landing. Philadelphia sends out the year with fireworks and more fireworks over the Delaware. Don't stay out too late, because tomorrow's the Mummers Parade!

Indexes

Entries for Philadelphia Restaurants and Lodgings also appear in the special indexes beginning on page 200.

GENERAL INDEX

Abyssinia, 185
Academy of Music, 45–46
Academy of Natural Sciences, 97
Adobe Cafe, 140
Adrienne, 59–60
Adventure Aquarium, 13
African American Museum, 25
AIA Bookstore, 59
Al Dana II, 147
Alison Building, 55
Amada, 33
American Swedish Historical
    Museum, 79
An Indian Affair, 163
Anam Cara Bed & Breakfast, 163
Anglecot, 151
Annenberg Center, University of
    Pennsylvania, 175–76
Anthropologie, 55
Antiquarian's Delight, 68
Antiques Row, 50
Arch Street Friends Meeting
    House, 20
Arden Theatre, 16
Art at Philadelphia International
    Airport, xii
Artisans on the Avenue, 148
Art Sanctuary, 120–21
Asociacion de Musicos Latino
    Americanos (AMLA), 124
Aspen, 93–94
Astral Plane, 62
Athenaeum, 28
Atwater Kent Museum, 26–27
Audrey Claire, 53–54
Avenue of the Arts, 44–50, 181
Awbury Arboretum, 158

Bambi Project, 114
Baptist Temple, 119
Barclay, 56
Barnes Foundation, 181–84
Belle Maison, 138
Belmont Mansion, 104–5
Belmont Plateau, 104
Benjamin Franklin Bridge, 14
Benjamin Franklin Parkway, 87–92
Best Western Center City, 108
Best Western Independence Park
    Inn, 32
Betsy Ross House, 19
Bhagya's Kitchen, 151
Biopond, University of
    Pennsylvania, 175
Bishop White House, 10
Bishop's Collar, 108
Black Cat, 173–74
Blendo, 50
Bliss, 48–49
Blue Horizon Boxing, 117
Boathouse Row, 100
Bob's Diner, 163
Book Corner, 90
Bourse, 22
Brandywine Workshop/Firehouse
    Arts Center, 50
Bredenbeck's Bakery and Ice Cream
    Parlor, 152
Brenner's Laff House, 68
Bridge: Cinema de Lux, 176
Buddakan, 22
Burholme Park, 127–29
Bushfire Theatre Company, 180–81

Cafette, 163
Calder Museum, 89

Calvary Center for Culture and Community, 180
Capital Grille, 44
Carpenter's Hall, 5
Caruso's Market, 148
Cathedral of Saints Peter and Paul, 89–90
Cedar Grove, 106
Center for Emerging Visual Artists, 56
Centro Musical, 124
Cereality Cereal Bar and Cafe, 172
Chamounix Mansion, 108
Cheesesteaks, 76
Chemical Heritage Foundation, 21
Chestnut Hill, 144–53
Chestnut Hill Farmers Market, 151
Chestnut Hill Historical Society, 146
Chestnut Hill Hotel, 151, 163
Chestnut Hill Welcome Center, 148
Chickie's and Pete's Cafe, 126–27
Chinatown, 41
Chinatown Mall, 41–42
Chink's, 133
Chloe, 33–34
Christ Church, 16, 23
Christ Church Burial Ground, 23
Chubby's, 140
Church of the Advocate, 120
Church of the Holy Trinity, 55
Cin Cin, 152–53
City Hall, 35, 37, 192
City Tavern, 11
Civil War and Underground Railroad Museum of Philadelphia, 51–52
Clarion Suites, 61
Clark Park, 178
Clay Studio, 17
Cliveden, 156–57
College Hall, University of Pennsylvania, 174
Coltrane House, 104
Comfort Inn, 32
Concord School House, 157
Condom Kingdom, 67
Congregation Rodeph Shalom, 116

Conwell Inn, 133
Country Club Restaurant & Pastry Shop, 133
Cresheim Cottage Cafe, 163–64
Cret, Paul Philippe, 14, 55, 179, 182
Cunningham Piano Company, 161
Curio Theater Company, 180
Curtis Center, 27
Curtis Institute of Music, 55–56

Dalessandro's Steaks, 140
D'Angelos Bros. Products, 75
Dante & Luigi's, 74
Dark Horse, 9–10
Dave and Busters, 131
DeBreaux's, 184
Delilah's, 40
Dental Museum, Temple University, 119
Deshler-Morris House, 161
Dibruno Brothers, 75
Dickens, Charles, 178–79
DiNic's, 40
Divine Lorraine Hotel, 116–17
Django, 84
Dmitri's, 70
Down Home Diner, 40
Draught Horse, 118–19
Drexel University, 169–70

Eakins Oval, 92
East Africa Resource and Study Center, 171
Eastern State Penitentiary, 94–95
Ebenezer Maxwell Mansion, 158–59
Effie's, 51
El Azteca Il Mexican, 34
Elfreth's Alley, 16–17, 190, 192
Ellen Phillips Samuel Memorial, 101
ENIAC, 175
Erogenous Zone, 67
Eye's Gallery, 67

Fabric Row, 69–70
Fabric Workshop and Museum, 39

Fairhill, 123–25
Fairmount, 92–98
Fairmount Park, 98–107, 192
Fairmount Water Works, 99–100
Fante's Cookware, 75–76
Farmicia, 34
Farm Journal, 29
Federal Reserve, 25
Figs, 93
Fireman's Hall Museum, 17
First Bank of the United States, 10
First Unitarian Church of
    Philadelphia, 60
Fisher Fine Arts Building, 174
Fisher's, 40
Fishtown, 113–14
Flotsam and Jetsam, 18
Flyers Skate Zone, 130
Fork, 20
Fort Mifflin, 82–83
Fosters Urban Homeware, 19
Fountain Restaurant, 98
Four Seasons Hotel, 98, 108
Fox Chase Farm, 129
Franklin Court, 21
Franklin Institute, 96–97
Franklin Mills Mall, 131
Franklin Square, 25
Free Library of Philadelphia, 90
Free Quaker Meeting House, 24
Freedom Theatre, 117
French Bakery and Cafe, 147
Friday Saturday Sunday, 54
Friends Hospital, 125
Frita's, 176
Furness, Frank, 38, 60, 76, 151, 169

Gables Bed & Breakfast, 185
Gallery at Market East, 42–43
Garden Gate Antiques, 151
Garden Gate Cafe, 151–52
Geno's, 76
German Society of Pennsylvania, 115
Germantown, 155–62
Germantown Avenue, 144–45

Germantown Historical Society,
    160–61
Germantown Mennonite Church, 159
Germantown Mennonite Historical
    Trust, 159
Germantown Theatre Guild, 162
Gershman Y, 49
Glen Foerd Mansion, 131–32
Gloria Dei Church, 71–72
Golden District, 123–24
Gowen Historic District, 153
Graff House, 26
Grand Army of the Republic Museum
    and Library, 126
Gravers Lane Station, 151
Great Plaza, 14
Green Tree Tavern, 160
Grey Lodge, 126
Grumblethorpe, 161–62
Guild House, 116

Halloween, 50
Head House Square, 9
Heinz, John, National Wildlife Refuge
    at Tinicum, 82
Hikaru, 164
Historic Bartram's Garden, 80–82
Historical Society of Pennsylvania, 46
Hockley, Thomas, House, 54
Holmesburg Prison, 132
Horace Jayne Mansion, 53
Horticultural Center, 105
Hotel Windsor, 108
House of Our Own Bookstore, 176
House of Tea, 68–69

Illuminaire, 109
Independence Hall, 4
Independence Living History
    Center, 10
Independence Seaport Museum, 12
Independence Visitor Center, 3
Indigo Arts, 18
InFusion, 154
Inn at Penn, 185

Insectarium, 127
Institute of Contemporary Art, 171
Intermission Gift Shop, 48, 148–49
Irish Memorial, 14
Italian Market, 73–76

Jack's Firehouse, 95
Jake's, 139
Jamaican Jerk Hut, 49
Jewelers Row, 27
Jim's Steaks, 68
John's Roast Pork, 73–74
Johnson House, 157–58
Johnny Brenda's, 114
Jones, 27
Joseph Fox Bookshop, 59

Kahn, Louis, 37, 51, 175
Kelly Writers House, 176
Kensington, 113–14
Khyber, 15
Killian Hardware, 148
Kimmel Center for the Performing
    Arts, 47–48
Klein Gallery, 171
Kosciuszko National Memorial, 9
Kosciuszko, Thaddeus, 9, 98
Kroiz Gallery, 174

La Comadre, 176
La Famiglia, 34
La Locanda del Ghiottone, 19
Lanza, Mario, Park and Museum, 71
LaSalle University, 120
La Terrasse, 186
Las Cazuelas, 134
Last Word Bookstore, 176
Latham Hotel, 61
Latitudes Fine Craft Gallery, 138
Lauletta's Grille, 85
Laurel Hill, 103
Laurel Hill Cemetery, 103
Le Bar Lyonnaise, 58–59
Le Bus, 139
Le Jardin, 56

Lee How Fook Tea House, 42
Lemon Hill, 101
Liacouras Center, 118
Liberties, 115
Liberty Bell Center, 3–4
Library Company of
    Philadelphia, 46
Library Hall, 5
Lincoln Legacy Mural, 27
Lit Brothers Building, 26
Littlest Streets, 46
Locks Gallery, 29
Logan Circle, 90
London Grill, 109
Louis Kahn Park, 51
LOVE sculpture, 89
Lovell, Benjamin, Shoes, 67
Ludwig's Garten, 62

Mace's Crossing, 98
Macy's, 43
Magic Garden, 70
Main Street, 137–39
Manayunk, 135–39
Manayunk Towpath, 137–38
Mantua Maker's Museum House, 17
Marconi Plaza, 78
Margaret Esherick House, 150
Marian Anderson Historical
    Residence and Museum, 78
Marigold Kitchen, 178
Market Square, Germantown, 160
Marriott Philadelphia, 61
Marvin Samson Center for the History
    of Pharmacy, 179
Mask and Wig Club, 51
Masonic Temple, 38
Material Culture, 131
Mayfair Diner, 127
McGillin's Olde Ale House, 43–44
McMenamin's Tavern, 154
McNally's Tavern, 146–47
Melrose Diner, 85
Memorial Hall, 106
Merchant's Exchange, 11

Merriam Theater, 47
Mineralistic, 67
Mitten Hall, Temple University, 119
Mixto, 51
Mokas, 186
Monkey Business, 147
Monk's Cafe, 62–63
Moore College of Art, 97
Morris Arboretum, 145–46
Moshulu, 14
Mother Bethel AME Church, 7
Mount Airy, 153–55
Mount Pleasant, 102
Mugshots, 95
Mum Puppettheatre, 15
Mummers Museum, 72–73
Mummers Parade, 72–73, 187
Mural Arts Program, xiii, 96
Muse Gallery, 16
Museum of Nursing History, 125–26
Mütter Museum, 60–61

Nan, 186
National Constitution Center, 3, 24
National Liberty Museum, 21–22
National Museum of American Jewish
    History, 22–23
Nifty Fifties, 130
Night Kitchen, 153
NorthBowl, 115
North by Northwest, 154
North Philadelphia, 116–23
Northeast Philadelphia, 125–33
Northern Liberties, 115–16

O'Doodles, 149
Old City, 15–20
Old Pine Presbyterian, 8
Old St. George's Methodist
    Church, 17–18
Old St. Joseph's Church, 6
Old St. Mary's Church, 7
Omni Hotel at Independence
    Park, 32
Ormiston, 103

Ortlieb's Jazz Haus, 115
Overbrook Farms, 184

Park Hyatt Philadelphia at the
    Bellevue, 45
Parrish, Maxfield, 28
¡Pasión!, 63
Pastorius Park, 149
Pat's, 76
Paul Peck Alumni Association
    Building, Drexel University, 169–70
Pavilion in the Trees, 105
Pearl's Oyster Bar, 40
Penn, William, ix, 35
Penn Relays, 172, 188
Penne, 186
Penn's Landing, 11–14
Pennsylvania Academy of the Fine
    Arts, 38
Pennsylvania Convention
    Center, 39–40
Pennsylvania Hospital, 29–31
Pennypack Environmental
    Center, 129
Pennypack Park, 129
Philadelphia Art Alliance, 56
Philadelphia Arts Bank, 50
Philadelphia Beauty Showcase
    National Historical Museum, 180
Philadelphia Clef Club of Jazz &
    Performing Arts, 50
Philadelphia Contributionship for
    the Insurance of Houses from
    Loss by Fire, 6
Philadelphia Cricket Club, 151
Philadelphia Doll Museum, 121
Philadelphia Ethical Society, 55
Philadelphia Folklore Project, 180
Philadelphia Jewish Sports Hall of
    Fame, 49
Philadelphia Museum of Art, 92
Philadelphia Museum of Jewish
    Art, 116
Philadelphia Print Center, 56–57
Philadelphia Sketch Club, 46–47

Philadelphia State Hospital for the
   Insane, 130
Philadelphia Theatre Company, 48
Philadelphia Zoo, 107
Philosophical Hall, 5
Physick House, 7
Pif, 85
Pink Rose Pastry, 68
Plastic Club, 47
Plays and Players, 51
Please Touch Museum, 96
Plough and the Stars, 15
Pod, 172
Poe, Edgar Allan, Historic Site,
   115–16
Poland Jewelers, 138
Polish American Cultural Center, 10
Pop's Water Ice, 78
Porcini, 63
Port Richmond, 113
Post Office, 20–21
Powel House, 10
Powelton Village, 170–71
Prince Music Theater, 44
Progress Plaza, 117
P S F S, 43

Ralph's, 85
Reading Terminal Market, 39–40
Real World House, 20
Rembrandt's, 109
Restaurant Row, 58
Restaurant School, 177
Rib Crib, 157
Richards Medical Research Building,
   University of Pennsylvania, 175
Ridgeland, 104
Ristorante La Buca, 29
Rittenhouse Hotel, 61
Rittenhouse Row, 58
Rittenhouse Square, 55–59
Rittenhouse Town, 142–43
Ritz Carlton, 44
Ritz 5, 11

RiverLink Ferry, 13
Robert W. Ryerss Library and
   Museum, 127–29
Robertson's, 148
Robeson House, 181
Rocco's, 40
Rocket Cat Cafe, 114
Rockland, 103
Rocky, 57, 69, 73, 80
Rodin Museum, 91
Romanian Folk Art Museum, 47
Rose Tattoo Cafe, 109
Rosenbach Museum and Library, 53
Roxborough, 140–41
Roxy Cinema, 59
Rx, 178

St. Augustine's Catholic Church, 18
St. Clement's Episcopal Church, 97
St. Mark's Episcopal Church, 57–58
St. Mark's Square, 177
St. Martin-in-the-Fields Episcopal
   Church, 150
St. Peter's Episcopal Church, 8–9
St. Philip Neri Church, 70–71
Salumeria, 40
Samuel S. Fleisher Art Memorial, 76
Sansom Street Oyster House, 59
Schuylkill Center for Environmental
   Education, 140–41
Second Bank of the United States, 5
Sedgwick Cultural Center, 154–55
Shampoo, 115
Shank and Evelyn's Luncheonette, 74
Sheraton Society Hill, 32
Sheraton University City, 185
Shippen Way Inn, 84
Shoe Museum, 23
Shofuso, 105–6
Show of Hands, 50
Silverstone Bed & Breakfast, 163
Skate Park, 79–80
Smith Civil War Memorial Arch, 106
Smith Memorial Playground, 101–2

Smokey Joe's, 176
Society Hill, 7–11
Society Hill Hotel, 34
Society Hill Towers, 11
Sofitel Philadelphia, 61
Solaris Grille, 164
South Philadelphia, 69–79
South Street, 65–69, 187
Southeastern Pennsylvania
   Transportation Authority (SEPTA), x
Southwark, 69
Sovalo, 134
Sparks Shot Tower, 72
Spirit of the Artist, 50
Sports Complex, 78
Stagecrafters Theater, 152
Standard Tap, 115
Stenton, 162
Strawberry Mansion, 104
Strikes Bowling Lounge, 176–77
Swann Memorial Fountain, 90
Sweetbriar, 107
Sweet Violet, 138

Tacconelli's Pizzeria, 132–33
Taller Puertorriqueño, 123
Tastykake, 128, 130
Temple University, 118
Theater of the Living Arts, 68
Thirtieth Street Station, 167, 169
Thomas Bond House, 32
Three Bears Park, 8
Tierra Colombiana, 124–25
Tin Angel, 15
Todd House, 6
Tomb of the Unknown Soldier, 28
Tony Luke's, 73–74
tour groups, xiii–xv
Tre Scalini, 77
Trocadero Theater, 41
Tulpehocken Historic District, 158

Ukrainian Catholic Cathedral, 116
Umbria, 154

Union League, 45
United States Mint, 23
U.S.S. *Becuna,* 13
U.S.S. *Olympia,* 13
University City, 167–77
University City Arts League, 178
University of Pennsylvania, 167
University of Pennsylvania
   Museum of Archaeology and
   Anthropology, 174
University of the Arts, The, 49
Upper Burying Ground, 157
Upsala, 155–56

Valley Green Inn, 142
Vanna Venturi House, 149
Venturi, Robert, 116, 149
Victor Cafe, 85
Vietnam, 42
Village of the Arts and
   Humanities, 121–23

Wagner Free Institute of
   Science, 119–20
Walk-A-Crooked-Mile Books, 153–54
Wanamaker's, 43, 192
Washington Square, 28–29
Water Works, 100
Water Works Restaurant, 99
Welcome Park, 11
Westphal Picture Gallery, 170
Wexler Gallery, 18
White Dog Cafe, 172–73
Wilma Theater, 49
Wissahickon Skating Club, 151
Wissahickon Valley, 141–43
Wistar Institute, 170
Women's Exchange, 148
Woodford, 103–4
Woodland Terrace, 179–80
Woodlands, 179–80
Woodmere Art Museum, 146
Wood Turning Center, 18
World Cafe Live, 170

World Sculpture Garden, 13
Worth Repeating, 153
Wyck, 159

Yards Brewing Company, 114
Yue Kee, 176

Zagar, Isaiah, 17, 67, 70
Zipperhead, 65
Zocalo, 171

RESTAURANTS

Abyssinia, 185
Adobe Cafe, 140
Al Dana II, 147
Amada, 33
An Indian Affair, 163
Aspen, 93–94
Astral Plane, 62
Audrey Claire, 53–54
Bishop's Collar, 108
Blendo, 50
Bliss, 48–49
Bob's Diner, 163
Bourse, 22
Buddakan, 22
Cafette, 163
Capital Grille, 44
Cereality Cereal Bar and Cafe, 172
Chickie's and Pete's Cafe, 126–27
Chink's, 133
Chloe, 33–34
Chubby's, 140
Cin Cin, 152–53
City Tavern, 11
Country Club Restaurant & Pastry
   Shop, 133
Cresheim Cottage Cafe, 163–64
Dalessandro's Steaks, 140
Dante and Luigi's, 74
Dark Horse, 9–10
Dave and Busters, 131
DeBreaux's, 184
Django, 84
Down Home Diner, 40
Dmitri's, 70
Draught Horse, 118–19

Effie's, 51
El Azteca II Mexican, 34
Farmicia, 34
Figs, 93
Fork, 20
Fountain Restaurant, 98
French Bakery and Cafe, 147
Friday Saturday Sunday, 54
Garden Gate Cafe, 151–52
Geno's, 76
Grey Lodge, 126
Hikaru, 164
Illuminaire, 109
InFusion, 154
Jack's Firehouse, 95
Jake's, 139
Jamaican Jerk Hut, 49
Jim's Steaks, 68
John's Roast Pork, 73–74
Johnny Brenda's, 114
Jones, 27
Khyber, 15
La Famiglia, 34
La Locanda del Ghiottone, 19
La Terrasse, 186
Las Cazuelas, 134
Lauletta's Grille, 85
Le Bar Lyonnaise, 58–59
Le Bus, 139
Le Jardin, 56
Lee How Fook Tea House, 42
Liberties, 115
London Grill, 109
Ludwig's Garten, 62
Mace's Crossing, 98

Marigold Kitchen, 178
Mayfair Diner, 127
McGillin's Olde Ale House, 43–44
McMenamin's Tavern, 154
McNally's Tavern, 146–47
Melrose Diner, 85
Mixto, 51
Mokas, 186
Monk's Café, 62–63
Moshulu, 14
Mugshots, 95
Nan, 186
Nifty Fifties, 130
North by Northwest, 154
¡Pasión!, 63
Pat's, 76
Penne, 186
Pif, 85
Plough and the Stars, 15
Pod, 172
Porcini, 63
Ralph's, 85
Rembrandt's, 109
Restaurant School, 177
Rib Crib, 157
Ristorante La Buca, 29

Rocket Cat Cafe, 114
Rose Tattoo Cafe, 109
Rx, 178
Sansom Street Oyster House, 59
Shank and Evelyn's Luncheonette, 74
Smokey Joe's, 176
Society Hill Hotel, 34
Solaris Grille, 164
Southwark, 69
Sovalo, 134
Standard Tap, 115
Tacconelli's Pizzeria, 132–33
Tierra Colombiana, 124–25
Tin Angel, 15
Tony Luke's, 73–74
Tre Scalini, 77
Umbria, 154
Valley Green Inn, 142
Victor Cafe, 85
Vietnam, 42
Water Works Restaurant, 99
White Dog Cafe, 172–73
Women's Exchange, 148
World Cafe Live, 170
Yards Brewing Company, 114
Zocalo, 171

LODGING

Anam Cara Bed & Breakfast, 163
Barclay, 56
Best Western Center City, 108
Best Western Independence
  Park Inn, 32
Chamounix Mansion, 108
Chestnut Hill Hotel, 151, 163
Clarion Suites, 61
Comfort Inn, 32
Conwell Inn, 133
Four Seasons Hotel, 98, 108
Gables Bed & Breakfast, 185
Hotel Windsor, 108
Inn at Penn, 185
Latham Hotel, 61

Marriott Philadelphia, 61
Omni Hotel at Independence
  Park, 32
Park Hyatt Philadelphia at the
  Bellevue, 45
Rittenhouse Hotel, 61
Ritz Carlton, 44
Sheraton Society Hill, 32
Sheraton University City, 185
Shippen Way Inn, 84
Silverstone Bed & Breakfast, 163
Society Hill Hotel, 34
Sofitel Philadelphia, 61
Thomas Bond House, 32

About the Author

Karen Ivory is a freelance writer in Philadelphia, where she lives with her husband and two children. She began her career as a broadcast journalist, writing and producing for ABC and CBS television stations in St. Louis, New York, and Philadelphia. The author of *Globe Trekker's World: What's on in the World and When* and *Eight Great American Rail Journeys: A Travel Guide,* she also worked on National Geographic guides to *America's Public Gardens, America's Great Houses,* and *Best Birdwatching Sites.*

Help Us Keep This Guide Up to Date

Every effort has been made by the author and editors to make this guide as accurate and useful as possible. However, many changes can occur after a guide is published—establishments close, phone numbers change, hiking trails are rerouted, facilities come under new management, etc.

We would love to hear from you concerning your experiences with this guide and how you feel it could be improved and be kept up to date. While we may not be able to respond to all comments and suggestions, we'll take them to heart, and we'll make certain to share them with the author. Please send your comments and suggestions to the following address:

The Globe Pequot Press
Reader Response/Editorial Department
P.O. Box 480
Guilford, CT 06437

Or you may e-mail us at: editorial@GlobePequot.com

Thanks for your input, and happy travels!